Tea-Time
at the
MASTERS®

a collection of recipes

The word "Masters®" is registered in
the U.S. Patent and Trademark Office
as a trademark and service mark of
Augusta National, Inc., Augusta, Georgia.

published by
The Junior League of Augusta, Georgia, Inc.
1977

1st Printing 10,000 Books — Oct., 1977	9th Printing 30,000 Books — Oct., 1986
2nd Printing 10,000 Books — Nov., 1977	10th Printing 15,000 Books — May, 1989
3rd Printing 10,000 Books — Feb., 1978	11th Printing 15,000 Books — June, 1990
4th Printing 20,000 Books — Feb., 1979	12th Printing 15,000 Books — June, 1991
5th Printing 20,000 Books — Feb., 1980	13th Printing 15,000 Books — July, 1994
6th Printing 30,000 Books — Feb., 1981	14th Printing 15,000 Books — July, 1996
7th Printing 30,000 Books — Jan., 1983	15th Printing 27,500 Books — July, 1998
8th Printing 30,000 Books — Dec., 1984	16th Printing 15,000 Books — Mar., 2002

The cover design is a progression from letterform "T's" through golf tees to tea-cups, a visual expression of the title pun, "Tea-Time at the Masters®". The feeling of the Masters®—the tradition of the tournament, the colorful crowds and flowers—is indicated by the conservative type treatment of the name "Masters®" and the bright colors against the "Masters® green." The design of a large cup below a red tee was initiated by, and echoes still, the Augusta National symbol of a golf flag above the United States.

Woody Kay, Cover Artist

To order copies of *Tea-Time at the Masters®*, send check for $22.95 (includes postage); Georgia residents add $1.60 tax. To order copies of *Second Round, Tea-Time at the Masters®*, send check for $20.95 (includes postage); Georgia residents add $1.47 tax.

Tea-Time at the Masters®
P.O. Box 40058
Augusta, Georgia 30909
Or call to charge your order:
1-888-JLT-TIME (toll free)
or 1-706-733-9098

International Standard Book Number: 0-918544-38-6

Published by:
Favorite Recipes® Press
an imprint of

FRP™

P.O. Box 305142
Nashville, Tennessee 37230

The growth of Augusta, Georgia, has not been totally dependent upon golf, nor has the ascension of golf relied on Augusta, but the two have been closely associated for a number of years. Founded in 1735 by General James Oglethorpe, Augusta somehow survived and even prospered without a golf course until 1897. In that year the Bon Air Golf Club, now the Augusta Country Club, completed a nine-hole course on the east side of Milledge Road. Two years later David Ogilvie, an assistant professional at the Royal and Ancient in St. Andrews, Scotland, was engaged as the head golf professional. By 1901 an eighteen-hole golf course and club house were constructed on the west side of Milledge Road, the present site of the Augusta Country Club.

During the 1920's there were two excellent golf courses in Augusta, the Augusta Country Club No. 1 Course and the Forest Hills-Ricker Hotel Course; there was also the Palmetto Golf Club in nearby Aiken, South Carolina. These courses received considerable play from an Atlanta golfer – Bobby Jones. Fortunately for Augusta and for golf, a frequent member of his foursome was his good friend, Mr. Clifford Roberts. These two men selected the site and formulated the plans for the Augusta National Golf Club, which opened for play in 1932. Two years later, in 1934, the now world-renowned Masters® Tournament began. The early years of the tournament were plagued by bad weather and even worse financial conditions, but Mr. Roberts, the members of the Augusta National Golf Club, and the business community never once compromised in their determined drive to establish a golf tournament complimentary to the name and compatible with the man – Bobby Jones. History reveals the deed unequivocally accomplished.

Also hard at work in Augusta during those formative years of the Augusta National and the Masters® was a group of young women who in 1925 formed an organization known as the Junior Workers. Their purpose was to recognize needs within the community and find solutions to these problems. Three years later, with a membership of 73, they were sponsored by Columbia, South Carolina, seconded by Charleston, South Carolina, and accepted into the Association of Junior Leagues of America. In 1974 a membership of 426 voted to undertake the publication of a cookbook which would not only do honor to culinary skills, but at the same time pay tribute to the area's most famous annual event.

Tea-Time at the Masters® should prove invaluable to those whose game is the kitchen as well as those for whom the kitchen is a game. The recipes provide something for every degree of expertise.

It is an absolute must for the serious collector of cookbooks as well as the avid golfer who views the kitchen strictly as the nineteenth hole. Scattered throughout the book are recipes submitted by well-known golf clubs, highlighted by the Royal and Ancient, Pebble Beach, Pinehurst and Firestone Country Club. Also included are numerous recipes from wives of Masters® participants, past and present. Each recipe in **Tea-Time** has been prepared over and over on the practice range and is therefore suitable for the big course under any playing conditions! There are no bogies, so "tea" it up and fire away; not only will you make the cut, but you will be right there with the leaders in the club house after the last bite is down.

Dr. Thomas Walter Blanchard

TABLE OF CONTENTS

Cookbook Committee

Mrs. Newton G. Quantz, Jr.

Mrs. William Hunter Baggs, Jr. Mrs. Harry T. Harper III
Mrs. William L. Clark, Jr. Mrs. Richard L. Magruder, Jr.
Mrs. Edwin L. Douglass, Jr. Mrs. Robinson W. Schilling, Jr.

Mrs. Thomas W. Blanchard

Mrs. Edward C. Austell Mrs. Benjamin Mason
Mrs. William W. Barrett Mrs. Finley Merry
Dr. Avis Brown Mrs. John C. Mitchell
Mrs. William L. Bruns Mrs. Eugene Neal
Miss Keith Claussen Mrs. Whitney C. O'Keeffe
Mrs. Ron Colton Mrs. Albert M. Pickett
Mrs. James Dale Mrs. John D. Reynolds III
Mrs. Rowland Dye Mrs. W. Wynn Riley
Mrs. S. Herbert Elliott Miss Geraldine Rinker
Mrs. S. Stetson Fleming Mrs. Richard B. Sasnett, Jr.
Mrs. Edward Forrester Mrs. Joseph L. Sheehan, Jr.
Mrs. Hugh P. Greene, Jr. Mrs. Samuel H. Sibley
Mrs. Danforth Hagler Mrs. Randall Strozier, Jr.
Mrs. David Hanks Mrs. William A. Trotter III
Mrs. William O. Kroeschell Mrs. J. Carleton Vaughn, Jr.
Mrs. William Maguire Mrs. James B. Wilkes

The purpose of the Junior League is exclusively educational and charitable and is to promote voluntarism; to develop the potential of its members for voluntary participation in community affairs; and to demonstrate the effectiveness of trained volunteers.

The recipes for "Tea-Time at the Masters®" have been tested for quality and edited for clarity and ease of preparation.

MASTERS MENUS

The annual spring festivities surrounding the Masters®offer the Augusta hostess unlimited opportunities for entertaining. A favorite of many is the brunch. The mid-morning hour is perfect. A brunch may be casual and simple in nature and your guests may go directly to the tournament, or it may be a seated, more formal affair if time permits.

Our menus would be just as appropriate for a pre-football game party or for a cold winter morning in a condominium by the ski slopes. There is an air of excitement over the forthcoming event and your guests will arrive in a gay mood of anticipation, armed with hearty appetites.

In these as in the following menus, we have chosen our favorite recipes. You may add to or simplify them as the occasion demands.

Masters' Saturday Morning Bloody Bull   Ha' Penny Snacks
Cheesy Ham Quiche   Broccoli Surprise
Spiced Peach Salad
Sausage Breakfast Bread
Fresh Apple Cake

Bull Shot   Scotch Eggs
Bourbon-glazed Ham
Blender Cheese Soufflé   Baked Tomatoes and Corn
Molded Asparagus Salad
Dilly Casserole Bread   Jan Smuts' Tea Cakes
Pickled Peaches
Orange Cake

Bloody Mary   Cheese Straws
                    Brunch Casserole
                    Mushroom Soufflé
Fresh Fruit Salad with   Hot Curried Fruit
Poppy Seed Dressing   or

                Honey Orange Braids
            Chocolate Peppermint Sticks

Milk Punch   Sausage Swirls
                    Eggs Hussarde
Broiled Tomato with   Hearts of Palm with
Dill Sour Cream   Dijon French Dressing
            Sylvester's "Six-Pack" Sour French Bread
                    Crêpes Fitzgerald

Usually, lunch during the Masters® is a quick sandwich on the course, but when the opportunity arises, men as well as women would enjoy these bountiful luncheons.

Ruby Red Punch   Crab Meat Spread
            Chicken and Wild Rice Casserole
Squash Stuffed with Spinach   Tomato Aspic
Sour Cream Muffins   Curry Slices
                Lemon Charlotte

Rhine Wine Aperitif   Mushroom Puffs
            Shrimp and Artichoke Casserole
                        on
            patty shells or toast points
        Hot Asparagus with lemon butter and almonds
Stuffed Beets   Mandarin Spinach Salad
            Wallace's Whole Wheat Rolls
                Chocolate Mousse

VIII.

Our selection of dinner and supper menus begins with a local favorite, the bird supper.

Heavenly Quail

Wild Rice and Peas   Broccoli Casserole

Perfection Salad

Tom's Rolls   Artichoke Relish

Scottish Trifle

For a casual, yet delicious supper, invite the neighbors over on Sunday night to enjoy . . .

Peanut Soup

Marinated Veal Shoulder Roast

Green Rice   Aunt Mary's Carrot Pudding

Marinated Bean and Artichoke Salad

Popovers

Strawberry Roll

A real family favorite that the children will request again and again . . . . . .

Steak Mozzarella over Noodles

Green Pea Casserole

Caesar Salad   Onion Cheese Supper Bread

Toffee Ice Cream Pie

For an elegant ending to a delightful day . . .

Steak Diane

Onion Pie   Stuffed Mushrooms

Connoisseur's Casserole

Spinach or Romaine Salad

Grandmother's Refrigerator Rolls

Cornelia's Mocha Log

A really grand presentation of your culinary talents . . .

Cup of Mock Turtle Soup
Crown Roast of Pork
Sweet Potato Pone   Green Beans with Sour Cream Sauce
Cucumber Ring Mold   Angel Biscuits
Mocha Baked Alaska
Irish Coffee

After a day at the Masters® complete the conviviality of the occasion with a sumptuous cocktail party.

Mushroom Appetizers
Sally's Roast Tenderloin   Envelope Rolls
Artichoke Dip   Cherry Tomato Appetizers
Sweet and Sour Sausage
Shrimp and Artichokes La Bretagne
Crabmeat Fingers   Parmesan Bites
The Now Famous Cheese Ring with crackers
Love Notes

Sausage Stuffed Mushrooms
Smoked Turkey   Angel Biscuits
Marinated Broccoli and Cauliflower
Chipped Beef Dip   Bacon Roll-ups
Maryland Shrimp Mousse with crackers
Assorted Cheeses and crackers
with Hot Pepper Jelly
Dot's Butterscotch Brownies

Appetizers

1

DIPS, SPREADS, MOLDS

Artichoke Dip

1 14-ounce can artichoke hearts
½ cup mayonnaise
1 teaspoon Worcestershire

1-2 teaspoons onion, grated
3 slices cooked bacon, crumbled
garnish: red pepper

Drain, then mash artichoke hearts with fork. Combine with remaining ingredients. Chill. Before serving, sprinkle red pepper on top. Serve with bland crackers or melba rounds. Yields 1 cup.

▼ Should be made a day ahead.

Herb Mayonnaise Dip

1 cup mayonnaise
½ teaspoon lemon juice
¼ teaspoon salt
¼ teaspoon paprika
¼ cup parsley, minced
1 tablespoon onion, grated

1 tablespoon chives, minced
⅛ teaspoon curry powder
½ teaspoon Worcestershire
1 garlic clove, minced
1 tablespoon capers, minced
½ cup sour cream

Mix all ingredients well. For full flavor, refrigerate overnight. Serve with selection of raw vegetables. Yields 1½ cups.
Adds special touch to roast beef or ham sandwiches.

Guacamole Dip

2 avocados, peeled and pitted
1 medium onion, finely chopped
2 green chili peppers, finely chopped
1 tablespoon lemon juice
1 teaspoon salt

½ teaspoon coarse black pepper
1 medium tomato, peeled and
   finely chopped
mayonnaise or salad dressing
corn chips or tortilla chips

Mash avocados with fork. Add onion, peppers, juice, salt and pepper. Beat until creamy. Fold in tomato. Spread top with thin layer of mayonnaise. Cover and chill. Just before serving, stir gently to mix. Serve with corn chips. Yields 2 cups.

▼ Make no more than 8 hours ahead.
Good appetizer for a Mexican meal.

Spinach Dip

1 10-ounce package frozen chopped
   spinach, thawed, WELL DRAINED
   (do not cook)
1 cup mayonnaise
1 cup sour cream

½ cup chopped parsley
juice of ½ lemon
⅓ cup green onion, minced
2 teaspoons dry dill weed
1 teaspoon salad herbs

Mix thoroughly and chill. Serve with crackers or chips. Yields 4 cups.
▼ Commercial salad herbs contain a mixture of basil, marjoram, tarragon,
  parsley, crushed dill seed and fennel seed.

Quick Spinach Dip

1 10-ounce package frozen chopped
   spinach, thawed, WELL DRAINED
   (do not cook)
1 cup sour cream

1 tablespoon mayonnaise
1 tablespoon onion, minced
1 0.4-ounce (small) package ranch
   style buttermilk dressing

Mix all ingredients well. Chill. Serve with corn chips.

Make dips a day ahead for full flavor.

Chipped Beef Dip

2 2½-ounce jars dried beef,
   minced
2 8-ounce packages cream cheese,
   softened
4 tablespoons milk
1 cup sour cream

1 medium onion, chopped
salt and pepper to taste
½ cup green pepper, chopped
   (optional)
garnish: 1 cup chopped
   sautéed pecans (optional)

Combine all ingredients. Mix well. Place in oven-proof serving dish. Bake at 350°
for 20-30 minutes. Garnish if desired. Serve hot with crackers. Serves 25.
Everybody's favorite.

Vegetable Dip

½ cup mayonnaise
1 8-ounce package cream cheese, softened
½ cup parsley, chopped
1 hard-boiled egg white, finely chopped

2 tablespoons onion, minced
1 garlic clove, minced
1 tablespoon anchovy paste
dash pepper
garnish: hard-boiled egg yolk, crumbled

Put all ingredients except egg yolk in blender and mix on high. Garnish. Serve with assorted raw vegetables. Yields 1½ cups.

Shrimp Spread

1 8-ounce package cream cheese
1 stick margarine
1 small onion, finely chopped
2 ribs celery, finely chopped
2 tablespoons mayonnaise

2 tablespoons lemon juice
dash Worcestershire
salt and pepper to taste
1 pound shrimp, boiled, cleaned and finely chopped

Soften cheese and margarine. Blend well. Add remaining ingredients and mix well. Chill. Serve at room temperature with crackers. Serves 16.
▼ Frozen shrimp work well in this recipe.

Crab Spread

¾ cup mayonnaise
1 cup crab meat, fresh or frozen

2 teaspoons capers
Cheddar cheese, grated

Combine first 3 ingredients. Sprinkle with cheese. Bake at 300° until bubbly. Serve hot with crackers.
Best made with homemade mayonnaise.

Crab Meat Spread

½ medium onion, grated with juice
4 3-ounce packages cream cheese, softened
2 tablespoons mayonnaise
2 tablespoons Worcestershire

1 tablespoon lemon juice
6 ounces chili sauce
1-2 cups crab meat, drained (preferably fresh)

Combine first 5 ingredients. Place in serving dish, cover with chili sauce and sprinkle with crab meat. Chill. Serve with Ritz crackers. Yields 3 cups.

Hot Clam Spread

2 8-ounce cans minced clams
2 teaspoons lemon juice
1 large onion, minced
1 large clove garlic, minced
1 stick butter
1½ teaspoons oregano
4 tablespoons reserved clam juice

¾ cup parsley, chopped
⅔ cup Italian seasoned
    bread crumbs
dash Tabasco, Worcestershire
½ teaspoon salt
grated Parmesan cheese

Bring clams and lemon juice to a boil. Drain and reserve liquid. Sauté onion and garlic in butter. Add remaining ingredients except cheese. Stir in clams. Put in small ovenproof dish. Top with cheese. Bake at 400° for 20 minutes. Serve hot with melba rounds. Serves 16.

Cheese Paste
Mrs. Arnold Palmer, wife of Masters' Champion 1958, 1960, 1962 and 1964

1 8-ounce package cream cheese
  at room temperature
6 ounces Kraft sharp processed
  cheese at room temperature
6 ounces pimiento cheese spread
  at room temperature

1 teaspoon MSG
1 teaspoon Worcestershire
1 drop Tabasco
3 tablespoons mayonnaise
juice from 1 clove garlic

garnish: 3 tablespoons chili powder, 3 tablespoons paprika and ½ cup finely chopped nuts.

Mix all ingredients together in mixer. CHILL. Form into 3 balls. Roll in garnish mixture. Yields 3 balls.

The "Now Famous" Cheese Ring

1 pound sharp Cheddar cheese,
  grated
1 cup pecans, chopped
¾ cup mayonnaise

1 medium onion, grated
1 clove garlic, pressed
½ teaspoon Tabasco
1 cup strawberry preserves

Combine all ingredients except preserves and mix well. Chill. Mold into ring. Fill with strawberry preserves. Serve with crackers.
An interesting combination of flavors.

5

Cheese-Pecan Ball

2 8-ounce packages cream cheese, softened
½ pound New York State sharp cheese, grated
1 large onion, grated
salt to taste
dash red pepper
½ cup parsley, chopped
½ cup pecans, chopped
paprika

Mix cheeses and onion by hand. Add salt and pepper. Mix again. Refrigerate several hours. Shape into ball. Roll in parsley and nuts. Sprinkle with paprika.
▼ May be frozen.

Barbara's Pineapple Cheese Ball

3 8-ounce packages cream cheese, softened
1 cup crushed pineapple, well drained
5 green onions, finely chopped
½ green pepper, chopped
½ cup pecans, chopped
dash of salt

Combine all ingredients. Shape into ball. Chill.
Goes well with ham at a cocktail party.

Salmon Mold

½ teaspoon salt
1½ tablespoons sugar
½ tablespoon flour
1 teaspoon dry mustard
dash cayenne
2 egg yolks
1½ tablespoons butter, melted
¾ cup milk
¼ cup vinegar
¾ tablespoon unflavored gelatin, softened in 2 tablespoons cold water
1 cup red salmon
1 cup celery, chopped
1 cup sour cream
garnish: olives (optional)

In top of double boiler, mix dry ingredients. Add egg yolks, butter, milk and vinegar. Cook, stirring until it thickens. Remove from heat and add gelatin, salmon and celery. Pour in oiled mold and chill. Glaze with sour cream and garnish. Serves 8-10 at cocktails.
Mold in individual molds and serve as a luncheon entrèe for four.

Chicken Mousse

3 cups cooked chicken,
   finely chopped
½ cup slivered almonds
2 cups celery, finely chopped
1 teaspoon salt
3 teaspoons onion juice
juice of 3 lemons

½ cup mayonnaise
2 tablespoons unflavored gelatin
   softened in 2 tablespoons water
½ cup chicken stock
½ pint whipping cream, whipped
paprika to taste
red and black pepper to taste

Mix first 6 ingredients. Add mayonnaise. Melt softened gelatin in hot stock. Pour over chicken and stir lightly to mix. Allow to cool. Fold in whipped cream. Add paprika and pepper to taste. Place in oiled 1½ quart mold or loaf pan. Chill. Unmold and serve with crackers. Serves 30.

Maryland Shrimp Mousse

1 10¾-ounce can tomato soup
1 envelope unflavored gelatin
   softened in ¼ cup cold water
1 cup mayonnaise
8 ounces cream cheese, softened
½ cup celery, chopped

½ cup onion, minced
5 4½-ounce cans shrimp, chopped
salt, Worcestershire to taste
¼ cup green pepper, chopped
   (optional)

Heat tomato soup. Add gelatin mixture. Cool. Cream mayonnaise with cream cheese. Add remaining ingredients. Mix well. Pour into 1½ quart mold or fish mold. Chill. Serves 25.

▼ Fresh or frozen shrimp may be used. Use 2 to 3 cups.

COLD FINGER FOOD

Marinated Broccoli

3 pounds fresh broccoli flowerets
1 cup cider vinegar
1 tablespoon sugar
1 tablespoon dill weed
1 tablespoon MSG

1 teaspoon salt
1 teaspoon coarse pepper
1 tablespoon garlic salt
½-1½ cups vegetable oil (as desired)

Broccoli may be blanched for a few minutes or left raw. Mix ingredients for marinade, pour over vegetables and refrigerate for at least 24 hours. Drain well before serving.

▼ Cauliflower may be added for contrast.

7

Cherry Tomato Appetizers

1 pint cherry tomatoes
⅓ pound blue cheese, mashed
⅓ cup sour cream
1 teaspoon lemon juice

salt to taste
dash Tabasco
garnish: paprika and parsley

Wash tomatoes, cut off tomato top and scoop out pulp. Drain well. Mix remaining ingredients. Stuff tomatoes with mixture. Garnish. Serve chilled. Yields approximately 25 tomatoes.

Beef Rolls

2 3-ounce packages cream cheese, softened
3 teaspoons onion, grated

2 teaspoons horseradish
dash Worcestershire
¼ pound packaged sliced beef

Combine first 4 ingredients. Mix well. Spread mixture on 1 slice of beef at a time. Roll beef up and refrigerate. When thoroughly chilled, the beef rolls may be cut into smaller pieces if desired. Serves 8 for cocktails.
Men love these!

Magnificent Mushrooms

1 pound mushrooms, halved (or sliced if very large)
½ cup dry vermouth
½ cup olive oil
½ cup red wine vinegar
1 garlic clove, crushed

2 tablespoons onion, chopped
1 tablespoon basil
1 teaspoon salt
½ teaspoon pepper
½ teaspoon sugar
½ teaspoon dry mustard

Put mushrooms in jar. Combine remaining ingredients and mix well. Pour over mushrooms. Seal and store in refrigerator. Will keep several weeks. Serves 8-10 for cocktails.

Pickled Shrimp

shrimp (any amount)
lemons, sliced
onions, sliced

1 3-ounce bottle of capers
cider vinegar
oil

Boil, peel and clean shrimp. Layer with lemons, onions and capers. Cover with vinegar and a small amount of oil. Marinate overnight in refrigerator. Serve chilled with toothpicks.

Marinated Shrimp

4 pounds medium shrimp, boiled, shelled and deveined
4 onions, sliced and ringed
4 lemons, thinly sliced
juice of 1 lemon
1 cup condensed tomato soup
1½ cups vegetable oil
¾ cup white vinegar
¼ cup sugar
½ teaspoon paprika
1 teaspoon cayenne
1 tablespoon dry mustard
1 tablespoon Worcestershire
2 teaspoons salt
¼ teaspoon Tabasco

Place shrimp, onions and lemons in large container. Mix remaining ingredients together. Pour over shrimp mixture. Marinate in refrigerator at least 24 hours. Serve in a bowl in marinade with toothpicks or drain and serve as a salad on a bed of lettuce.

Use Kraft Zesty Italian dressing, sliced lemons and sliced onions for an easy marinated shrimp appetizer.

Shrimp and Artichokes La Bretagne

2 pounds shrimp
1 teaspoon seafood seasoning
2 14-ounce cans artichoke hearts, halved
1 6-ounce can pitted black olives
¾ cup olive oil
2 tablespoons tarragon vinegar
2 cloves garlic, crushed
1½ teaspoons salt
1½ teaspoons dry mustard
1 teaspoon sugar
½ teaspoon black pepper, freshly ground
leaf or Bibb lettuce
watercress

Cook shrimp in boiling water with seafood seasoning until done (about 5 minutes). Cool and clean shrimp. Combine shrimp, artichokes and olives. Combine oil, vinegar and seasonings. Pour over shrimp mixture. Marinate in refrigerator for several hours or overnight. Serve as a first course on a bed of lettuce topped with a sprig of watercress. May serve as hors d'oeuvres with toothpicks in a large iced compote. Serves 12 as first course or 16 for hors d'oeuvres.

Shrimp Arnaud

⅞ cup vegetable oil
⅞ cup cider vinegar
1⅓ cups prepared mustard
½ cup catsup
2 tablespoons celery, chopped

2 tablespoons onion, chopped
2 tablespoons parsley, chopped
salt, pepper to taste
4 pounds shrimp, boiled and cleaned

Combine all ingredients except shrimp. Blend well. Pour over shrimp and marinate in refrigerator. Serves 25 at cocktails.

▼ Serve on bed of lettuce and garnish with tomato wedges for a tangy first course for 12.

Marinate broccoli flowerets in Good Seasons Italian dressing at least 24 hours for a zesty vegetable hors d'oeuvre.

Double Cheese Wafers

¾ cup butter
½ cup Cheddar cheese, grated
⅓ cup bleu cheese
½ clove garlic, minced

1 teaspoon parsley, chopped
1 teaspoon chives, chopped
2 cups sifted flour
½ teaspoon salt

Cream butter and cheeses. Add remaining ingredients. Shape in 1½-inch (diameter) rolls and chill. Slice and bake at 375° for 8-10 minutes. Yields 3 dozen.

Ha'Penny Snacks

½ cup butter
½ pound sharp cheese, grated
1 cup plain flour

½ envelope onion soup mix
½ teaspoon salt

Let butter and cheese come to room temperature and mix thoroughly. Add remaining ingredients and blend. Shape into about 3 rolls 1-inch in diameter. Wrap in wax paper and chill. Slice rolls into slices ¼-inch thick. Bake on ungreased cookie sheet at 375° for 10-12 minutes or until slightly browned on edges. Keeps well in air-tight container. Yields 6 dozen.

Parmesan Bites

1 cup plain flour
1-2 dashes cayenne pepper
⅔ cup grated Parmesan cheese

½ cup butter or margarine,
    softened
cream or evaporated milk

Sift flour into mixing bowl. Stir in pepper and cheese. Cut in butter with pastry blender, then work dough with hands until it holds together. Roll out on floured surface to ⅓-inch thickness. Cut into 1 or 1½-inch squares. (A pastry wheel gives a nice edge.) Transfer to ungreased baking sheet. Brush tops with cream or evaporated milk. Bake at 350° for 12-15 minutes. Do not overbake. Yields 30 appetizers.

▼ Freezes well. Will keep in an air-tight container.

Cheese Straws

1 pound New York State sharp
    cheese, grated
4 sticks corn oil margarine

4½ cups plain flour
¾ teaspoon cayenne pepper
salt, several dashes

Cream cheese and margarine together. Add flour, pepper and salt. Blend well. Squeeze through a cookie press onto an ungreased cookie sheet. Bake at 350° for 12-15 minutes. Yields 6 dozen straws.

▼ These freeze beautifully.

HOT FINGER FOOD

Cheese Puffs
Mrs. J. Cole, mother of Bobby Cole, South Africa

1 cup flour
2 teaspoons baking powder
¼ teaspoon cayenne pepper
1 egg

¾ cup milk
4 tablespoons vegetable oil
1 cup Cheddar cheese, grated

Sift dry ingredients together. Beat egg, milk and oil together. Add cheese to flour, then add egg mixture and mix to a very soft consistency. Put in patty tins and bake at 425° for about 10 minutes.

Easy Cheese Puffs

1 loaf unsliced white bread
1 3-ounce package cream cheese
4 ounces sharp Cheddar cheese, broken

1 stick butter or margarine
2 egg whites, beaten
dash of dry mustard, cayenne

Cut bread into 1-inch cubes. Melt cheeses and butter in double boiler. Fold egg whites and seasonings into mixture. Dip bread into cheese mixture. Put on cookie sheet and brown under broiler. Yields 60-80 puffs.

▼ To prepare ahead, place on cookie sheet and freeze. Place in plastic bags. Thaw to cook.

For an easy yet popular appetizer, serve hot pepper jelly on Roquefort, Brie or cream cheese with crackers.

Pierre's Stuffed Mushrooms
Chef Pierre, Firestone Country Club

2 pounds ground chuck
2 teaspoons salt
5 tablespoons parsley, minced
1½ teaspoons garlic salt
3 whole eggs

Breading mixture:
2 cups flour
½ teaspoon celery salt
½ teaspoon paprika
¼ teaspoon garlic salt
¼ teaspoon MSG

¾ to 1 cup fine bread crumbs
1 large onion, minced
3 stalks celery, minced
3 pounds medium mushrooms, stems removed

¼ teaspoon white pepper
2 cups Golden Dipt or fine bread crumbs
1½ cups milk
2 whole eggs

Season meat with salt, parsley, garlic salt, eggs and bread crumbs. Sauté onions, celery and 1 cup of chopped stems of mushrooms until soft. Add to meat mixture. Mix well. Stuff mushrooms with this mixture. Chill for 1 to 2 hours. Season flour with celery salt, paprika, garlic salt, MSG and pepper. Mix eggs with milk and beat. Take stuffed mushroom and gently put it in the flour mixture, then into the egg batter and then into Golden Dipt. Bread it well. Chill. Fry in deep fryer at 350° until golden brown. Drain on absorbent paper. Serve hot. Serves 50 at cocktails.

Hot Sausage Balls

1 pound hot sausage
1 16-ounce can shredded sauerkraut
3 ounces cream cheese, softened
1 egg, beaten

½ cup milk
¾ cup bread crumbs
1 tablespoon parsley (optional)

Crumble sausage. Cook and drain well. Drain sauerkraut and snip into pieces. Combine sausage, sauerkraut and cream cheese. Refrigerate until cool. Roll into balls. Dip each ball in egg and milk mixture. Roll in bread crumbs (may add parsley to crumbs for color). Bake at 350° for 10 minutes. Serve hot. Yields 30-40 balls.

Crab Meat Bacon Fingers

½ cup tomato juice
1 egg, beaten
1 cup dry bread crumbs
½ teaspoon salt
dash pepper
1 teaspoon parsley, chopped

1 teaspoon celery leaves, chopped
1 6½-ounce can crab meat, flaked
12 slices bacon, cut in half

Mix first 8 ingredients thoroughly. Roll into finger lengths and wrap each with ½ slice bacon. Secure with toothpicks. Broil until brown on all sides for about 10-15 minutes, turning several times. Drain on paper. Serve immediately. Yields 2 dozen.

May be frozen and baked at the last minute.

Bacon Roll-ups

¼ cup butter or margarine
½ cup water
1½ cups packaged herb stuffing mix

1 egg, slightly beaten
¼ pound bulk pork sausage
½ to ⅔ pound sliced bacon

Melt butter in water in a saucepan. Remove from heat; stir into stuffing, then add egg and sausage. Blend thoroughly. Chill for about an hour for easier handling. Shape into small oblongs. Cut bacon strips into thirds. Wrap bacon around dressing mixture and fasten with toothpicks. Place on rack in shallow pan. Bake at 375° for 35 minutes or until brown and crisp. Turn at halfway point in cooking. Drain. Serve hot. Yields 3 dozen.

13

Mushroom Puffs

Pastry:
3 ounces cream cheese,
  softened

½ cup butter, softened
1½ cups flour

Filling:
1 onion, minced
3 tablespoons butter
½ pound fresh mushrooms, minced
¼ teaspoon thyme

½ teaspoon salt
pepper to taste
2 tablespoons flour
¼ cup sour cream

For pastry, mix cheese and butter. Stir in flour and blend well. Chill. For filling, sauté onion in butter until golden. Add mushrooms and cook 3 minutes. Add seasonings. Sprinkle flour over mixture. Add sour cream. Cook until thickened. DO NOT BOIL. Roll chilled dough very thin on floured board. Cut 3-inch rounds and place 1 teaspoon filling on each. Fold edges over and press together. Prick with fork. Bake on ungreased sheet at 450° for 15 minutes. Yields 50 puffs.
▼ May be frozen before baking. Allow more time for baking.

Mushroom Appetizer

Croustades:
24 slices fresh thin-sliced
   white bread
1 3-inch plain cookie cutter

2 tablespoons butter, softened
2 12-muffin (miniature) tins

Mushroom filling:
3 tablespoons shallots, minced
4 tablespoons butter
½ pound mushrooms, minced
2 level tablespoons plain flour
1 cup whipping cream
½ teaspoon salt

⅛ teaspoon cayenne
1 tablespoon parsley, minced
1½ tablespoons chives, minced
½ teaspoon lemon juice
2 tablespoons grated
  Parmesan cheese

Croustades: Cut 3-inch rounds from each slice bread. Heavily butter muffin tins. Carefully fit bread into tins. Mold GENTLY from center. Bake at 400° for 10 minutes.
Mushroom filling: Sauté shallots in butter in heavy skillet for 4 minutes. Add mushrooms. Cook 10 to 15 minutes. Remove from heat. Sprinkle in flour and mix well. Add cream. Bring to boil stirring constantly. Simmer 2 minutes longer. Add remaining ingredients except Parmesan. Fill croustades mounding slightly. Top with cheese. Bake at 350° for 10 minutes before serving. Yields 24.
▼ Filling and croustades may be made ahead and frozen separately. Assemble just before baking.

Easy Sausage Swirls

2 8-ounce cans crescent
  dinner rolls

2 tablespoons hot mustard
1 pound hot pork sausage

Separate rolls into 4 rectangles and spread with mustard. Spread with thin layer of sausage. Roll and chill until ready to serve. Thinly slice each roll (10 swirls to a roll) and place on ungreased pan. Bake at 400° for 18-20 minutes. Serve hot. Yields 80 swirls.

Sausage Swirls

4 cups sifted flour
¼ cup cornmeal
¼ cup sugar
2 tablespoons baking powder

1 teaspoon salt
⅔ cup vegetable oil
⅔ to 1 cup milk
2 pounds hot bulk sausage

Sift dry ingredients together. Blend in oil. Add enough milk to make a stiff dough. Thinly roll out dough on lightly floured board into two 10x18-inch rectangles. Spread on sausage and roll up lengthwise. Chill well. Slice. Bake at 350° for 15-20 minutes. Yields 6 dozen.

Spinach Balls

2 10-ounce packages frozen
  chopped spinach
2-2½ cups packaged herb stuffing
¾ cup margarine or
  butter, melted
6 eggs

½ cup grated Parmesan cheese
2 small onions, minced
salt, pepper, garlic powder
  and thyme to taste

Cook and drain spinach VERY WELL. Combine all ingredients and roll into balls (1 teaspoon each). Bake at 350° for 20 minutes on greased cookie sheet. Remove from cookie sheet at once and drain on paper. Serve hot. Yields 75 balls.

▼ May be frozen after cooking. Reheat 3-5 minutes at 400°.

Sausage Stuffed Mushrooms

30-40 large, fresh mushrooms,
    stemmed
3 tablespoons butter, melted
1 pound bulk sausage, cooked

½ cup bread crumbs, toasted
½ cup pizza or spaghetti sauce
1 egg
Mozzarella cheese

Dip mushrooms in butter. Stuff with mixture of sausage, bread crumbs, sauce and egg. Top with a 1-inch square of sliced Mozzarella cheese. Bake at 425° for 15 minutes. Serve at once.

▼ Large canned mushrooms may be used.

Stuffed Mushrooms

½ pound medium mushrooms
½ cup onion, minced
2 cloves garlic, minced
2 tablespoons parsley, chopped
¾ teaspoon salt

¼ teaspoon oregano
½ cup butter
½ cup dry bread crumbs
¼ cup grated Parmesan cheese

Remove stems from mushrooms and chop finely. Sauté mushroom stems, onion, garlic, parsley, salt and oregano in butter until onion is tender. Stir in crumbs and cheese. Spoon mixture into mushroom caps and broil until tender (8 minutes). Serves 4-6.

CHAFING DISH

Artichoke Hearts

½ stick butter
2 ounces blue cheese

2 14-ounce cans artichoke
hearts, well drained

Melt butter and cheese together over low heat. Cut artichoke hearts into bite-size pieces. Add to cheese mixture. Serve in chafing dish. Serves 12.

Hot Artichoke Spread

1 14-ounce can artichoke hearts,
finely chopped
1 cup Hellmann's mayonnaise

6-8 ounces Parmesan cheese,
freshly grated
cayenne, Tabasco, salt to taste

Mix all thoroughly. Bake at 350° for 30 minutes. Serve warm in ovenproof dish with plain crackers. Serves 20-25.

Chicken Livers in Wine

1 pound chicken livers
½ cup plain flour
½ teaspoon pepper
¾ teaspoon salt

¼ cup salad oil
½ cup dry white wine
1 tablespoon Worcestershire

Wash, drain and section livers. Combine flour, pepper and salt. Coat livers with flour mixture. Sauté in oil until brown. Add wine and Worcestershire. Cover skillet tightly and simmer 30 minutes. Serve in chafing dish. Serves 8-10 for cocktails.

Cocktail Meatballs

Meatballs:

3 pounds ground beef
½ cup seasoned bread crumbs
2 onions, minced
4 teaspoons horseradish

4 garlic cloves, crushed
1½ cups tomato juice
4 teaspoons salt
pepper to taste

Sauce:

¼ cup butter or margarine
2 onions, chopped
¼ cup flour
3 cups beef broth
1 cup red wine
¼ cup brown sugar

¼ cup catsup
2 tablespoons lemon juice
6 ginger snaps, crumbled
   (optional)
2 teaspoons salt
pepper to taste

Combine all ingredients for meatballs and shape into one inch balls. Place on cookie sheet with sides and brown in oven for 10 minutes at 450°. Drain well. For sauce, melt butter in large skillet. Sauté onions until golden. Blend in flour. Add broth, stirring until smooth. Stir in remaining ingredients and simmer over low heat for 15 minutes. Add meatballs to hot sauce. Serve in chafing dish. Yields 100 meatballs.

▼ May freeze meatballs in sauce. To serve, heat covered in 300° oven.

Always serve cheese at room temperature.

Mock Oysters Rockefeller

2 10-ounce packages frozen
   chopped broccoli
1 medium onion, grated
½ pound fresh mushrooms, sliced
   (may use canned)
½ cup butter
1 10¾-ounce can condensed cream
   of mushroom soup

1 6-ounce roll garlic cheese
dash Tabasco
2 teaspoons lemon juice
1 teaspoon Worcestershire
sliced almonds (optional)
small patty shells or
   jumbo Fritos

Cook broccoli as directed. Drain well. Sauté onion and mushrooms in butter in heavy pan. Add soup. Mix with broccoli, cheese (crumbled) and seasonings. Allow cheese to melt. Add almonds. Serve hot from a chafing dish. Serve with patty shells or Fritos. Serves 25 for cocktails.

▼ Freezes well.

Rumaki

1 pound chicken livers
½ cup soy sauce
1 8-ounce can water chestnuts
¾ cup brown sugar
bacon

Marinate chicken livers, cut in bite-sized pieces, in soy sauce for several hours. Put piece of water chestnut in each piece of liver and roll in brown sugar. Wrap each piece in half strip of bacon. Secure with toothpick and roll in brown sugar again. Bake at 350° for 20-30 minutes.

▼Can freeze before cooking. Serve with bottled sweet and sour sauce.

Hot Crab Dip

8 ounces cream cheese, softened
1 tablespoon milk
1 tablespoon sauterne
2 teaspoons Worcestershire
2 tablespoons green onion, chopped
1 6½-ounce can crab meat or shrimp

In a small saucepan, combine first 4 ingredients and stir over heat until melted. Stir in onion and crab. Heat, stirring occasionally, on medium heat until blended. Reduce to low for holding. Serve in chafing dish with bland crackers. Yields 2 cups.

Sweet and Sour Sausage

2 pounds bulk sausage or cocktail sausage links
1¼ cups ketchup
¼ cup dark brown sugar
1 tablespoon soy sauce
1 tablespoon lemon juice
1 15-ounce can pineapple chunks, drained

Shape sausage in small balls. Fry at medium heat until golden and drain well on paper towels. Pour off grease. Return sausage to skillet and add all ingredients except pineapple. Simmer, covered, 10 minutes. Just before serving, add pineapple and put in chafing dish. Yields 5 dozen.

▼ Ground chuck may be substituted for sausage.
Delicious yet easy.

CANAPÉS & SANDWICHES

Tangy Toasted Cheese Sandwiches

1 pound sharp cheese, grated
1 teaspoon Worcestershire
dash Tabasco
juice of ½ lemon

1 medium onion, grated
salt to taste
bread
butter

Combine first 6 ingredients. Chill at least 24 hours. Have at room temperature before spreading. Make sandwiches, toast on each side and butter top before serving. Serve hot. Yields at least 10 sandwiches.
Good with hearty soup.

Ham-Asparagus Broil

4 slices bread, toasted on
  one side
2 teaspoons prepared mustard
4 slices ham
1 14½-ounce can asparagus
4 ounces Swiss cheese, grated

4 tablespoons green onions,
  chopped
2 tablespoons pimiento, chopped
1 tablespoon sesame seeds,
  toasted

Spread untoasted side of bread with mustard. Top with ham and asparagus. Combine remaining ingredients and sprinkle over asparagus. Broil until cheese melts, 2-3 minutes. Serves 4.

Hot Crab Meat Canapé

½ pound crab meat
6 tablespoons mayonnaise
½ teaspoon salt
½ teaspoon MSG
1 tablespoon onion, grated

2 tablespoons lemon juice
1 tablespoon Worcestershire
½ cup Parmesan, freshly grated
toast rounds
paprika

Combine first 8 ingredients. Spread on toast rounds and sprinkle with paprika. Place under broiler until bubbly and slightly brown (about 5-7 minutes). Yields 3 dozen.

Cucumber Sandwiches

2 cucumbers, peeled and chopped
1 small white onion, grated
½ cup slivered almonds, toasted and finely chopped

salt and pepper to taste
mayonnaise to bind
bread with crusts removed

Drain cucumbers well. Mix with next 4 ingredients. DRAIN AGAIN. Spread at last minute and cut into finger sandwiches.

Turkey Delight

2 .3-ounce packages smoked turkey or 2 cups turkey, chopped
1 apple, unpeeled and chopped
1 small onion, finely chopped
6 ounces Swiss cheese, grated

½ cup walnuts, chopped
mayonnaise
salt and pepper to taste
delicatessen rolls or French bread, buttered

Bind first 5 ingredients with mayonnaise. Season to taste. Spread on rolls. Wrap tightly in foil. Bake at 350° for 20 minutes. Serves 4-6.

Cheese Mushroom Puffs

16 pieces white bread
2 tablespoons butter, melted
2 3-ounce cans mushroom buttons
4 hard-boiled egg yolks, grated

1 3-ounce package cream cheese, softened
dash paprika
dash red pepper

Cut rounds from bread (2 per slice) and brush with butter on one side. Toast on buttered side. Place a mushroom on untoasted side. Mix remaining ingredients and put teaspoon of mixture on each mushroom. Place under broiler until it puffs. Serve at once. Yields 32 puffs.

Hot Onion Canapé

½ cup onion, minced
½ cup mayonnaise
4 drops Tabasco

1 teaspoon paprika
salt and pepper to taste
32 saltine crackers

Combine first 5 ingredients and spread on saltines. Brown on top rack at 400° until bubbly. Yields 32.
Easy yet delicious.

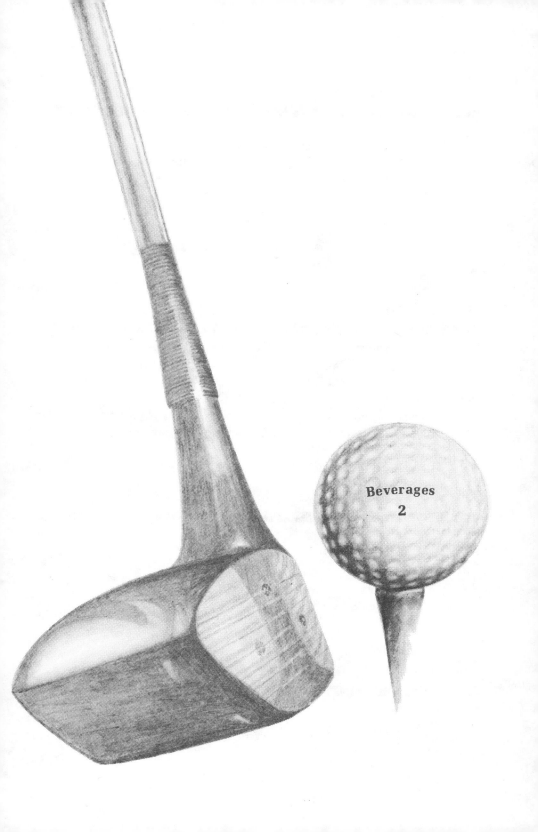

Masters' Saturday Morning Bloody Bull

1 quart tomato juice
1 10½-ounce can beef bouillon
1 teaspoon salt
½ teaspoon black pepper
1 tablespoon Lea and Perrins
  Worcestershire

¼ teaspoon Tabasco
1 tablespoon lime juice
2 tablespoons lemon juice
dash MSG
dash celery seed

Combine all ingredients and chill. Put large jigger of vodka or gin over ice in glass, and add above mixture. Yields 8-10 (6-8 ounce) servings.

Bloody Mary

1 quart Clamato juice
1 cup vodka
2 lemons, juice and rinds
¾ teaspoon salt

¼ teaspoon pepper
6 dashes Tabasco
lemon-pepper
lime slices

Combine first 6 ingredients, stir, and chill 1 hour. Fill glasses with ice, sprinkle with lemon-pepper. Pour liquid. Garnish with limes. Yields 6-8 drinks.

Bull Shot

2 ounces vodka
5 ounces cold beef bouillon
  (½ soup can)

dash Tabasco
dash salt
celery or cucumber stick

Mix first 4 ingredients. Pour over ice in 8-ounce glass and garnish with celery or cucumber stick. Yields 1 drink.

Milk Punch

4 scoops rich vanilla ice cream
2 cups milk
1 teaspoon vanilla

3 ounces bourbon
nutmeg, grated

Put all ingredients except nutmeg in blender. Blend on high 10 seconds. Pour in highball glasses. Sprinkle nutmeg on top. Yields 2 drinks.

Peach Fuzz Buzz

1 large ripe peach,
  chopped
6 ounces gin or vodka

1 6-ounce can frozen pink
  lemonade concentrate
2 cups ice, cracked

Put all ingredients in blender. Blend well. Serve in champagne glasses. Yields
5-6 drinks.
Delicious summer drink.

Sugar does not dissolve well in alcohol. Add it to water or fruit juice first.

Rhine Wine Aperitif

2 oranges
1 lemon
½ cup pineapple juice
¼ cup pineapple preserves
¼ cup sugar

2 bottles Rhine wine, chilled
8 pineapple wedges
8 orange slices
8 mint sprigs

Cut peels of oranges and lemon into narrow strips. In a saucepan, cover strips
with water and blanch about 1 minute. Drain. Add strips to juice of oranges and
lemon, pineapple juice, preserves and sugar. Bring to a boil and simmer 5
minutes. Cool. Chill. Mix with wine and serve over ice in 8-ounce stemmed
glasses. Garnish with pineapple wedge, orange slice, and mint. Yields 8
8-ounce drinks.

Red Sangria

1 cup sugar
6 quarts red wine or rosé
6 ounces Triple Sec
6 ounces brandy
juice of 6 lemons
juice of 6 oranges

1 apple, thinly sliced
1 fresh peach, thinly sliced
1 orange, thinly sliced
36 ounces club soda
garnish: fruit slices

Dissolve sugar in wine. Add Triple Sec, brandy, juices, apple slices, peach
slices and orange slices. Let stand overnight in refrigerator. Immediately before serving, add soda and mix well. Pour over cracked ice in tumblers. Garnish. Serves 25.

Ruby Red Punch

¼ cup sugar
½ cup boiling water
1 pint cranberry juice
1 cup orange juice

¼ cup lemon juice
1 fifth white champagne
   (or 2 7-ounce bottles of
   ginger ale)

Boil sugar in water until dissolved. Add juices, mix and chill. Just before serving, add champagne. Yields 15 4-ounce servings.
Lovely Christmas punch.

To make a Spritzer, drop a lemon peel spiral in a highball glass. Add 2 or 3 ice cubes, 6 ounces dry white wine, and 4 ounces club soda.

Sherry Punch

2 fifths dry sherry, chilled
1 16-ounce bottle whiskey sour mix

maraschino cherries
mint sprigs

Combine sherry and sour mix. Pour over ice ring in punch bowl or ice cubes in glasses. Garnish with cherries and mint. Serves 10-12.
"Potent!"

White Sangria

1 orange
1 fifth dry white wine
2 slices lemon
2 slices lime
1 ounce cognac

2 tablespoons sugar
1 stick cinnamon
8 large strawberries, hulled
   and halved
6 ounces club soda, chilled

Cut entire peel of orange in a single strip, beginning at stem end and continuing until spiral reaches bottom of fruit. White part should be cut along with outer peel, so that orange fruit is exposed. Carefully place orange in glass pitcher, fastening top end of peel over rim. Pour wine into pitcher. Add lemon, lime, cognac, sugar, cinnamon and strawberries. Stir gently to dissolve sugar. Let mixture sit at room temperature at least 1 hour. Add soda and 1 tray of ice cubes immediately before serving and stir. Serves 4-6.

Christmas Champagne Punch

2 fifths claret
2 fifths pink champagne

2 28-ounce bottles
ginger ale

Chill well before mixing. Just before serving, place large pieces of ice in a punch bowl. Add all ingredients and mix gently. Serve in champagne glasses. Yields 36 4-ounce servings.
Good all year long!

Coffee Punch

1 gallon strong hot coffee
½ cup sugar
1 quart whipping cream, whipped

2 quarts vanilla ice cream
whipping cream, whipped

Sweeten coffee with sugar. Let coffee cool. Add 1 quart whipped cream and ice cream to very cold coffee. Float more whipped cream on top. Serves 16-20.

▼ May add 1 teaspoon each vanilla extract and almond extract, if desired.

Hot Spiced Tea Mix

2⅓ cups orange breakfast drink
   powder
1¼ cups instant dry tea
½-1 cup sugar (to taste)

1-2 packages (5¾-ounces)
   lemonade mix (to taste)
2 teaspoons cinnamon
2 teaspoons ground cloves

Mix all ingredients together. Store in an air-tight container. Use 2 heaping teaspoons for each cup of boiling water.

▼ Add bourbon at end of day.

Iced Spiced Tea

2 cups sugar
2 cups water
1 quart hot water
8 tea bags

2 quarts cold water
2 cups orange juice
¾ cup lemon juice
garnish: mint sprigs

Boil sugar and 2 cups water for five minutes. Add hot water and tea bags. Steep for 5 minutes. Discard tea bags. Add remaining ingredients, mixing thoroughly. Serve over ice. Garnish. Yields 1 gallon.

Egg Nog I

12 egg yolks
pinch of salt
¾ cup sugar

1-2 cups bourbon or dark rum
12 egg whites, stiffly beaten
1 pint whipping cream, whipped

In a bowl, beat yolks adding salt and sugar slowly. Add bourbon or rum very slowly while beating. Fold in whites, then fold in cream. Chill before serving. Yields approximately 2 quarts.

Egg Nog II

24 eggs, separated
2 pounds powdered sugar
2 pints brandy
1 pint light rum

1 pint peach brandy
6 pints milk
2 pints whipping cream
nutmeg, grated

Beat yolks with sugar. SLOWLY add brandy, rum and peach brandy. Stir in milk and cream. Beat egg whites until stiff. Fold into egg nog. DO NOT STIR. Top with nutmeg. Yields 35 6-ounce servings.

Rum Louis

1 ounce light rum
1 ounce dark rum
2 ounces canned mixed pineapple
  and grapefruit juice

2 ounces orange juice
juice of 1 lemon
orange slices
maraschino cherries

Combine all liquids and serve over cracked ice. Garnish with orange slice and cherry. Yields 1 drink.

Wine Sherbet Cooler

1 quart lemon sherbet (may use
  lime, orange or pineapple)
12 ounces chablis

1 12-ounce can diet lemon-lime
  soda

Mix half the sherbet, wine and soda in blender. Blend on high speed 15 seconds. Pour into glasses and repeat. Serves 8 6-ounce old-fashioned glasses.

▼ This is just as good without wine. Just double the amount of soda.

May be made in larger quantity and served in punch bowl.

Holiday Wassail

3 large oranges
72 whole cloves
1 gallon apple juice
½ cup lemon juice

10 cinnamon sticks
2 cups vodka
¼ cup brandy

Stud oranges with cloves. Bake uncovered in shallow pan at 350° for 30 minutes. Heat apple juice until bubbly at edge. Add lemon juice, cinnamon sticks and baked oranges. Simmer, covered, 30 minutes. Remove from heat. Add vodka and brandy. Mix well. Use oranges and cinnamon sticks as garnish in punch bowl. Serve warm. Serves 36 4-ounce cups.
A festive, Christmas punch.

Hot Buttered Rum Mix

1 stick margarine (not butter)
1 pound light brown sugar
1 heaping teaspoon cinnamon
1 heaping teaspoon nutmeg

½ teaspoon angostura bitters
⅛ teaspoon ground allspice
¼ teaspoon ground ginger
dark rum

Mix all ingredients except rum thoroughly. Refrigerate until ready to use. For drink: combine 1 heaping teaspoon mix, 2 ounces dark rum and about 4 ounces boiling water.
▼ Will keep in refrigerator for several months.

Mint Julep

Syrup:
3 cups sugar
1 cup water

fresh mint sprigs

Beverage:
crushed ice
3 ounces whiskey, per glass
stemmed cherries

powdered sugar
garnish: mint sprigs

To make syrup, add sugar to water in a 2 quart saucepan. Fill pan to top with mint. Boil about 5 minutes or until syrup is green. Strain mixture into bottle. Chill. For one mint julep, fill 10-ounce glass with crushed ice. Add 3 ounces whiskey and 1 ounce prepared syrup. Top with a cherry which has been coated with powdered sugar. Garnish. Syrup should be prepared ahead and chilled.

"Stymie"
Royal and Ancient Golf Club of St. Andrews, Fife, Scotland

Take a 24, 25 or 26 ounce bottle (e.g., an empty whiskey bottle). Put in ½ bottle of gin, approximately 13 ounces. Add practically 11 ounces Martini or Cinzano Bianco (dry vermouth). Add 2 ounces brandy (Hennessy or Martel). Colour with Martini or Cinzano Rosso (sweet vermouth) until contents are the colour of whiskey.

Serve with ice (on the rocks) with a slice of lemon. This is normally served in a measure of 2 ounces. Yields 13 2-ounce drinks.
▼ Should be prepared at least 48 hours before use.

Frozen Banana Daiquiri

1 6-ounce can frozen limeade concentrate
6 ounces light rum
1 or 2 bananas to taste
1 tray ice cubes, crushed
maraschino cherries

Place first 4 ingredients in blender. Blend until consistency of snow. Serve topped with a cherry. Serves 4.
▼ May substitute peaches or strawberries for bananas.

For a delicious drink, a Kir, mix 1 tablespoon cassis with 6 ounces dry white wine. Serve over ice cubes with a twist of lemon peel.

Sun Ray Fizz
Del Monte Lodge, Pebble Beach, California

2 ounces half-and-half
2 ounces fresh orange juice
1 ounce Holland House Sweet and Sour Mix
1½ ounces gin
½ teaspoon vanilla
1 egg white
2 tablespoons sugar (or to taste)
¾ cup crushed ice
garnish: ¼ of fresh orange

Mix above ingredients well in a blender. Garnish. Yields 1 drink.
One of the more popular drinks at Del Monte Lodge.

Golden Dream

1 ounce Galliano	½ ounce orange juice
½ ounce Triple Sec or Cointreau	½ ounce cream

Mix all ingredients. Shake well with cracked ice. Strain into cocktail glass. Yields 1 drink.

Fruits used in beverages should be fully ripe, especially when used in a milk drink.

Irish Coffee

1½ ounces Irish whiskey	sugar
black coffee, hot and strong	whipped cream

Pour Irish whiskey into stemmed glass or mug. Fill to within ½ inch of brim with black coffee. Add sugar to taste and stir well. Top with whipped cream. DO NOT STIR. Flavor is obtained by drinking coffee and whiskey through the cream. Yields 1 drink.

▼ Sanka may be substituted for coffee and Cool Whip for cream.

Use freshly drawn cold water to brew coffee. Never boil coffee.

Velvet Hammer

1 pint rich vanilla ice cream	1½ ounces brandy
1 ounce Cointreau	1 ounce white crème de cacao

Combine all ingredients in blender. Blend well. Yields 2 drinks.

Soups

3

Bouillabaisse

⅓ cup olive oil
2 cups onion, diced
½ cup celery, sliced
2 cloves garlic, minced
½ medium green pepper, diced
3-4 carrots, sliced, pre-cooked
1 16-ounce can tomatoes
1 16-ounce can tomato sauce or
    tomato juice
1 teaspoon thyme

1 bay leaf
2 tablespoons parsley, chopped
1 teaspoon basil, crumbled
1 teaspoon salt
1 teaspoon black pepper
1 pound fresh shrimp, cleaned
½ pound scallops, fresh or frozen
1 cup dry white wine
6½ ounces crabmeat, fresh, frozen
    or canned

In a large kettle, heat oil and sauté onion, celery, garlic, green pepper and carrots. Stir in tomatoes, tomato sauce, seasonings, shrimp and scallops. Bring to a boil. Simmer 30-60 minutes. Add wine and crabmeat. Warm only. Serves 6.

▼ May be frozen.

Isle of Hope Crabmeat Soup

1 pound crabmeat, fresh, frozen
    or canned
2 hard-boiled eggs
2 cups milk
3 tablespoons margarine
3 tablespoons flour
2 tablespoons onion, chopped
¼ cup celery, diced

¼ cup butter
½ lemon
¼ teaspoon MSG
8 whole allspice
salt and pepper to taste
1 cup whipping cream
2 cups milk
¼ cup sherry or more to taste

Flake crabmeat and remove shell fragments. Chop egg whites and yolks separately and set aside. Make a thin white sauce of 2 cups milk, margarine and flour. Set aside. In a 2-quart saucepan, sauté onion and celery in butter for 5 minutes. Add crabmeat, lemon and seasonings. Cook slowly for 10 minutes, covered. Add cream, white sauce, milk and chopped egg whites. Heat slowly. DO NOT BOIL. When ready to serve, remove lemon and allspice (count them). Add chopped egg yolks and sherry. Serve at once. Serves 4-5.

A meal with salad and dessert.

31

Crab Bisque

1 10¾-ounce can condensed
   cream of mushroom soup
1 10½-ounce can condensed
   cream of asparagus soup
1½ soup cans milk

1 cup half-and-half
1 7½-ounce can (1 cup)
   crabmeat, flaked
¼ cup dry white wine
   or dry sherry

Blend soups. Stir in milk and cream. Heat just to boiling. Add crab. Heat through. Stir in wine just before serving. Serves 6-8.

She Crab Soup

"Town Tavern," Augusta, Georgia

2 tablespoons butter
2 tablespoons plain flour
1 quart milk
2 cups white lump crabmeat
½ teaspoon salt

⅛ teaspoon pepper
4 tablespoons dry sherry
4 hard-boiled egg yolks,
   finely crumbled

Melt butter in top of double boiler. Blend in flour. Add milk gradually, stirring constantly. As mixture begins to thicken, add crabmeat, salt and pepper. When soup is of preferred consistency, remove from heat. Add sherry. Garnish with egg yolks. Yields 1 quart.

Velvet Corn Soup

¼ cup onion, finely chopped
¼ cup butter
3 cups fresh corn
   (approximately 6 ears)

4 cups half-and-half
1 egg, beaten
salt and pepper to taste
3 tablespoons sherry (optional)

Sauté onions in butter until soft. Add corn, cream and egg. Cook until mixture begins to boil, stirring constantly (about 3-4 minutes). Add seasonings. Let cool slightly. Put in blender and whip until creamy. Strain, reheat and adjust seasonings. DO NOT OVERHEAT. Add sherry if desired. May be served cold. Serves 8-10

Cream of Broccoli Soup
Martha Fleming, "The Cookery," Augusta, Georgia

1 bunch fresh broccoli or
  2 10-ounce packages frozen
  broccoli
3 cups chicken stock
½ onion, chopped
4 tablespoons butter

5 tablespoons flour
half-and-half cream
salt, white pepper to taste
garnish: paprika, croutons
  and parsley

Cook broccoli in stock with onion until soft. Place in blender and blend quickly. Leave small pieces of broccoli. Make a roux using butter and flour. Cook 3 minutes, stirring constantly. Add broccoli and stock to roux. To avoid lumps, stir constantly until thickened. Thin to preferred consistency with cream. Add seasonings. Garnish. Serves 6.

Cream of Carrot Soup

1 cup carrots, sliced
1 medium onion, sliced
1 rib celery with leaves, sliced
1½ cups chicken broth

1 teaspoon salt
pinch cayenne pepper
½ cup cooked rice
¾ cup whipping cream

Put carrots, onion, celery and ½ cup broth in a pan. Bring to a boil. Simmer uncovered for 15 minutes, cover and simmer 15 more minutes. Place in blender with salt, pepper and rice. Blend until smooth. Blend in remaining broth. Return to pan, heat, and add cream. DO NOT BOIL. Serves 6.

Cream of Cauliflower Soup
Martha Fleming, "The Cookery," Augusta, Georgia

1 head cauliflower, washed
3 cups chicken stock
4 tablespoons butter
5 tablespoons flour

salt, white pepper, nutmeg
  to taste
half-and-half cream
garnish: paprika, parsley

Chop cauliflower into small pieces. Cook in stock until tender. Blend cauliflower and stock in blender until smooth. Make a roux, using butter and flour. Cook 3 minutes, stirring constantly. Add cauliflower mixture. Add seasonings. Thin to preferred consistency with cream. Garnish. Serves 6.

▼ If texture is preferred, reserve about ½ cup flowerets, chop and cook separately. Add to finished soup.

33

Cream of Pimiento Soup
Martha Fleming, "The Cookery," Augusta, Georgia

2 7-ounce cans pimientos
  and juice

3 cups whole milk
2 chicken bouillon cubes

garnish with one of the following: sour cream, red caviar, chopped shrimp, paprika or parsley

Blend pimientos, juice and milk in blender until smooth. Heat mixture gently. Add bouillon cubes and stir until dissolved. Garnish. Serves 4-6.

▼ Prolonged heat will curdle soup. Run soup through blender to smooth again.

Quick and easy.

Creamy Potato Soup

6 slices bacon
1 cup onion, chopped
2 cups potatoes, cubed
1 cup water
1 teaspoon salt

2 10¾-ounce cans condensed
  cream of mushroom soup
2 soup cans milk
2 tablespoons parsley, snipped

In a saucepan, cook bacon until crisp; set bacon aside. Pour off all but 3 tablespoons fat. Add onion and brown. Add potatoes and water. Cook covered 15 minutes or until potatoes are tender. Stir in salt, soup and milk. Heat but DO NOT BOIL. Garnish with bacon and parsley. Serves 4.

This is a hearty soup.

Cream of Spinach Soup
Martha Fleming, "The Cookery," Augusta, Georgia

2 10-ounce packages frozen
  chopped spinach
⅓ cup onion, chopped
3 cups chicken stock
4 tablespoons butter
5 tablespoons flour

1 cup half-and-half
½-1 teaspoon tarragon
1 scant teaspoon salt
⅛ teaspoon white pepper
garnish: chopped egg,
  bacon bits or croutons

Cook spinach with onion in chicken stock until just tender. (Overcooking will make spinach lose its bright green color.) Blend until smooth. Make a roux, using butter and flour. Cook 3 minutes stirring constantly. Add blended mixture. Thin to preferred consistency with cream. Add remaining seasonings. Garnish. Serves 6-8.

Cold Avocado Soup

1 cup half-and-half
1 10¾-ounce can condensed
   cream of chicken soup
dash Worcestershire
½ teaspoon salt
¼ teaspoon white pepper

¼ teaspoon MSG
¼ teaspoon ground nutmeg
3 ripe medium avocados
⅓ medium white onion, chopped
garnish: sour cream and
   chopped chives

Mix first 7 ingredients together. Chill well. Just before serving, prepare avocados. Place in blender with onion and above mixture. Blend well. Garnish with dollop of sour cream and chives. Serves 6-8.

Cucumber Soup

1 medium cucumber, peeled
   and sliced
1 10¾-ounce can condensed cream
   of chicken soup
¾ cup milk

1 cup sour cream
celery salt, pepper to taste
dash curry powder
garnish: fresh chives

Put cucumber, soup, milk, sour cream and seasonings in blender. Blend 1 minute. Chill several hours. To serve, stir, and pour into small bowls or cups. Garnish. Serves 6.

Gazpacho

4 cups tomatoes, strained, or
   4 cups V-8 juice
½ cucumber, peeled and chopped
1 onion, chopped
1 bell pepper, chopped
⅓ cup olive or vegetable oil
⅓ cup red wine vinegar
1½ teaspoons salt

⅛ teaspoon black pepper
⅛ teaspoon paprika
1 clove garlic, chopped
3 tablespoons lemon or lime
   juice
½ teaspoon red pimiento
1 teaspoon chives, chopped
¼ teaspoon Worcestershire

garnish: lemon slice, chopped cucumbers, croutons, bacon bits, parsley and chopped hard-boiled eggs

Blend tomatoes in blender and set aside. Combine remaining ingredients and blend in blender. Add to tomatoes. Chill several hours. To serve, top with lemon and cucumber. Pass garnish in separate bowls. Serves 6.

White Gazpacho

1 10¾-ounce can chicken broth
3 spring onions
few sprigs of parsley
1 8-ounce carton sour cream

2 tomatoes, finely chopped
1 large cucumber, finely chopped
salt and pepper to taste
slivered almonds, toasted

In blender, mix first 3 ingredients on medium high. Add sour cream and blend on low. Remove from blender. Add tomatoes and cucumber. Season to taste. Serve ice cold garnished with almonds. Serves 4.

▼ Better if made the day before.

Mock Vichyssoise

2 13¾-ounce cans chicken broth
2 10¾-ounce cans cream of
   potato soup

2 8-ounce cartons sour cream
2 teaspoons onions, finely minced
garnish: chopped chives

Combine broth, soup, sour cream and onion. Chill for several hours. Garnish generously. Serves 8.
Better than the real thing!

Minestrone

2 pounds boneless chuck, cut
   into small cubes
2 tablespoons salt, divided
1 16-ounce can peeled tomato
   wedges, undrained
1 medium onion, chopped
2 stalks celery, cut into
   ½ inch pieces
½ cup parsley, divided
½ teaspoon oregano

⅛ teaspoon pepper
1 clove garlic, minced
2 cups zucchini, sliced
2 cups cut green beans
1 cup carrots, sliced
1 cup cabbage, chopped
2 cups tomato juice
1 cup elbow macaroni, uncooked
1 cup grated Parmesan cheese,
   divided

Put meat in heavy saucepan. Cover with 2½ quarts boiling water. Add 1 tablespoon salt and simmer until meat is tender. Remove meat from broth. Add 1 tablespoon salt, tomatoes, onion, celery, ¼ cup parsley, oregano, pepper and garlic to broth. Simmer 20 minutes stirring occasionally. Add meat, remaining vegetables, tomato juice and macaroni. Simmer 30 minutes or until vegetables are tender. Before serving, add remaining parsley and ½ cup cheese. Use remaining cheese as garnish. Serves 10.

▼ Can be frozen.
A meal by itself.

Onion Soup Gratiné
Augusta Country Club

3 pounds onions, thinly sliced
¾ cup butter
1 tablespoon plain flour
6 cups Campbell's beef broth
  (48 ounces)
⅓ cup dry red wine
½ teaspoon thyme, crushed

salt and pepper to taste
8 thick slices French Bread,
  toasted
1½ cups Muenster cheese, grated
1½ cups Swiss cheese, grated
½ cup grated Parmesan cheese

In a large heavy saucepan, sauté onions in butter 40-45 minutes, until caramel-colored. Sprinkle flour over onions and cook, stirring, 2 minutes. Stir in broth, wine, thyme, salt and pepper. Cover and simmer 30 minutes. Divide the soup in 8 flameproof bowls or ramekins. Top each bowl with a slice of French bread, topped with 3 tablespoons each of Muenster and Swiss cheese, then 1 tablespoon Parmesan cheese. Put under broiler 1-2 minutes, or until cheese melts and is lightly browned. Serves 8.

Harbor Chowder
Pinehurst Country Club, Pinehurst, North Carolina

4 ounces salt pork, diced in
  ¼-inch cubes or 6 slices
  bacon, diced
1 onion, finely diced
1 carrot, finely diced
2 stalks celery, finely diced
1 pint fresh clams, minced, or
  1 quart whole clams
flour

4 tablespoons butter, melted
1 quart water
½ cup dry white wine
1 teaspoon caraway seeds
6 medium potatoes, diced
1 quart half-and-half (hot)
3 teaspoons salt (or to taste)
¼ teaspoon white pepper
  (or to taste)

Place salt pork or bacon in heavy bottomed pot. Render over medium heat for 3-4 minutes. Add onion, carrot and celery. Sauté until onion is tender. In a small pot, bring clams and their juice to a quick boil. Set aside. Stir enough flour into butter to make a paste as thick as heavy cream. Add to vegetables. Cook, stirring constantly, for 1-2 minutes. Add juice from clams plus 1 quart water, wine and caraway seeds. Stir well. Simmer 30 minutes stirring occasionally to prevent vegetables from sticking. Add potatoes. Simmer 30 minutes. Add clams and cook until potatoes are done. Add cream. Season to taste. Yield ½ gallon (10-12 servings).
▼ This can be halved.

Mock Turtle Soup

1 pound veal, cut into 1-inch cubes
1 cup shortening
1 cup onions, diced
1 cup celery, diced
6 cloves garlic, chopped
1 cup flour (browned in oven)
1 15-ounce can tomato sauce
3 quarts warm water
2 ounces Bovril beef broth base
2 teaspoons celery salt
4 bay leaves
12 cloves
1 teaspoon thyme
½ cup parsley, chopped
⅓ cup Lea and Perrins Worcestershire
salt and pepper to taste
1 cup dry sherry

garnish: 2 lemons, thinly sliced and 2 hard-boiled eggs, chopped

Sauté veal in shortening until very brown. Add onions, celery, and garlic. Cook 10 minutes. Blend in flour and cook 5 minutes. Slowly add tomato sauce, water and broth base. Add all ingredients except sherry, and simmer about 2 hours or until soup is thick and meat is tender and shreds. Just before serving, add sherry and heat a few minutes. Discard bay leaves and cloves. Garnish. Serves 16. May be frozen.

To brown flour, place flour in pan and bake at 350° for about 10-15 minutes or until light brown. Stir occasionally.

Bovril broth base can be found in specialty shops and gourmet shops.
A hearty, spicy soup!

Black Bean Soup

4 cups black beans
3 stalks celery, finely chopped
3 large onions, finely chopped
½ cup butter (not margarine)
2½ tablespoons flour
½ cup parsley, finely chopped
rind and bone of a cooked smoked ham
3 leeks, thinly sliced
2 bay leaves
salt to taste
freshly ground pepper
1 cup dry Madeira
garnish: thin lemon slices

Soak beans overnight in enough cold water to cover. Drain. Add 5 quarts cold water and cook beans on low heat for 1½ hours. In a soup kettle, sauté celery and onion in butter. Blend in flour and parsley. Cook, stirring, for 1 minute. Gradually stir in beans and liquid. Add ham rind and bone, leeks, bay leaves, salt and pepper. Simmer 4 hours. Remove and discard rind, bone and bay leaves. Force beans through a sieve. Combine beans, broth and Madeira. Heat soup. Garnish. Yields approximately 6 quarts.

Senate Bean Soup

1½ cups dry Idaho Great
   Northern beans
1 smoked ham hock
1 medium potato, finely chopped
1 onion, chopped

½ cup celery, chopped
1 clove garlic, minced
salt and pepper to taste
garnish: parsley, chopped

Soak beans overnight in 1 quart of water. Drain beans and measure water, adding enough water to make 2 quarts. Place beans, water and ham hock in kettle. Cover and simmer for 2 hours. Add potato, onion, celery and garlic. Simmer 1 hour. Remove ham hock and cut up meat. Remove 1 cup of beans and some liquid and puree in blender. Return meat and beans to soup. Heat. Season to taste. Garnish. Serves 8.

Dutch Pea Soup

3 pounds pork spareribs
1 pound dried split peas
2 quarts water
½ cup onion, chopped
4 teaspoons salt

⅛ teaspoon pepper
1 16-ounce can tomatoes
2 cups cabbage, chopped
½ teaspoon celery seed
½ teaspoon thyme

Cut spareribs into serving pieces. Place spareribs, peas, water, onion, salt and pepper in Dutch oven. Cover and bring to a boil. Simmer 2 hours. Cool, then chill in refrigerator 6 hours or more to allow fat to harden. Remove fat and bones and discard. Add remaining ingredients, cover, and bring to a boil. Simmer ½ hour or until cabbage is tender. Serves 8-10.

Peanut Soup
Mrs. Rosalynn Carter

¼ cup yellow onion, finely
   chopped
1 tablespoon butter
½ cup creamy peanut butter

1 10¾-ounce can condensed
   cream of chicken soup
2¼ cups milk, room temperature
¼ cup salted peanuts, chopped

garnish: chopped salted peanuts, parsley sprigs and paprika

Sauté onion in butter until tender but not browned. Fold in peanut butter. Cook several minutes more. Blend in soup and milk. Add peanuts. Heat thoroughly. DO NOT BOIL. Garnish. Serves 6.

Salads,
Salad Dressing
4

Apricot Salad

1 17-ounce can apricots, drained
and quartered (reserve juice)
1 4-ounce bottle maraschino
cherries, halved (reserve
juice)

¼ cup cider vinegar
3 sticks cinnamon
1 tablespoon whole cloves
1 3-ounce package lemon gelatin
1 cup nuts, chopped.

Add enough water to apricot juice, cherry juice and vinegar to make 2 cups liquid. Simmer with cinnamon and cloves for 15 minutes. Cover. Strain. Add gelatin and stir until dissolved. Cool. Add fruits and nuts. Pour into individual molds. Chill. Serves 4-6.
Delicious served with Poppyseed Dressing (see index).

Bing Cherry Salad

1 3-ounce box lemon gelatin
1 17-ounce can pitted dark
sweet cherries (reserve
juice and add enough water
to make 1¾ cups liquid)

1½ teaspoons unflavored gelatin
¼ cup cold water
½ cup dry sherry
juice of 1 lemon
1 cup pecans or walnuts, chopped

Dissolve lemon gelatin in heated juice. Soften unflavored gelatin in cold water. Add to juice. When cool, add sherry and lemon juice. Chill until slightly thick. Add cherries and nuts. Chill until firm. Serve on lettuce with home-made mayonnaise. Serves 8.

Strawberry-Sour Cream Salad

2 3-ounce packages strawberry
gelatin
2 cups boiling water
2 10-ounce packages frozen
strawberries, not drained

1½ cups crushed pineapple, drained
2 large bananas, sliced
1 cup sour cream
1 cup nuts, chopped

Dissolve gelatin in boiling water in large bowl. Add strawberries, pineapple and bananas. Stir well. Pour half of mixture into 8x8x2-inch pan. Chill until firm. Combine sour cream and nuts. Spread over chilled gelatin mixture. Cover with remaining gelatin mixture that is at room temperature. Chill*. Cut in squares to serve. Serves 10-12. *Do not prepare more than 1 day in advance because bananas will darken.

Old-Fashioned Cranberry Salad

1 tablespoon unflavored gelatin
¼ cup cold water
2 cups boiling water
1 6-ounce box raspberry gelatin
1 3-ounce box orange gelatin
1 pound fresh cranberries
3 cups water

½ to ¾ cup sugar (optional)
grated rind of 1-2 oranges
4 oranges, sectioned
1 20-ounce can crushed
    pineapple, undrained
3 cups celery, finely chopped
1 cup pecans, chopped

Soften unflavored gelatin in ¼ cup cold water. In large bowl, pour boiling water over other gelatin. Stir in unflavored gelatin until all is dissolved. In blender, chop cranberries using 3 cups water. Add to gelatin along with remaining ingredients. Pour into 2 9x9-inch pans. Chill until firm. Serves 18.
A colorful holiday salad!

Always sprinkle gelatin on top of a cold liquid, then dissolve in a hot liquid.

Spiced Peach Salad

4 oranges, peeled, sectioned, and
    chopped (reserve ½ cup juice)
1 28-ounce jar spiced peaches,
    chopped (reserve juice)

2 3-ounce packages lemon gelatin
½ cup pecans, chopped
⅓ cup maraschino cherries,
    chopped

Prepare oranges. Heat peach juice and pour over gelatin to dissolve. Add all ingredients. Pour into 2-quart mold. Chill until firm. Serves 12.

Creamy Lime Salad

1 3-ounce package lime gelatin
1 5.3-ounce can evaporated milk
1 8¼-ounce can crushed pineapple,
    undrained
1 tablespoon lemon juice

1 cup cream-style cottage cheese
½ cup broken nuts (optional)
½ cup celery, finely cut
½ cup mayonnaise

Dissolve gelatin in ¾ cup boiling water. Cool slightly, then stir in milk. Chill until thick but not set. Stir in remaining ingredients. Pour in 8-inch square pan or mold. Chill until firm. Serves 8.

Molded Asparagus Salad

¾ cup sugar
½ cup vinegar
1 cup water
1 teaspoon salt
2 envelopes unflavored gelatin,
   dissolved in ½ cup cold water

1 tablespoon onion, minced
1 5-ounce can water chestnuts,
   thinly sliced
1 cup celery, chopped
1 14½-ounce can cut green
   asparagus, drained
1 4-ounce jar pimientos, sliced

Combine sugar, vinegar, water and salt. Bring to a boil and dissolve sugar. Remove from heat. Add gelatin and onion to boiled mixture. Cool. Combine remaining ingredients and add to liquid. Pour mixture in large greased mold or individual molds. Chill. Serves 6-8.

For salads, use cider vinegar unless otherwise indicated.

Cucumber Ring Mold

2 envelopes unflavored gelatin
¼ cup cold water
1 8-ounce package cream cheese
2 cups cucumbers, pared, grated
   and drained

1 cup mayonnaise
¼ cup onion, finely minced
¼ cup parsley, finely minced
½ teaspoon salt
juice of ½ lemon

Soften gelatin in cold water. Dissolve over hot water in double boiler. In separate bowl, stir cheese to soften. Add remaining ingredients. Mix well. Stir gelatin into cheese mixture. Pour in 5-cup ring mold. Chill until firm. Serves 8.

Emerald Salad

1 3-ounce package lime gelatin
¾ cup hot water
¾ cup cucumber, unpeeled and
   shredded

2 tablespoons onion, grated
1 cup cottage cheese
1 cup mayonnaise
⅓ cup slivered almonds, toasted

Dissolve gelatin in hot water. Chill. Strain cucumber and onion. Mix with remaining ingredients. Fold into gelatin. Pour into mold. Chill. Serves 8-10.

Frozen Cranberry Salad

1 16-ounce can jellied cranberry
  sauce
3 teaspoons lemon juice
1 cup whipping cream, whipped

¼ cup real mayonnaise
½ cup confectioners sugar
1 3-ounce package cream cheese
1 cup walnuts, chopped

Combine first 2 ingredients. Mash with fork. Pour into greased pan or mold. Mix remaining ingredients, pour over cranberry mixture and freeze for 8 hours. Cut in squares or unmold. Serve on lettuce. Serves 6-8.
Pretty salad for Thanksgiving or Christmas.

Whip cream to a medium consistency (soft piles, not soft peaks) if it is to be blended with a gelatin mixture.

Frozen Fruit Salad

1 pint sour cream
¾ cup sugar
2 tablespoons lemon juice
1 banana, sliced
¼ cup nuts, chopped

1 8¼-ounce can crushed pineapple,
  drained
¼ cup maraschino cherries, chopped
⅛ teaspoon salt

Mix sour cream and sugar together. Add remaining ingredients. Stir. Freeze*. Slice and serve on lettuce with mayonnaise. Serves 8-10.
*Must be prepared at least a day ahead.

Perfection Salad

2 envelopes unflavored gelatin
½ cup sugar
1 teaspoon salt
1½ cups boiling water
1½ cups cold water
½ cup vinegar
2 tablespoons lemon juice
garnish: carrot curls and ripe olives

2 cups cabbage, finely shredded
  (have cold to shred)
1 cup celery, chopped
¼ cup green pepper, chopped
¼ cup pimientos, diced
½ cup stuffed green olives, sliced
1 tablespoon onion juice

Combine gelatin, sugar and salt. Add boiling water and stir to dissolve gelatin. Add cold water, vinegar and lemon juice. Chill until partially set. Add remaining ingredients. Pour into 8½ x 4½ x 2½ loaf pan. Chill until firm. Garnish. Serves 8-10.

Tomato Aspic

4 cups tomato juice	Worcestershire, Tabasco to taste
½ cup onion, chopped	pepper, paprika to taste
¼ cup celery leaves, chopped	3 envelopes unflavored gelatin
2 tablespoons brown sugar	¼ cup cold water
1 teaspoon salt	3 tablespoons fresh lemon juice
2 small bay leaves	1 cup celery, chopped
4 whole cloves	½ cup green olives, sliced

garnish: snipped parsley and mayonnaise

In a saucepan, combine tomato juice, onion, celery leaves, sugar, salt, bay leaves, cloves, Worcestershire, Tabasco, pepper and paprika. Simmer 5 minutes. Strain. Soften gelatin in cold water; add to hot mixture. Add lemon juice. Chill until partially set. Add celery and olives. Chill in 1½-quart, 8-inch ring mold or individual small molds. Garnish. Serves 8.

Mustard Ring
Byron Nelson (1937, 1942 Masters' Champion)

4 whole eggs	¼ teaspoon salt
¾ cup sugar	1 cup water
1 envelope unflavored gelatin	½ cup cider vinegar
1½ tablespoons dry mustard	1 cup whipping cream
½ teaspoon turmeric	

Beat eggs in top of double boiler. Mix sugar and gelatin thoroughly. Stir in mustard, turmeric and salt. Add water and vinegar to eggs, then stir in sugar mixture and cook over boiling water until slightly thickened. Stir constantly (important). Cool until quite thick. Whip cream and beat into thick cool mixture. Turn into 1½ quart ring mold and let it become firm. Unmold and, if desired, fill center with cole slaw or fresh fruit. Garnish with greens. Serves 8.

Five Cup Ambrosia

1 cup mandarin oranges	1 cup miniature marshmallows
1 cup coconut, grated	1 cup sour cream
1 cup pineapple chunks	

Combine all ingredients. Refrigerate. Let sit one day before serving. Serves 6.
Quick and easy.

24 Hour Salad

2 eggs, beaten
2 tablespoons sugar
¼ cup cream or fruit syrup
dash salt
1 tablespoon butter
1 cup whipping cream, whipped
1 teaspoon lemon juice
1 teaspoon vanilla
½ cup pecans, chopped

2 cups pitted white cherries, drained and halved
1 11-ounce can crushed pineapple, drained
1 cup mandarin oranges, drained and halved
2 cups marshmallows, cut in fourths
lettuce cups

Combine first 5 ingredients. Cook over hot water until thick. Cool completely. Add whipped cream, lemon juice and vanilla. Stir in nuts, fruit and marshmallows. Pour into an 11x13x2 inch dish. Refrigerate one day before serving. Cut in squares and serve on lettuce cups. Serves 10-12.
A beautiful, white salad to have at Easter.

Bahamian Orange and Onion Salad

3 sweet oranges
2 medium onions, (yellow or white) thinly sliced
2 teaspoons marjoram

juice of 1 lime
3 tablespoons vegetable or olive oil
salt and pepper to taste

Squeeze juice from 1 orange. Set aside. Peel the other oranges, removing all the white, and slice. Mix oranges, onions, and marjoram. Combine orange juice, lime juice, oil, salt and pepper. Pour over salad. May be served on a bed of lettuce on salad plates. Serves 6.
Excellent with fowl or game.

Cucumber and Onion Salad

3 cucumbers
salt

2 red onions, thinly sliced

Dressing:
⅓ cup sour cream
¼ cup sugar

⅓ cup white vinegar

Peel cucumbers leaving some green skin. Thinly slice and salt cucumbers. Toss. Let sit in refrigerator for 1 hour. Rinse and drain. Add onion. Pour dressing over all. Toss. Chill 4 hours. Serve cold. Serves 6-8.

Miss Bessie's Marinated Cole Slaw

¾ cup vegetable oil
1 cup sugar
1 cup cider vinegar
1 teaspoon salt
1 teaspoon dry mustard

½ teaspoon celery seed
¾ teaspoon turmeric (optional)
1 large head cabbage, chopped
1 large onion, chopped
1 large bell pepper, chopped

In a saucepan, mix first 7 ingredients. Bring to a boil and pour over remaining ingredients. Marinate in refrigerator at least 1 day. Will keep a week. Serves 8. *Good for picnics!*

Marinated Sauerkraut

⅓ cup water
⅔ cup cider vinegar
⅓ cup vegetable oil
1¼ cups sugar
2 16-ounce cans sauerkraut
1 cup celery, diced

1 cup bell pepper, diced
1 cup onion, diced
1 4-ounce jar pimientos, chopped
1 8-ounce can water chestnuts, sliced

Heat water, vinegar and oil. Dissolve sugar in mixture. Pour over vegetables. Chill.* Serves 14-16.
*May be prepared ahead and kept indefinitely in refrigerator.
▼ Can be used with any meat as a salad substitute.

Marinated Zucchini Salad

Marinade:
⅔ cup salad oil
¼ cup vinegar
1 small clove garlic, minced
1 teaspoon sugar

¾ teaspoon salt
¾ teaspoon dry mustard
dash black pepper, freshly ground

Salad:
1 16-ounce can sliced carrots, drained
1 14-ounce can artichoke hearts or hearts of palm, drained

1 medium zucchini, thinly sliced (2 cups)
Bibb lettuce
2 ounces blue cheese, crumbled

Combine ingredients for marinade. Shake well. Pour over carrots, artichoke hearts and zucchini. Chill overnight. To serve, drain vegetables, arrange on lettuce and top with cheese. Serves 8.

Marinated Bean and Artichoke Salad

Salad:
1 14-ounce can artichoke
   hearts, sliced
1 6-ounce jar green olives,
   sliced
2 small onions, sliced and
   ringed

1 6-ounce can sliced mushrooms
1 9-ounce package frozen French-
   style green beans, cooked
   (may use 1 16-ounce can
   French-style green beans)

Dressing:
1 clove garlic, crushed
½ cup red wine vinegar
¾ cup salad oil

1 teaspoon salt
¼ teaspoon pepper

Combine salad ingredients and toss lightly. Mix dressing, shake and pour over vegetables. Marinate overnight in refrigerator. Serves 6-8.

Marinated Green Bean and Pea Salad

Salad:
2 15½-ounce cans French style
   green beans
1 17-ounce can LeSueur peas
   (no substitutions)
1 16-ounce can sliced carrots

1 large onion, sliced
1 cup celery, chopped
½ cup ripe olives, sliced
   (optional)
½ cup mayonnaise (or more)

Marinade:
¾ cup salad oil
⅓ cup white vinegar
2 tablespoons sugar

2 teaspoons salt
1 teaspoon pepper

Drain canned vegetables well. Place in a large mixing bowl. Place onions on top. Combine marinade ingredients, beating well with mixer. Pour over vegetables. Chill overnight. Drain well in colander for several hours. Stir occasionally. Remove onion. Add celery, olives and enough mayonnaise to bind together. (Good without mayonnaise, also.) Serves 10-12.

▼ Must be prepared at least one day ahead.
Great with cookouts and cold plates.

Marinated Mushroom Salad

1 pound fresh mushrooms
4½ tablespoons Dijon mustard
4½ tablespoons red wine vinegar
½ teaspoon dried tarragon
½ teaspoon salt

½ teaspoon dried oregano
¼ teaspoon pepper, freshly ground
¾ cup salad oil
1 head Boston lettuce, separated
into leaves

garnish: 1 avocado peeled and thinly sliced, ½ cup giant black olives, and 3 tablespoons parsley, chopped

Slice mushrooms evenly and set aside. In a separate bowl, combine mustard and vinegar. Add tarragon, salt, oregano and pepper. Add oil and blend thoroughly with a whisk. Pour dressing over mushrooms making sure each slice is thoroughly coated. Chill 2 to 3 hours. Serve on a bed of Boston lettuce. Garnish. Serves 6-8.

Garnish for Salad

1 14-ounce can hearts of palm, drained and sliced
1 14-ounce can artichoke hearts, (plain) drained and quartered
1 6-ounce can sliced mushrooms, drained
2 red onions, thinly sliced

2 green peppers, cut in strips
1 bottle Good Seasons Italian dressing made with red wine vinegar
½ cup white vinegar
salad greens
cherry tomatoes

Combine all ingredients except greens and tomatoes. Marinate overnight in refrigerator. Toss with salad greens and tomatoes. Serves 12.

Tomatoes Piquant

6 ripe tomatoes, peeled and quartered
⅔ cup salad oil
¼ cup tarragon vinegar
¼ cup parsley, snipped
1 garlic clove, minced
¼ cup green onions, sliced

½ teaspoon dried thyme or 2 teaspoons fresh thyme, snipped
1 teaspoon salt
¼ teaspoon pepper, freshly ground
lettuce
garnish: parsley, snipped

Put tomatoes in deep bowl. In jar, combine remaining ingredients. Shake well. Pour over tomatoes. Chill 3 hours or overnight. Spoon marinade over tomatoes occasionally. To serve, drain tomatoes, place on lettuce and garnish. Serves 6.

Greek Salad

6 ripe tomatoes, quartered
2 red onions, sliced
2 cucumbers, peeled and sliced
4 ounces black Progresso olives
1 head romaine lettuce

1 cup salad oil
⅓ cup wine vinegar
salt and pepper
½ pound Feta cheese, crumbled

Mix first 4 ingredients and place on bed of lettuce. Pour dressing made of oil, vinegar and seasonings over salad. Top with cheese. Serves 6.

Green Goddess Salad

1 head lettuce
1 head endive

3 tomatoes, diced (optional)

Dressing:
1 tablespoon chives, minced
8 tablespoons tarragon vinegar
¾ tube anchovy paste
2 tablespoons parsley, minced

1 green onion, minced
1 clove garlic, pressed
1 pint mayonnaise

Prepare salad greens. Place in a bowl. Add tomatoes and toss with dressing which has been mixed well in a blender. Serves 10-12.

▼ Dressing makes a delicious raw vegetable dip.

Shell Salad With Marinated Sprouts

2 cups cooked seashell macaroni
½ cup spring onions with tops, chopped
½ cup fresh parsley, chopped
mayonnaise to bind
2 tablespoons white wine vinegar

¼ cup sour cream
salt and white pepper to taste
½ cup Oil and Vinegar Marinade (see index)
2 10-ounce packages frozen baby Brussels sprouts, cooked, drained and cooled

Toss macaroni with next 6 ingredients. Season to taste. Chill several hours. Pour Oil and Vinegar Marinade over Brussels sprouts. Chill overnight. To serve, arrange pasta salad on platter and surround with drained sprouts. Serves 6.

Hot Potato Salad

5 cups potatoes, cooked and diced
½ pound bacon, fried and crumbled
⅓ cup reserved bacon drippings
⅓ cup cider vinegar
3 tablespoons water
1 egg, slightly beaten
1 teaspoon sugar
¼ teaspoon pepper
1 teaspoon dry mustard

1 teaspoon salt
½ cup onion, chopped
¼ cup chives, snipped (optional)
2 tablespoons bell pepper,
minced (optional)
2 eggs, hard-boiled and diced
(optional)
2 tablespoons pimiento, diced
(optional)

While potatoes and bacon are still hot, combine bacon drippings, vinegar, water, egg, sugar, pepper, mustard and salt. Stir over low heat until thickened. Toss with potatoes, bacon, onion and any optional ingredients desired. Heat. Serves 8-10.

May vary recipe by placing salad in a casserole, sprinkling with 2 cups grated sharp Cheddar cheese and heating under the broiler until cheese is bubbling.

Never cut salad greens; tear them.

Korean Salad

Dressing:
1 cup vegetable oil
¼ cup vinegar
⅓ cup ketchup
¾ cup sugar

1 teaspoon Worcestershire
1 medium onion, grated
salt and pepper

Salad:
½ bag or bunch spinach
½ large head romaine or
2 heads Bibb lettuce
3 hard-boiled eggs, grated

5 strips bacon, fried and crumbled
1 16-ounce can bean sprouts, drained
1 8-ounce can water chestnuts,
thinly sliced

Put all dressing ingredients in blender. Mix well. Chill. Prepare salad greens. Add eggs, bacon, bean sprouts and water chestnuts. Toss greens with desired amount of dressing. Serve at once. Serves 8.

51

Peg's Layered Salad

1 head lettuce, broken
½ cup green pepper, chopped
1 onion, diced
½ cup celery, diced
1 10-ounce package frozen green peas, thawed but not cooked

2 cups Hellmann's mayonnaise mixed with 2 tablespoons sugar
1 4-ounce package Cheddar cheese, grated
6-8 strips bacon, fried and crumbled
salt
Parmesan cheese, grated

In a bowl, layer first 8 ingredients in order given. Chill for 24 hours. When ready to serve, salt to taste, toss and top with Parmesan cheese. Serves 8-10.
▼ Must be made a day ahead.
A filling salad.

Mexican Salad

1 large head iceberg lettuce
1 15-ounce can ranch-style or kidney beans
2 tomatoes, diced
½ red onion, finely chopped

1 10-ounce package sharp cheese, coarsely grated
6 ounces Kraft Catalina Dressing
1 9½-ounce package corn chips, crushed

Prepare lettuce for salad. Drain, wash and chill beans. Add beans, tomatoes, onion, cheese and dressing to lettuce. Chill 1 hour. Just before serving, add chips and toss. Serves 12.
A great picnic dish!

Stuffed Lettuce

1 head iceberg lettuce
2 ounces Roquefort or bleu cheese
1 8-ounce package cream cheese

2-3 tablespoons milk
1 tablespoon onion, grated
Basic French Dressing (see index)

Hollow out center of lettuce leaving at least a 1-inch shell. Beat cheeses and milk until smooth. Add onion and mix thoroughly. Stuff lettuce with mixture. Chill until firm. To serve, cut into crosswise slices and serve with Basic French Dressing. Serves 4-6.
A man's favorite.

Caesar Salad

2 large heads romaine lettuce
  (or 3 medium heads)
1 egg, beaten
juice of 2 medium lemons
½ cup grated Parmesan cheese
salt to taste

black pepper, freshly ground
1 cup vegetable oil or top grade
  olive oil
2 cloves garlic, crushed
2½ cups plain croutons
anchovies

Prepare greens for salad. Combine egg, lemon juice, cheese, salt and pepper. Set aside. Combine oil and garlic. Sauté croutons in ¼ oil mixture. Combine remaining oil mixture with lemon mixture. Chill. After dressing is sufficiently chilled, place about ¾ of it in salad bowl. Add greens and 2 cups of croutons. Toss. More dressing may be added if needed. Garnish with anchovies and remaining croutons. Serves 10-12.

Home-Made Croutons

For delicious home-made croutons, cube 2 hot dog buns. Toast at 225° for 15 minutes. Remove from oven and let sit 1 hour. Sauté in mixture of 2 tablespoons salad oil and 1 large clove garlic, crushed. Store in air-tight container. Yields 2 cups.

Watercress Salad

2 4-ounce bunches watercress,
  cleaned
1 3-ounce package slivered almonds,
  sautéed in 1 tablespoon butter

1 pound fresh mushrooms, sliced
3-5 stalks of hearts of palm,
  sliced

Vinaigrette Dressing:
1 cup Wesson oil
⅓ cup cider vinegar
2 teaspoons sugar
1 tablespoon salt
1 tablespoon capers

2 tablespoons onion, grated
½ tablespoon dried parsley
1 hard-boiled egg, grated
  or minced
dash of red pepper

Just before serving, toss vegetables with Vinaigrette Dressing. Serves 8-10.

Cauliflower Salad

1 cup real mayonnaise
1 cup grated Parmesan cheese
1 garlic clove, crushed
salt, pepper to taste

1 head romaine lettuce
1 head leaf or iceberg lettuce
1 head cauliflower, grated

For dressing, combine mayonnaise, cheese, garlic, salt and pepper. Set overnight in refrigerator. Dressing must be prepared a day ahead. For salad, prepare greens. Add cauliflower. Toss with dressing. Serves 8-10.

Mandarin Spinach Salad

1 1-pound bag fresh spinach
1 11-ounce can mandarin orange
  sections, drained
1 bunch spring onions, sliced
  (bottoms only)
4-5 slices bacon, fried and
  crumbled

½ pound fresh mushrooms, washed
  and sliced
salt and freshly ground black
  pepper to taste
French Dressing (see index)

Prepare spinach for salad. Chill. To serve, add orange sections, onions, bacon, mushrooms and seasonings. Toss with French Dressing. Serves 4-6.

Spinach Salad

2 pounds fresh spinach
3 hard-boiled eggs, grated
8 strips bacon, fried and crumbled
sesame seeds

1 red onion, sliced
1 bottle Old Dutch Sweet
  and Sour Dressing

Prepare spinach for salad. Sprinkle eggs, bacon, sesame seeds and onion over spinach. Pour dressing over salad and toss. Serves 12.

Spinach or Romaine Salad

1 pound fresh spinach or romaine
1 onion, diced
2 large tomatoes, quartered
1 green pepper, diced
1 pimiento, diced

¼ pound bleu or Roquefort cheese, crumbled
2 slices rye bread, slightly stale and diced

Dressing:
½ cup cider vinegar
½ of 10½-ounce can condensed tomato soup
1 cup salad oil
1 tablespoon onion, minced

1 teaspoon salt
1 tablespoon sugar
⅛ teaspoon black pepper, freshly ground
1 tablespoon dry mustard

Prepare salad greens. Combine vegetables and cheese. Chill. Mix dressing. Chill. Just before serving, toss, then add bread. Serves 10.

Do not soak greens when washing them. Crisp by placing briefly in ice water.

Spinach and Mushroom Salad

Dressing:
¾ cup salad oil
¼ cup fresh lemon juice
¾ teaspoon salt

coarse black pepper to taste
1 clove garlic, crushed
2 teaspoons Dijon mustard

Salad:
1 10-ounce bag spinach
1 medium red onion, sliced
½ pound fresh mushrooms, sliced

2 ounces blue cheese, crumbled
2 cups croutons (see index)

Make dressing in advance. Combine all dressing ingredients. Mix well. Store covered in refrigerator. Prepare chilled spinach for salad. Place in salad bowl. Add onion, mushrooms and blue cheese. Toss with desired amount of dressing. Add croutons. Toss. Serves 8.

▼ Parmesan cheese may be substituted for blue cheese.

Molded Turkey or Chicken Salad

2 envelopes unflavored gelatin
1 cup cold water
1 10¾-ounce can condensed cream of celery soup
½ teaspoon salt
2 tablespoons lemon juice

1 tablespoon onion, grated
¾ cup mayonnaise
¾ cup sour cream
1 cup celery, diced
3 cups turkey or chicken, cooked and diced

Dissolve gelatin in water over low heat stirring constantly. Remove from heat. Add soup, salt, lemon juice, onion, mayonnaise and sour cream. Chill until thick but not set. Add celery and turkey. Pour into mold. Chill until firm. Garnish as desired. Serves 6-8.

Tuna Mousse

1 envelope unflavored gelatin
2 tablespoons lemon juice
½ cup chicken broth, boiling
½ cup Hellmann's mayonnaise
¼ cup milk
2 tablespoons parsley, chopped

1 tablespoon green onion, minced
1 teaspoon prepared mustard
1 teaspoon dried dill weed
¼ teaspoon pepper
1 7-ounce can tuna, drained and flaked
½ cup cucumber, shredded

Soften gelatin in lemon juice in large bowl. Add broth and stir to dissolve gelatin. Add mayonnaise, milk, parsley, onion, mustard, dill weed and pepper. Beat until frothy. Fold in tuna and cucumber. Turn into 2-cup mold. Chill 3 hours. Serves 4.
▼ Best prepared a day ahead.

Carole Brewer's Tuna Salad
Mrs. Gay Brewer – Wife of 1967 Masters' Champion

Dressing:
1 cup mayonnaise
1 tablespoon lemon juice

1 teaspoon soy sauce
⅛ teaspoon curry powder

Salad:
2 6½-ounce cans tuna, drained
1 3-ounce jar cocktail onions, drained and halved
1 cup celery, chopped

1 10-ounce package frozen peas, defrosted
1 3-ounce can chow mein noodles
lettuce

Mix dressing ingredients in large bowl. Add first 4 salad ingredients and mix well. When ready to serve, add noodles and toss. Serve on lettuce. Serves 6-8.

Shrimp and Rice Salad

1 cup shrimp, cooked and cleaned	½ teaspoon salt
3 cups cooked rice	¼ teaspoon pepper
¼ cup celery, sliced	3 tablespoons mayonnaise
¼ cup pimiento-stuffed olives, sliced	crisp lettuce
	2 tomatoes, wedged
¼ cup green pepper, chopped	½ cup Basic French Dressing
¼ cup pimientos, chopped	(see index)
¼ cup onion, minced	1 lemon, wedged

Split each shrimp lengthwise. Combine shrimp, rice, celery, olives, green pepper, pimientos and onion. Cover and chill. Just before serving, combine salt, pepper and mayonnaise. Toss with shrimp mixture. Spoon shrimp onto lettuce. Garnish with tomato wedges and whole shrimp if desired. Serve with Basic French Dressing and lemon wedges. Serves 6.

▼ Crabmeat or lobster may be substituted for shrimp.
Good luncheon for ladies.

Spanish Paella Salad

1½ cups saffron rice, uncooked	1 pound shrimp, peeled and deveined
8 half-breasts chicken, skinned and boned	1 medium onion, chopped
6 tablespoons olive oil	1 garlic clove, chopped
¼ cup white wine or dry vermouth	1½ cups pimiento stuffed green olives
1½ teaspoons salt	

Sauce:

¾ cup mayonnaise	1 teaspoon lemon juice (or more to taste)
1 tablespoon brandy (or more to taste)	

garnish: 1 sliced, ripe avocado, tomato wedges, lemon wedges, lettuce.

Cook rice. Set aside. In skillet, cook chicken in 3 tablespoons oil for about 5 minutes coating each piece well. Add wine. Sprinkle chicken with salt. Simmer 15 minutes. Turn chicken. Add shrimp. Simmer uncovered for 10 minutes or until shrimp turns pink. Remove both and set aside. In same skillet, sauté onion and garlic in remaining oil until tender. Add onion and garlic to rice. Cut chicken into diagonal pieces. Add shrimp, chicken and olives to rice, and toss. Cool, then chill. Garnish. Serve with sauce. Serves 6-8.

Fresh Fruit Salad

Arrange assorted fruits, such as strawberries, blueberries, melon balls, fresh pineapple, grapefruit and orange sections, seedless grapes and sliced bananas in a fruit boat or on bed of lettuce. Serve with your choice of fruit salad dressing.

Fresh Fruit Dressing

1 tablespoon poppy seed (or celery seed)
1/3 cup sugar
1/4 teaspoon dry mustard
1/2 teaspoon paprika
1/2 teaspoon salt

1/2 cup smooth applesauce
1/4 cup honey
3 tablespoons lemon juice
1 tablespoon vinegar
1/4 teaspoon lemon rind, grated
1/2 cup oil

Put all ingredients in blender. Mix well. Chill. Yields 2 cups.
Delicious served over fresh fruit.

Celery Seed Fruit Salad Dressing

1 cup sugar
2 teaspoons dry mustard
2 teaspoons salt
1/2 teaspoon MSG
4 tablespoons cider vinegar

2 teaspoons onion, grated
2 cups Wesson oil
5 more tablespoons cider vinegar
2 tablespoons celery seed
1 tablespoon paprika

Mix together first 6 ingredients. Slowly add oil, beating constantly. Beat until thick and light. Continue beating and slowly add remaining vinegar. Quickly and lightly, stir in celery seed and paprika. Yields 2½ cups.
Good on all fresh fruit.

Poppy Seed Dressing

2/3 cup honey
1 teaspoon salt
dash white pepper
3/4 cup cider vinegar

6 tablespoons prepared mustard
2 cups Wesson oil
3-4 tablespoons poppy seeds
1 medium onion, grated

Mix honey, salt, pepper, vinegar and mustard in electric mixer. SLOWLY add oil. Mix until thickened and oil disappears. Add poppy seeds and onion. Stir. Yields 1 quart.
Delicious over fresh fruit.

Whipped Cream Dressing

⅔ cup sugar
2 tablespoons flour
2 tablespoons Wesson oil
3 tablespoons lemon juice

4 tablespoons orange juice
1 cup unsweetened pineapple juice
2 eggs, beaten
½ pint whipping cream, whipped

Combine first 6 ingredients in top of double boiler. Cook until it begins to thicken. Add small amount of mixture to eggs, then carefully add eggs to hot mixture. Cook 3-5 minutes. When cool, fold in whipped cream. Yields approximately 1½ cups.
Can be made 1 day before using.
Very good served on fruit which has been put in a scooped-out watermelon shell. Freeze watermelon shell for several hours before using.

Pineapple and Ginger Dressing

1 3-ounce package cream cheese
½ of 8¼-ounce can crushed
   pineapple, drained

¼ cup candied ginger,
   finely chopped

Soften cream cheese. Add pineapple and ginger. Mix together until preferred consistency. Serves 6.
Use on sweet molded salads. Good with chicken, turkey or ham.

Bacon Salad Dressing

8 strips lean bacon
¾ cup red wine vinegar
1 cup sugar

1 teaspoon salt (or to taste)
½ cup water

Fry bacon, drain and crumble. Pour bacon grease into saucepan. Add remaining ingredients. Keep warm until served. Do not prepare ahead because grease will solidify. Serves 8-10.
  ▼ Serve on spinach or other salad greens for a wilted salad.

Basic French Dressing

¾ teaspoon dry mustard
½ teaspoon black pepper
½ teaspoon paprika

½ teaspoon sugar
2 ounces cider vinegar
6 ounces salad oil

Mix dry ingredients. Add vinegar. Shake well. Add oil. Shake thoroughly before using. Yields 1 cup.

Dijon French Dressing

½ cup salad oil
1 tablespoon green onion, chopped
1 tablespoon parsley, snipped
2 teaspoons lemon juice
2 tablespoons salad vinegar

¼ teaspoon salt
1 clove garlic, crushed
1 teaspoon Dijon mustard
black pepper, freshly ground

Combine all ingredients. Shake. Chill. Yields ¾ cup.

Harry's Blue Cheese Dressing

1 cup sour cream
2½ heaping tablespoons
   mayonnaise
juice of ½ lemon

dash Tabasco
few drops cider vinegar
¼ teaspoon salt
3 ounces blue cheese, crumbled

Mix ingredients together well. Store covered in refrigerator. Yields 1½ cups.

Oil and Vinegar Marinade

½ cup olive oil
2 tablespoons tarragon vinegar
2 cloves garlic, crushed
1 teaspoon salt

1 teaspoon dry mustard
½ teaspoon sugar
¼ teaspoon black pepper

Combine all ingredients. Chill. Yields ⅔ cup.

Seafood

5

Crêpes Newburg

Mrs. Amelia Cartledge, Adult Homemaking Division, Richmond County Schools, Augusta, Georgia

Filling:
1 pound crab meat, flaked
1 8-ounce can sliced mushrooms
4 tablespoons butter
6 tablespoons flour
3 cups half-and-half
2 chicken bouillon cubes
¾ teaspoon prepared mustard
1 clove garlic, finely minced

1 teaspoon salt
¼ teaspoon black pepper
¼ teaspoon red pepper
⅛ teaspoon ginger
⅛ teaspoon nutmeg, freshly grated
1 tablespoon soy sauce
⅓ pound sharp cheese, grated

Combine crab meat with well-drained mushrooms. Refrigerate until ready to fill crêpes. To make sauce for filling, melt butter in saucepan. Remove from heat; add flour and stir to a smooth paste. Return to heat and cook for a few minutes. Remove from heat again and slowly blend in hot cream. Add remaining ingredients. Return to heat, stirring constantly until mixture boils. Adjust seasonings. This can be made a day ahead and stored in the refrigerator. If filling is made ahead, reheat in double boiler. Add crab meat and mushrooms to sauce when ready to assemble crêpes.

Newburg sauce:
2 pounds shrimp, cooked and cleaned
1 cup cooked lobster, cut in bite-size chunks (optional)
4 tablespoons butter
4 tablespoons flour

2½ cups whipping cream
1 teaspoon salt
1 teaspoon paprika
pinch red pepper
3 egg yolks, beaten
½ cup sherry

Refrigerate shrimp and lobster until ready to add to sauce. Using the same method as in the filling, make a cream sauce with butter, flour, cream, salt, paprika and pepper. This can be made the day before and refrigerated. If sauce is made ahead, reheat in double boiler. Just before serving, add egg yolks, sherry, shrimp and lobster. Stir sauce as little as possible after seafood is added.
To assemble Crêpes Newburg (see index for crêpe recipe), place about 3 tablespoons of filling on unbrowned side of each crêpe. Roll up and place in buttered baking dish or greased cookie sheet. Bake at 350° until crêpes are heated through. Spoon hot Newburg sauce over crêpes just before serving. Sauce and filling is enough to serve 12.

Crab Casserole

Mrs. Jack Nicklaus – wife of Masters' Champion 1963, 1965, 1966, 1972 and 1975

8 slices white bread
butter
8 slices American cheese
1 pound fresh crab meat
½ pound fresh mushrooms,
    sliced and sautéed in butter

1 onion, chopped
4 eggs, beaten
2½ cups milk
1 teaspoon dry mustard
1 teaspoon salt

Remove crusts from bread. Butter both sides of bread. Put 4 slices bread in bottom of 8-inch square pan. Top with 4 slices of cheese, then crab, mushrooms and onion. Top onion layer with remaining cheese and end with bread. Combine eggs, milk, mustard and salt. Pour over casserole. Cover and soak overnight or several hours in refrigerator. Bake uncovered at 350° for 45-60 minutes. Serves 4.

▼ Must be prepared a day ahead.

Crab Meat Florentine

2 10-ounce packages frozen chopped
    spinach, thawed
3 tablespoons butter
1 tablespoon onion, minced
1 teaspoon lemon juice
½ teaspoon salt
2 tablespoons flour
1½ cups milk
¼ cup dry sherry

½ cup Swiss cheese, grated
    dash Worcestershire
salt and pepper to taste
1 pound crab meat, fresh or
    frozen
1 cup fine dry bread crumbs
grated Parmesan cheese
paprika
butter

Drain spinach and press out water. Melt 1 tablespoon butter in a small skillet, add onion and cook until limp. Add spinach, lemon juice and salt. Cover and cook 1-2 minutes, only until spinach is hot. Remove from heat and spoon into 8 ramekins. Flatten spinach out to completely cover bottom of ramekin. Melt remaining butter in saucepan, add flour and stir over low heat for 4-5 minutes. Slowly add milk and stir until thickened. Add sherry and cheese, stirring until cheese melts. Add Worcestershire, salt and pepper. Remove from heat and add crab. Spoon mixture over spinach. Top with bread crumbs, Parmesan, paprika and dot with butter. Bake at 350° for 20 minutes or until thoroughly heated. Place under broiler until lightly browned. Serves 8.

It's as pretty to look at as it is to eat.

Artichoke Crab Casserole

1 9-ounce package frozen
   artichoke hearts, cooked
1 cup sharp cheese, grated
2 tablespoons onions, minced
¼ cup butter
2 tablespoons flour
¼ teaspoon curry powder

½ teaspoon salt
1 cup milk
1 tablespoon lemon juice
12 ounces crab meat, fresh or
   frozen
½ cup bread crumbs
2 tablespoons butter, melted

Place artichokes in 1-quart casserole. Sprinkle with cheese. Sauté onions in butter. Add flour, curry and salt. Stir in milk and stir until sauce thickens. Add lemon juice and crab. Pour over artichokes. Mix bread crumbs with butter and sprinkle over casserole. Bake at 350° for 30 minutes. Serves 4.

▼ Lobster may be substituted for crab. Freezes well.

Rena's Deviled Crab

2 eggs, beaten until light
1 pound crab meat
pinch of dry mustard
1 tablespoon lemon juice

few drops Worcestershire
2 cups white sauce
2 cups fine bread or cracker crumbs
½ stick butter, melted

Fold eggs into crab and add seasonings. (If more than a few drops of Worcestershire is added, the flavor of the crab will be destroyed.) Combine mixture with white sauce while sauce is hot. Put a heaping portion in each crab shell and top with crumbs. Pour butter over each. Bake at 350° for 45 minutes. Serves 6-8, depending on size of shell used.

Commander's Palace Crab Meat Imperial

1 green pepper, finely diced
2 pimientos, finely diced
1 tablespoon English mustard
1 teaspoon salt
½ teaspoon white pepper

2 eggs
1 cup mayonnaise
2 pounds lump crab meat
mayonnaise
paprika

Mix green pepper and pimientos. Add mustard, salt, white pepper, eggs and mayonnaise. Mix well. Add crab meat and mix with fingers so that lumps are not broken. Lightly heap mixture into 8 crab shells or casseroles. Top with thin layer of mayonnaise. Sprinkle with paprika. Bake at 350° for 15 minutes. Serve hot or cold. Serves 8.

Asparagus Crab Soufflé

8 slices white bread
2 cups fresh crab meat or
  2 6½-ounce cans
½ cup mayonnaise
1 small onion, chopped
1½ cups cooked or canned
  asparagus with tips

4 eggs, beaten
3 cups milk
1 10¾-ounce can condensed cream
  of mushroom soup
½ cup Cheddar cheese, grated
paprika

Dice 4 slices of bread and place in large buttered baking dish. Combine crab meat, mayonnaise and onion. Spread over bread. Top with asparagus. Trim crusts from remaining bread and place over asparagus. Combine eggs and milk. Pour over all. Cover and refrigerate overnight. To serve, bake at 325° for 15 minutes. Remove from oven and pour soup over top. Sprinkle with cheese and paprika. Continue baking for about 50 minutes. Serves 8.
▼ Must be prepared ahead.

Always carefully pick through fresh or canned crab meat to remove shell and cartilage before using.

Bahama Crab Meat Casserole

2 6-ounce packages frozen
  king crab meat
2 10-ounce cans frozen shrimp
  soup, thawed
1 6-ounce can sliced mushrooms,
  drained
¼ cup onion or green onion,
  finely chopped
½ cup green pepper,
  finely chopped

1-2 tablespoons butter
few drops Tabasco
1 teaspoon Worcestershire
  (or to taste)
salt and pepper to taste
cracker crumbs or potato
  chips, finely crushed
grated Parmesan cheese

Flake crab meat. Add soup. Sauté mushrooms, onion and green pepper in butter. Add to crab mixture. Add seasonings. Pour into individual shells or 1½-quart casserole. Top lightly with crumbs (or chips) and cheese. Bake at 325° for 15 minutes in shells or 25-30 minutes in casserole. Serves 8.
Easy yet delicious.

Crab Meat Au Gratin

½ stick butter
1 heaping tablespoon plain flour
1½ cups half-and-half
1 heaping tablespoon green
  onion, chopped
1 heaping tablespoon parsley,
  chopped

1 cup Cheddar cheese, grated
salt, pepper, Tabasco and
  Worcestershire to taste
1 pound lump crab meat (fresh)
Cheddar cheese, grated
bread crumbs
parsley

In top of double boiler, make a white sauce with butter, flour and cream. Add onion, parsley, cheese and seasonings. Mix well. Gently add crab meat. Pour into casserole or individual baking shells. Sprinkle with cheese and bread crumbs mixed together. Bake at 350° for about 30 minutes or until hot and cheese is browned. Sprinkle with parsley. Serves 4-6.

Hot Seafood Salad

1 pound shrimp, cooked, cleaned
  and deveined
½ pound fresh crab meat
½ cup bell pepper, chopped
1 cup celery, chopped

½ cup onion, chopped
1 cup Miracle Whip salad dressing
salt and pepper to taste
Worcestershire to taste
bread crumbs

Combine all ingredients except bread crumbs and mix well. Put in a buttered casserole, sprinkle with crumbs and bake at 400° for 30 minutes. Serves 4.

Clam Casserole

6 tablespoons butter
1 cup fine bread crumbs, plain
  or with herbs
milk or cream

1 8-ounce can minced clams
  (reserve juice)
2 tablespoons plain flour
1 egg

Melt 3 tablespoons butter in skillet and brown crumbs. Set aside. Add enough milk to clam juice to make 1½ cups liquid. Melt remaining butter and add flour. Add clam juice and milk mixture. Boil 1 minute, stirring constantly. Cool COM-PLETELY. Beat in egg and clams with a wire whisk. Put half of crumbs into 1-quart greased baking dish, then add clam mixture. Top with remaining crumbs. Bake at 350° for 30 minutes. Serves 3.
Inexpensive.

Seafood Casserole
Mrs. Henry G. Picard, wife of 1938 Masters' Champion

6 slices bacon
1¼ cups onion, finely chopped
1¼ cups bell pepper, finely
    chopped
6 slices dry white bread
4 eggs
1 13-ounce can evaporated milk
⅔ cup water
1 teaspoon salt
½ teaspoon pepper

2 tablespoons catsup
2 teaspoons Worcestershire
dash Tabasco
1 18-ounce jar seafood
    cocktail sauce
½ cup sherry
2 pounds shrimp, cooked
    and cleaned
2 cups crab meat

Fry bacon until very crisp. Crumble and set aside. Sauté onion and bell pepper in small amount of bacon grease. Cut bread into small pieces. Combine remaining ingredients except seafood. Beat until well mixed. Add bacon crumbs, onion, bell pepper, bread crumbs and seafood. Spread in large, shallow greased casserole. Bake uncovered at 325° for 1 hour or until knife inserted comes out clean. Serves 8-12.

Wilma's Seafood Casserole

½ cup green pepper, chopped
½ cup onion, chopped
½ cup celery, chopped
½ cup margarine
⅔ cup flour
½ teaspoon garlic, minced
½ teaspoon salt
¼ teaspoon paprika
dash of red pepper
1 10¾-ounce can Campbell's
    shrimp soup
2 cups milk

1 7-ounce can crab meat or
    1 6-ounce package frozen
    snowflake crab meat, drained
1 12 or 18-ounce package frozen
    shrimp
1 8-ounce can water chestnuts,
    sliced
1 4-ounce can sliced mushrooms
2 tablespoons butter, softened
½ cup sharp Cheddar cheese,
    grated
½ cup bread crumbs

Sauté green pepper, onion and celery in margarine. Stir in flour and cook 1 minute. Add seasonings. Stir in soup. Add milk and stir until thick. Combine crab meat, shrimp, water chestnuts and mushrooms. Mix well. Place in a 2-quart casserole. Pour sauce on top. Combine butter, cheese and crumbs. Sprinkle over casserole. Bake at 350° for 30-35 minutes. Serves 6.

▼ May be prepared ahead and refrigerated or frozen.
Worth the effort!

Shrimp Crêpes
Martha Fleming, "The Cookery," Augusta, Georgia

Lemon Sauce:
2 sticks butter
1½ cups plain flour
10 cups rich chicken stock

juice of 3-4 lemons
salt and pepper to taste
tarragon to taste (optional)

White Wine Sauce:
2 sticks butter
1½ cups plain flour
8 cups milk
1 cup dry white wine

1 cup cream
1 tablespoon salt
1 teaspoon white pepper
¼ teaspoon nutmeg

Filling:
2 pounds shrimp
seasoned salt
Gruyère cheese, grated
fresh mushrooms, sautéed in
    butter
artichoke hearts, quartered

bacon, cooked and finely chopped
grated Parmesan cheese
paprika
garnish: thin lemon slices and
    sliced pimientos

Lemon Sauce: Make a roux using butter and flour. Cook at least 3 minutes, stirring constantly. Do not let brown. Add remaining ingredients and stir until thick.

White Wine Sauce: Make a roux using butter and flour. Cook until frothy, at least 3 minutes, stirring constantly. Add hot milk to roux in a steady stream, stirring constantly. When sauce is thickened, add remaining ingredients.

Filling: Partially cook shrimp. Clean and devein shrimp. Season with seasoned salt.

To assemble crêpes: Fill each crêpe (see index for crêpe recipe) with small amounts of shrimp, Gruyère cheese, mushrooms and 2 tablespoons Lemon Sauce. Fold crêpe over and place in baking dish. Place artichoke hearts around crêpe. Top with White Wine Sauce. Sprinkle bacon, Parmesan cheese and paprika on top of crêpe. Garnish. Bake at 450° for about 12 minutes or until bubbly and slightly brown. Filling serves 6-8. Lemon Sauce and White Wine Sauce yields enough for 20 crêpes.

When boiling shrimp, add fresh celery leaves to minimize odor.

Creole Jambalaya

2 onions, chopped
½ cup green onions, chopped
4 tablespoons butter
1 14-ounce can tomatoes, chopped (reserve juice)
1 6-ounce can tomato paste
2 ounces water
4 cloves garlic, chopped
2 stalks celery, chopped
¼ bell pepper, chopped
2 tablespoons parsley, chopped

¼ teaspoon thyme
1 bay leaf
3 cloves, chopped
2 pounds raw shrimp, peeled
1 pound bulk hot sausage, cooked and drained
3½ cups cooked rice
salt, pepper, cayenne
1½ cups chicken, cooked and diced
garnish: snipped parsley

Sauté onions in butter for 5 minutes. Add tomatoes, juice, tomato paste and water. Cook 5 minutes, stirring constantly. Add garlic, celery, bell pepper, parsley, thyme, bay leaf and cloves. Stir well. Add shrimp and sausage. Cook 30 minutes, stirring frequently. Remove bay leaf. Stir in rice. Season to taste. Gently stir in chicken.* Bake in buttered casserole at 350° for 30 minutes. Garnish. Serves 10.
*Prepare ahead to this point.
▼ Ham may be substituted for chicken.
A fabulous dish for a crowd!

Sea Island Shrimp Mull

Herman Yursick, Chef, The Cloister, Sea Island, Georgia

½ cup bacon fat
1 cup onion, chopped
1 cup green pepper, diced
4 garlic cloves, minced
4 bay leaves
½ cup sugar
2 tablespoons chili powder
¼ cup flour
1 cup water
salt, Tabasco to taste

1 6-ounce can tomato paste
2 tablespoons Worcestershire
1 cup dry white wine
½ cup vinegar
1 cup chili sauce
1 cup catsup
½ cup Dijon mustard
4 pounds raw shrimp, peeled and deveined
cooked rice

In a large pot, place first 7 ingredients. Cook until all juices are gone and vegetables are light brown, stirring occasionally. Add flour, mix well and cook 5 more minutes. Add remaining ingredients, except shrimp and rice, and bring to a boil. Add shrimp and cook 15 minutes. If too thin, thicken with a little cornstarch. Serve over rice. Serves 8.

Rachel's Shrimp Creole

4-6 slices bacon
½ cup onion, chopped
¼ cup bell pepper, chopped
¼ cup celery, chopped
2 16-ounce cans tomatoes
1½ teaspoons salt

1 tablespoon Worcestershire
3 tablespoons catsup
2 pounds green shrimp, peeled
    and deveined
1 tablespoon sugar
hot cooked rice

Brown bacon in iron skillet. Remove bacon and set aside. Sauté onion, bell pepper and celery in bacon drippings. Add tomatoes, salt, Worcestershire and catsup. Crumble bacon and return to skillet. Simmer sauce uncovered for 45 minutes to 1 hour or until thickened. Add shrimp a few at a time. Add sugar. Simmer about 10 minutes after last shrimp has been added. Serve over rice. Serves 6-8.

Cretan Shrimp

6 tablespoons olive oil
¼ cup onion, finely chopped
1½ cups canned tomatoes,
    drained and chopped
½ cup dry white wine
2 tablespoons parsley, finely
    chopped

½ teaspoon oregano
1 teaspoon salt
freshly ground black pepper
1½ pounds raw shrimp,
    cleaned
2 ounces Feta cheese, cut in
    ¼-inch cubes

Heat oil over medium heat in a heavy 10 to 12-inch skillet. Add onion and cook until soft and transparent, about 5 minutes, stirring frequently. Stir in tomatoes, wine, 1 tablespoon parsley, oregano, salt and pepper. Bring to boil and cook briskly, uncovered, until mixture thickens to a purée. Add shrimp. Cook over moderate heat for 5 minutes. When shrimp are pink and firm, stir in cheese. Sprinkle remaining parsley on top. Serves 4.

Daisy's Fried Shrimp

1 pound green shrimp, cleaned
1 egg, beaten
24 Ritz crackers, finely crushed

salt and pepper to taste
Crisco
garnish: lemon wedges

Dip shrimp in egg. Dredge in cracker crumbs that have been seasoned with salt and pepper. Fry in heavy skillet in 2 inches of very hot shortening for 3 minutes, turning once. Serves 2.

Shrimp Mosca

1 stick butter (not margarine)
6 large cloves garlic, minced
1 teaspoon black pepper,
   coarsely ground
1 teaspoon oregano

2 tablespoons rosemary
3 bay leaves
1 cup white wine
1½ pounds large shrimp
   in the shell

Melt butter. Add remaining ingredients, adding shrimp last. Sizzle mixture until most of liquid is gone and butter has browned on shrimp shells. Serves 4. Do not prepare ahead.
This is messy but fun to eat. Give everyone a fingerbowl filled with cold water, an ice cube and a slice of lemon.

Low Country Southern Gumbo

1 cup vegetable oil
1 cup plain flour
8 stalks celery, chopped
3 large onions, chopped
1 green pepper, chopped
2 cloves garlic, minced
½ cup parsley, chopped
1 pound okra, sliced
2 tablespoons shortening
2 quarts chicken stock (less
   for thicker gumbo)
2 quarts water (less for
   thicker gumbo)
½ cup Worcestershire
Tabasco to taste

½ cup catsup
1 large ripe tomato, chopped
4 slices bacon or ham, chopped
2 tablespoons salt
1-2 bay leaves
¼ teaspoon rosemary
¼ teaspoon thyme
red pepper to taste
2 cups chicken, cooked and diced
1 to 2 pounds crab meat
4 pounds shrimp, boiled and cleaned
1 pint oysters, drained
1 teaspoon molasses or brown sugar
juice of 1 lemon
cooked rice

Heat oil in iron pot on medium heat. Add flour slowly, stirring constantly with wooden spoon for 30-40 minutes until medium brown. Add celery, onions, green pepper, garlic and parsley. Cook 45 minutes, stirring constantly. Fry okra in shortening until brown and add to gumbo. Stir over low heat for a few minutes. Add stock, water, Worcestershire, Tabasco, catsup, tomato, bacon and seasonings. Simmer 2-3 hours. About 30 minutes before serving, add chicken, crab and shrimp. Add oysters last 10 minutes of simmer period. Add molasses and check seasonings. Add lemon juice. Serve over rice. Serves 12 generously. Freezes well.

Two tablespoons filé may be substituted for bay leaves, rosemary, thyme and red pepper. However, do not add filé until gumbo is removed from heat and ready to serve. Allow 5 minutes after adding filé before serving.

Shrimp in Sour Cream

3 pounds green shrimp	1½ teaspoons salt
2 tablespoons salt	¼ teaspoon pepper
1 tablespoon vinegar	1 cup sour cream
1 cup onion, minced	1 cup milk
½ cup butter	½ cup sherry
½ pound mushrooms, sliced	Tabasco, Worcestershire (optional)
4 tablespoons flour	cooked rice

Cover shrimp with water containing 2 tablespoons salt and 1 tablespoon vinegar. Bring to boil. Boil 5 minutes. Remove from heat and drain. Clean shrimp. Sauté onion in butter. Add mushrooms. Cook 5 minutes. Blend in flour, 1½ teaspoons salt and pepper. Add sour cream and milk. Cook until thick, stirring constantly. Add shrimp. Remove from heat. Stir in sherry and seasonings if desired. Cook on low for a few minutes. Serve on rice. Serves 6-8.

Cindy's Shrimp Stroganoff

½ stick butter	pepper to taste
2 pounds fresh shrimp, cleaned	1 teaspoon Worcestershire
(may use frozen)	dash Tabasco
¼ cup green onions, chopped	1 cup sour cream
¼ cup almonds, slivered or sliced	3 tablespoons pimiento, sliced
1 cup English peas	1 teaspoon lemon juice
1½ teaspoons salt	cooked rice or noodles
1 teaspoon sugar	

Melt butter. Add shrimp, onions and almonds. Heat until shrimp are thoroughly cooked. Add peas, salt, sugar, pepper, Worcestershire and Tabasco. Mix and heat thoroughly. Fold in sour cream, pimiento and lemon juice. Heat. Serve over rice or noodles. Serves 4-6.

Sweet and Sour Shrimp

1 15¼-ounce can pineapple chunks	2 tablespoons brown sugar
1 medium green pepper, cut in strips	4 teaspoons cornstarch
	1 tablespoon cold water
¼ cup green onions, sliced with tops	2 teaspoons vinegar
1 vegetable or chicken bouillon cube	2 pounds cooked shrimp, peeled and deveined
	1 3-ounce can chow mein noodles

Drain pineapple chunks, reserving juice. Add enough water to make 1⅓ cups liquid. In saucepan, combine juice, pineapple, green pepper, onion and bouillon cube. Heat to boiling. Simmer covered for 3-4 minutes. Blend brown sugar, cornstarch, cold water and vinegar. Add to pineapple mixture. Cook and stir until thick and bubbly. Fold in shrimp. Heat through. Serve over chow mein noodles. Serves 6.

French Shrimp

4 tablespoons butter
  or margarine
3 tablespoons plain flour
1½ cups milk
½ teaspoon salt
dash pepper, paprika

¼ cup dry sherry
1 pound (2 cups) small
  shrimp, cooked and cleaned
  (may use lobster or crab)
5 tablespoons grated
  Parmesan cheese

Melt butter or margarine in saucepan. Stir in flour. Add milk. Stir until thickened. Stir in salt, pepper, paprika, sherry and shrimp. Pour into 5 baking shells or ramekins. Sprinkle each with 1 tablespoon cheese. Place 3 to 4 inches under broiler until cheese browns. Serves 5.

▼ May be served over rice or toast points or in patty shells as an entrée.

Tabby's Egg and Shrimp Casserole

2½ pounds shrimp, boiled and
  cleaned
8 hard-boiled eggs, halved
  lengthwise
1 3-ounce package cream cheese
salt and red pepper to taste
8 tablespoons butter
9 tablespoons plain flour
1 quart milk

½ cup sharp cheese, grated
1 tablespoon Worcestershire
1 tablespoon dry mustard
1 tablespoon catsup
1 tablespoon salt
2 tablespoons parsley, chopped
¼ cup dry sherry
2 3-ounce cans Chinese noodles

Cut shrimp in half. Stuff eggs with mixture of yolks, cream cheese, salt and red pepper. Make cream sauce of butter, flour and milk. Add cheese, Worcestershire, mustard, catsup, salt and parsley. Stir sherry in last. Place eggs in casserole. Add shrimp and cream sauce. Put noodles on top. Bake at 350° for 30 minutes.* Serves 8-10.

*May be prepared a day ahead.

Shrimp and Artichoke Casserole

6½ tablespoons butter
4½ tablespoons flour
1 cup whipping cream
½ cup half-and-half
salt and pepper to taste
1 14-ounce can artichoke hearts
1½-2 pounds shrimp, cooked and
    cleaned

½ pound fresh mushrooms
¼ teaspoon flour
¼ cup dry sherry
1 tablespoon Worcestershire
¼ cup grated Parmesan cheese
paprika

Melt 4½ tablespoons of butter. Stir in flour. Add creams, stirring constantly. When thick, add salt and pepper. Drain artichokes and cut in half. Place on bottom of casserole. Place shrimp over artichokes. Sauté mushrooms in remaining butter. Sprinkle ¼ teaspoon flour over mushrooms. Stir. Scatter mushrooms over shrimp. Add sherry and Worcestershire to cream sauce. Pour over casserole. Top with cheese and paprika. Bake at 375° for 20 minutes. Serves 6.

You cannot get enough of this dish!

Shrimp Supreme

½ cup butter
1 tablespoon onion, grated
½ cup flour
2 cups milk, scalded
½ cup whipping cream
3 egg yolks
2 tablespoons parsley,
    finely chopped
½ cup mushrooms, sliced and
    sautéed
½ teaspoon paprika
1 teaspoon prepared mustard

1 teaspoon Worcestershire
2 pounds shrimp, cooked, cleaned
    and deveined
1 4-ounce can ripe olives,
    slivered
2 hard-boiled eggs, chopped
salt and pepper to taste
4 dashes Tabasco
3 tablespoons sherry or to taste
3 tablespoons Swiss cheese, grated
bread crumbs

Melt butter. Add onion and flour. Gradually pour in milk and cream. Cook over very low heat, stirring until sauce is very thick and smooth. Stir in egg yolks, parsley, mushrooms, paprika, mustard and Worcestershire. Then add shrimp, olives, eggs, seasonings and sherry. Heat well but DO NOT BOIL. Pour in casserole. Top with cheese and bread crumbs. Bake at 350° until bubbly. Serves 6-8.

Really rich and delicious.

Shrimp and Rice Almondine

¾ cup raw rice, cooked
2½ pounds shrimp, cooked, cleaned
   and deveined
1 tablespoon lemon juice
3 tablespoons salad oil
¼ cup onion, minced
2 tablespoons margarine
1 teaspoon salt

⅛ teaspoon pepper
dash cayenne
1 10¾-ounce can condensed
   tomato soup
1 cup whipping cream
½ cup dry sherry
¾ cup slivered almonds,
   blanched and toasted

Spread rice in a 2½-quart greased casserole. Arrange shrimp on top and sprinkle with lemon juice and oil. Sauté onion in margarine for about 5 minutes or until soft, but not brown. Stir in salt, pepper, cayenne, soup, cream,* sherry and half the almonds. Pour over shrimp and stir gently to mix. Bake at 350° for 35 minutes. Sprinkle remaining almonds on top and bake 5 more minutes. Serves 6-8.
*Can be prepared ahead and frozen minus sherry and almonds. Let casserole thaw at room temperature. Add sherry and almonds and bake.

Curried Shrimp Casserole

1½ cups raw rice
1 small onion, grated
1½ sticks butter
1 teaspoon curry
1 teaspoon white pepper
1 teaspoon celery salt

2½ pounds shrimp, cooked, cleaned
   and deveined
½ cup slivered almonds
¾ cup raisins
6 pieces bacon, cooked and
   crumbled

Cook rice as directed. Sauté onion in butter. Add curry, pepper and celery salt. Add rice and shrimp to butter sauce. Add almonds and raisins. Put in large casserole. Heat thoroughly at 350°. Sprinkle bacon on top before serving. Serves 8-10.

Baked Oysters with Almonds

4 tablespoons butter, at
   room temperature
4 tablespoons almonds, ground
1 small clove garlic, minced

1½ teaspoons brandy
dash cayenne pepper
salt to taste
1 dozen oysters, drained

Cream butter and almonds together. Add garlic, brandy, pepper and salt. Fill oyster shells or ramekins with oysters and top each with a teaspoon of mixture. Bake at 450° for 5 minutes. Then place under broiler for 2-3 minutes to toast almonds. Serves 2 as a first course.

Baked Oysters Maxine
Chef Arthur Person, Grand Hotel, Point Clear, Alabama

1 tablespoon dry shallots, chopped
butter
1 pound lump crab meat
2 tablespoons ripe olives, chopped
1 quart Mornay sauce
1 heaping tablespoon Creole mustard
salt to taste
rock salt
oysters on the half-shell
white wine
grated Parmesan cheese

Sauté shallots in butter. Add crab meat, olives, Mornay sauce and mustard. Salt to taste. Remove from heat and keep warm. Fill small baking dish with rock salt. Heat rock salt under broiler. Place open-shell oysters on rock salt. Sprinkle with wine. Place under broiler. Poach oysters for 3-4 minutes. Cover each oyster with crab meat mixture and sprinkle with Parmesan cheese. Place under broiler to brown. Serve at once.

Wild Rice with Oysters

½ cup raw wild rice
½ cup butter, melted
2 cups cracker crumbs
1 cup oysters (reserve liquor)
2 tablespoons butter
chicken broth

Cook rice as directed. Combine melted butter and crumbs. In a buttered baking dish, arrange in layers, half the crumbs, half the rice and all of the oysters. Dot oysters with 2 tablespoons butter and top with remaining rice. Add enough chicken broth to oyster liquor to make 1½ cups. Pour over contents of baking dish. Sprinkle with remaining crumbs. Bake covered at 350° for 30 minutes. Uncover and bake 15 minutes or until crumbs are golden. Serves 4.

Lobster and Artichoke Casserole

1 9-ounce package frozen
artichoke hearts or
1 14-ounce can
3 tablespoons butter
2 teaspoons onion, chopped
¼ teaspoon garlic salt
1 10¾-ounce can condensed cream
of mushroom soup
3 tablespoons sherry (do not use
cooking sherry)
1 cup lobster, cut in small pieces
¾ cup Cheddar cheese, grated

Cook artichoke hearts. Drain. Melt butter in iron skillet. Add onion and let soften. Add salt, soup and sherry. Let simmer 3 minutes. Arrange lobster and artichokes in 1-quart baking dish. Pour soup mixture over lobster. Top with cheese. Bake at 400° for 20 minutes. Serve with wild rice or on toast points. Serves 6-8.

▼ Shrimp or king crab may be substituted for lobster.

The Doctor's Bass

Stuffing:

1 heaping cup bread crumbs
   (Arnold's or Pepperidge Farm)
½ cup dry sherry
3 tablespoons butter
½ cup onion, finely chopped
½ cup celery, chopped

½ cup fresh mushrooms, chopped
2 tablespoons fresh parsley,
   chopped
¼ teaspoon salt
¼ teaspoon pepper
cayenne pepper to taste

Fish:

1 freshly caught 4½-5 pound bass
   or red snapper
4 strips bacon
3 tablespoons butter, softened

salt and white pepper to taste
butter
water
paprika

To make stuffing, mix crumbs and sherry. Let stand 10 minutes. Melt butter and sauté onion and celery for 3 minutes. Drain excess sherry from crumbs. To crumbs, add all stuffing ingredients and mix well. For a more attractive dish, leave bass whole. Replace eyes with olives before baking. Pat fish dry. Make three 2-inch diagonal cuts on one side of bass. Cut 2 strips of bacon into pieces and place in the diagonal cuts. Mix butter with salt and pepper and dab over top of fish. Put remaining bacon on bottom of baking dish. Put fish on top of bacon. Use wooden spoon to stuff fish. Bake at 325° on center rack of oven for 1 hour. Baste with mixture of 1 part melted butter to 1 part water about every 20 minutes. When fish is done, transfer to serving platter by using 2 spatulas, approaching fish from head to tail to keep it intact. Sprinkle with paprika. Serves 4-6.

Stuffed Flounder

1 large or 2 small flounder
salt
½ cup green onion, chopped
¼ cup green pepper, minced
½ cup celery, minced
1 clove garlic, minced
4 tablespoons butter
1 cup chicken bouillon

2 cups plain stuffing mix
1 tablespoon parsley, chopped
1 egg, beaten
1 cup small shrimp, cooked
salt and pepper to taste
paprika
lemon juice
garnish: parsley

Make a pocket in side of flounder. Season with salt. Sauté onion, pepper, celery and garlic in 2 tablespoons butter. Set aside. Bring bouillon to boil. Add stuffing mix and parsley to bouillon and toss. Let cool slightly. Add egg. Mix with sautéed vegetables and shrimp. Season to taste with salt and pepper. Stuff fish. Place in buttered pan and cover with foil. Bake at 350° for 30 minutes. Brush with remaining butter. Sprinkle with paprika and lemon juice. Bake 10 more minutes uncovered. Garnish. Serves 2.

Sweet and Sour Halibut

Mrs. Bobby Nichols

Sauce:
1 cup white vinegar
1 cup apricot nectar
1 cup brown sugar
1 teaspoon Worcestershire
½ cup catsup

1 teaspoon cornstarch mixed
  with 1 teaspoon water
2 cups pineapple chunks
1 cup green pepper, diced
2 medium tomatoes, peeled and
  cut in wedges

Fish:
3 tablespoons cornstarch
3 tablespoons water
1 tablespoon Kikkoman soy sauce

1½ pounds halibut, cut into
  ¾-inch cubes
salt and pepper to taste

Sauce: Combine first 5 ingredients. Simmer 30 minutes. Thicken with cornstarch mixture. Add pineapple, green pepper and tomatoes. Keep hot.
Fish: Mix cornstarch, water and soy sauce to form a paste. Dip halibut cubes in paste to coat lightly. Sprinkle with salt and pepper. Deep fat fry until golden brown. Place on serving dish and cover with sauce. Serves 6.

▼ Any firm, white boneless fish could be substituted.

Fillet of Sole with Spinach

1 pound fresh spinach or
  1 10-ounce package frozen
  spinach
2 tablespoons butter

2 cups white wine
salt, pepper to taste
4 fillets of sole
grated Parmesan cheese

Béchamel Sauce:
1 tablespoon onion, chopped
2 tablespoons butter
2 tablespoons flour
3 cups half-and-half, warmed

¼ teaspoon salt
white pepper to taste
sprig parsley, chopped
pinch of nutmeg

Wash and cook spinach. DRAIN WELL. Heat butter, wine, salt and pepper in skillet. Poach fillets for 5 minutes. To prepare Béchamel sauce, sauté onion in butter. Add flour and cook, stirring constantly. Add cream. Stir with whisk. Add salt, pepper, parsley, nutmeg and wine from skillet. Cook slowly for about 30 minutes or until smooth and reduced by ⅓. (This may take longer.) Strain. This makes about 2 cups sauce. Spread ½ of sauce in bottom of buttered baking dish. Place fillets on top. Add spinach. Cover with remaining sauce. Sprinkle with Parmesan cheese. Bake at 350° for 15-20 minutes. Serves 4.

▼ Flounder may be substituted for sole. This may be made a day ahead.
This is elegant and delicious.

Salmon Tetrazzini

4 ounces uncooked spaghetti
1 16-ounce can (2 cups) Red
   Sockeye salmon and liquid
milk
2 tablespoons butter
2 tablespoons flour
¼ teaspoon salt

dash pepper, nutmeg
2 tablespoons dry sherry
1 3-ounce can broiled sliced
   mushrooms, drained
4 tablespoons dry bread crumbs
4 tablespoons grated
   Parmesan cheese

Cook spaghetti according to package directions. Drain. Drain salmon, reserving liquid. Remove any bones or large pieces of skin. Break salmon into large pieces. Add enough milk to salmon liquid to make 2 cups. Melt butter and blend in flour, salt, pepper and nutmeg. Add liquid mixture all at once. Cook over medium heat, stirring constantly, until thick and smooth. Add sherry. Stir in spaghetti, mushrooms and salmon. Place in greased 1-quart casserole. Top with mixture of bread crumbs and cheese. Bake at 350° for about 40 minutes. Serves 4-6.

Baked Whole Shad

1 whole shad
milk
salt and pepper to taste

bacon strips, uncooked
lemon slices

Place shad in roasting pan. Cover almost completely with milk. Season shad and top with bacon and lemon slices. Bake at 250° for 8 hours covered. Cooking shad in milk dissolves the bones. The roe can be fried in butter just before serving the shad.

Fish Fillet in Wine Sauce

1½ pounds broccoli (optional)
1½ pounds fish fillets
juice of 1 lemon
1 cup white wine
1 cup fresh mushrooms, sliced

2 tablespoons butter
2 tablespoons flour
½ cup half-and-half
½ teaspoon salt
1 cup sharp Cheddar cheese, grated

Cook broccoli until tender. Sprinkle fish with lemon juice. Let stand a few minutes. Drain fish. Poach in heated wine. Place broccoli at each end of shallow baking dish. Place fish in center of dish. Sauté mushrooms lightly in butter. Blend in flour. Stir in cream and ½ cup wine in which fillets were poached. Cook and stir until thickened. Blend in salt and cheese. Stir over very low heat until cheese melts. Pour over fish. Bake at 350° for 20-30 minutes. Serves 4.

Tuna Taipei
Mrs. Jimmy Demaret, wife of Masters' Champion 1940, 1947 and 1950

2 6½ or 7-ounce cans tuna
½ cup green onion, chopped
¼ cup salad oil
4 cups cooked rice, unsalted

3 tablespoons soy sauce
2 eggs, beaten
1 5-ounce can water chestnuts, drained and coarsely chopped

Drain and flake tuna. Sauté onion in oil until tender. Add rice and soy sauce. Stir over low heat until rice is hot. Push rice to one side. Pour in eggs and cook, stirring frequently. Add water chestnuts and tuna. Mix well. Serves 6-8.
Quick and easy.

Seaman's Pie

1 6-ounce package noodles, cooked
1 7-ounce can tuna, drained
¼ cup onion, chopped
2 eggs, boiled and chopped
1 10¾-ounce can condensed cream of mushroom soup

½ teaspoon salt
pepper to taste
1 teaspoon Worcestershire
dash Tabasco
1 tablespoon parsley, chopped
¼-½ cup sharp cheese, grated

Put layer of noodles in square casserole. Add layer of tuna, onion and eggs. Mix soup with seasonings and pour over all. Sprinkle cheese on top. Bake at 350° for 30 minutes.* Serves 4-6.
*May be prepared a day ahead.
Children love it.

Tuna Quick Casserole

1 8-ounce package noodles, cooked
½ pint sour cream
¾ cup onion, chopped
½ pint cottage cheese
2 7-ounce cans tuna, drained

seasoning salt to taste
Tabasco to taste
1 tablespoon Worcestershire
grated Parmesan cheese
paprika

In a baking dish, combine noodles, sour cream, onion, cottage cheese, tuna, salt, Tabasco and Worcestershire. Mix well. Sprinkle Parmesan cheese and paprika on top. Bake at 350° for 30 minutes. Serves 6.

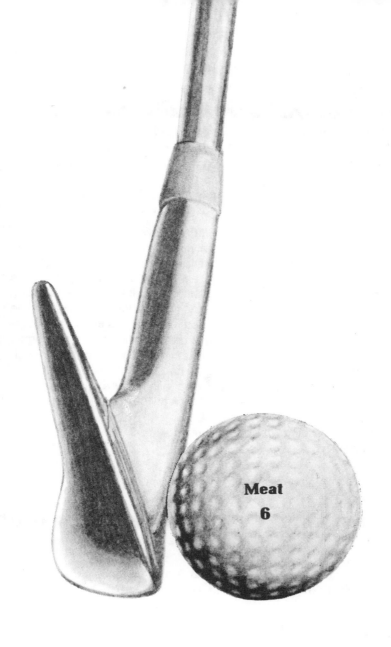

Bert's Beef Wellington

1 5-7 pound beef tenderloin
1 stick butter, melted
½ pound mushrooms, minced
1 pound cooked ham, ground
¼ cup sherry or white wine
2 tablespoons tomato paste
½ cup water
2 10-ounce packages frozen
  Pepperidge Farm patty shells
flour
1 egg yolk
2 teaspoons water

Trim all fat from meat and fold tail under to form an even-shaped roast. Brush meat with 4 tablespoons butter and roast 35 minutes at 425°. Remove from pan and cool. Sauté mushrooms in remaining butter until soft. Combine mushrooms, ham, wine, tomato paste and ½ cup water. Set aside. For crust, allow patty shells to thaw 20-30 minutes until just pliable but not sticky. Stack 2 deep in 2 rows and roll out using a minimum amount of flour to keep from sticking. Crust should be large enough to cover meat completely. Tear off rough edges to make decoration and set aside. To assemble, place ham mixture in center of crust in approximate dimensions of roast. Place roast top-side down on mixture and fold dough over meat. Pinch edges together. Wet fingers if necessary to seal dough. Turn over. Cut out decoration and place on top. Brush with mixture of egg yolk and water. Place roast on rack in clean roaster and cook at 450° for 30-35 minutes for rare to medium rare. Serves 8-10.

▼ Can sit an hour after being wrapped before cooking.
For very special company.

Tournedos of Beef

4 mushroom caps
butter
red wine
2 tablespoons shallots,
  finely chopped
¾ cup beef broth
1 tablespoon cornstarch
4 ½-inch slices eggplant, peeled
flour
salt and pepper to taste
4 (3-4 ounces each) tournedos
  (beef tenderloin)
4 slices prosciutto ham

Lightly brown mushroom caps in 2 tablespoons butter. Sprinkle with 2 tablespoons red wine and cook 3-4 minutes. Set aside. For sauce, sauté shallots in 1 tablespoon butter. Combine beef broth with cornstarch and ⅓ cup red wine and stir into shallots. Simmer 3-4 minutes until thickened. Set aside. Dredge eggplant in flour and season with salt and pepper. Brown on both sides in 4 tablespoons butter. Dust meat with flour, season with salt and pepper and sauté in butter to desired doneness. To assemble tournedos, arrange slices of eggplant on warmed serving platter, top each with a slice of prosciutto, tournedo and a mushroom cap. Spoon sauce on top. Serves 4.

Beef Strips in Tomato Cream Sauce
Mrs. Bruce Crampton

4-6 pounds sirloin steak, cut
   in thin strips
1 cup plain flour (or more if
   desired)
1 tablespoon salt
ground pepper to taste
½ cup salad oil (more if
   needed)
2 cups onion, chopped
4 cloves garlic, crushed

2 cups green pepper, diced
1 pound mushrooms, sliced and
   sautéed in butter
2 10¾-ounce cans tomato soup,
   undiluted
1 beef bouillon cube dissolved
   in 1 cup boiling water
2 tablespoons Worcestershire
4 cups sour cream (or less to
   taste)

Dredge beef strips in mixture of flour, salt and pepper. Brown meat in oil, remove and set aside. In same skillet, sauté onion, garlic and green pepper. Add mushrooms, soup, bouillon and Worcestershire. Add sirloin and heat. Remove from heat and add sour cream. Place in 2-quart casserole and keep warm until ready to serve. Do not boil after adding sour cream. Serve with parsley rice. Serves 16-24.

Sally's Roast Tenderloin

1 (5-8 pound) tenderloin roast
   (may use rib eye or any tender
   cut of roast)
garlic powder (not garlic salt)
coarse black pepper or lemon-
   pepper

1½-2 cups soy sauce
½-¾ cup bourbon
powdered horseradish (if available)
bacon or salt pork (optional)
1 onion, sliced (optional)
1 bell pepper, halved (optional)

Wipe surface of meat with paper towel. Sprinkle entire surface with generous amounts of garlic powder and pepper. Place roast in 2 large plastic bags (double thickness). If large garbage size plastic bags are used, roast can be turned easily by rotating bag. Add soy sauce, bourbon and horseradish. Marinate at least 2 hours at room temperature or overnight in refrigerator. Allow roast to come to room temperature before roasting. If roast is very lean, have butcher lard it or add strips of bacon or salt pork on top. Preheat oven to 450°. Put meat on rack in open roasting pan. Pour marinade over roast and put onion and bell pepper in pan. Reduce heat to 400° and roast 35-50 minutes or until internal temperature reaches 135° on meat thermometer for a rare roast.

▼ Fresh mushrooms which have been sliced and sautéed may be added to liquid in pan and thickened slightly for gravy.
A favorite at Augusta cocktail parties.

83

Steak Medallions Mignon

Bordelaise Sauce:
1 tablespoon butter
1 tablespoon flour
1 cup beef stock
1 clove garlic, minced
1 tablespoon onion, minced
1½ teaspoons catsup

1½ teaspoons Worcestershire
¼ teaspoon celery salt
1 bay leaf
salt, pepper and paprika
   to taste
1 tablespoon sherry

Medallions:
1½ pounds beef tenderloin
4 tablespoons butter
½ teaspoon salt
dash of pepper

¼ teaspoon garlic salt
½ cup onion, diced
1 cup mushrooms, sliced

For sauce, melt butter and add flour, stirring until brown. Gradually add stock, garlic, onion, catsup, Worcestershire, celery salt and bay leaf. Simmer 5 minutes. Season with remaining ingredients. Remove bay leaf. Set sauce aside and keep warm. Prepare tenderloin by cutting in 1-inch cubes. Sauté in 2 tablespoons butter in a hot skillet. Season to taste with salt, pepper and garlic salt. Add onion and mushrooms. Cook over low heat about 5 minutes. Add Bordelaise sauce. Serve immediately. Serves 4.

Beef Stroganoff

1 pound sirloin, cut in
   ¼-inch strips
½ teaspoon salt
4 tablespoons plain flour
4 tablespoons butter
1 4-ounce can sliced mushrooms

½ cup onion, chopped
1 tablespoon catsup
1 10½-ounce can beef broth
1 cup sour cream
2 tablespoons cooking sherry
cooked rice or noodles

Dredge meat in mixture of salt and 1 tablespoon flour. Melt 2 tablespoons butter in a hot skillet, add meat and quickly brown on all sides. Add mushrooms and onion. Cook 3-4 minutes or until onion is barely tender. Transfer skillet contents to a bowl and keep warm. Add 2 tablespoons butter to pan drippings. Blend in 3 tablespoons flour and catsup. Slowly add beef broth. Cook, stirring constantly, until mixture thickens. Return meat mixture to pan and stir in sour cream and sherry. Heat briefly. Serve over rice or noodles. Serves 4.

Filet of Beef with Brandy Sauce

4 tablespoons sweet butter, or as
  needed to fry steaks
1 clove garlic, chopped
⅛ teaspoon rosemary
⅛ teaspoon thyme
4 8-ounce filets

6 ounces whipping cream
2 ounces dry white wine
1 tablespoon Dijon mustard
1 teaspoon Worcestershire
2 ounces brandy (or to taste)

Melt butter in heavy skillet and sauté garlic, rosemary and thyme. Remove as much of garlic and herbs as possible. Cook filets to desired doneness in same butter. Remove filets and excess butter. Keep warm. Add remaining ingredients to skillet and boil for 5-7 minutes. Return filets to skillet. Heat through. Pass sauce when serving. Serves 4.

Steak Diane

4 sirloin strip steaks, ½ inch thick
salt to taste
black pepper, freshly ground
4 teaspoons dry mustard

4 tablespoons butter
3 tablespoons lemon juice
2 teaspoons chopped chives
1 teaspoon Worcestershire

With a mallet, pound steaks to ⅓-inch thick. Sprinkle both sides with salt, pepper and mustard. Pound into meat. Heat butter in skillet. Cook steak 2 minutes on each side. Transfer to hot serving dish. Add remaining ingredients to skillet. Bring to a boil. Pour over meat. Serves 4.

▼ If desired, garnish with stuffed mushrooms (see index).
Elegant when cooked at the table using a chafing dish.

Steak Nolan

2 bell peppers, sliced
2 onions, sliced
1 pound fresh mushrooms, sliced
  (or left whole, if small)
4 tablespoons butter
salt and pepper

6 ounces brandy, or more to taste
1 cup consommé
¼ cup flour mixed with ¼ cup water
sirloin steak (1½ inches thick), cooked
  as desired

Sauté pepper, onions and mushrooms in butter. Add salt and pepper. Stir in an ounce or two of brandy. Set aside. In a saucepan, heat consommé. Add flour-water mixture and 2 ounces of brandy. Simmer until thickened. Add sautéed vegetables. Season with more brandy, if desired. Serve over sirloin sliced into long, thin, ¼-inch pieces on preheated dinner plates.

▼ Be bold with brandy.

Lindy's London Broil

1 cup soy sauce
1 small onion, minced
1 teaspoon MSG
1 teaspoon lemon-pepper
½ teaspoon garlic powder

2 teaspoons ground ginger
3 thin slices lemon
2½-3 pound top round or
   flank steak

Combine first 7 ingredients. Bring to a boil. Pour immediately over meat and refrigerate 8 hours. Broil over charcoal, about 10 minutes per side for rare. Baste frequently with sauce while cooking. Cut thin slices on the diagonal. Serves 6.

▼ Make your own lemon-pepper by combining 1 teaspoon grated lemon rind and ½ teaspoon freshly ground black pepper.

Marinated Flank Steak

½ cup oil
⅓ cup dry burgundy
3 tablespoons green onions
   with tops, minced
1 garlic clove, minced
1 teaspoon dry mustard
¼ cup soy sauce

2 teaspoons red wine vinegar
1-2 tablespoons brown sugar
½ teaspoon basil
¼ teaspoon pepper
⅛ teaspoon marjoram
1½ pound flank steak

Mix first 11 ingredients. Pour over steak in a plastic or glass bowl. Marinate overnight. Grill or broil steak no more than 5 minutes per side. Cut in thin diagonal slices. Serve warmed marinade with steak. Serves 4.

Florida Marinated Flank Steak

6 tablespoons frozen orange
   juice concentrate
¼ cup vinegar
½ cup vegetable oil
2 tablespoons soy sauce
1 small onion, sliced
salt and pepper to taste

½ teaspoon rosemary (optional)
½ teaspoon celery salt
½ teaspoon leaf thyme
1 small garlic clove, sliced
2½-3 pounds flank, top round
   or sirloin steak

Combine marinade ingredients and pour over meat. Marinate in refrigerator for 8-12 hours. Cook on grill, basting with marinade while cooking. Serves 6-8.

Boeuf Bourguignon

3 pounds lean boneless beef,
  cut in 1-inch cubes
3-4 tablespoons olive oil
1 cup burgundy
1 bay leaf
½ teaspoon thyme
1 clove garlic, minced
½ teaspoon salt

1-2 tablespoons tomato paste
2 cups beef broth
2 tablespoons flour
4 tablespoons butter
1 pound fresh mushrooms, sliced
2 tablespoons vegetable oil
1 16-ounce jar whole small onions
cooked rice

In a skillet, brown beef cubes in oil. Transfer to a Dutch oven. Pour wine into skillet. Scrape up brown bits and pour over beef. Add seasonings, tomato paste and broth to meat. Cover and bring to a boil. Transfer to oven. Bake at 325° for 2-3 hours. Discard bay leaf. Remove beef. Make a roux of flour and 2 tablespoons butter. Sauté mushrooms in 2 tablespoons butter and oil. Add both to the Dutch oven along with the beef and onions. Mix well. Serve over rice. Serves 6-8.
▼ Freezes well.

Sauerbraten

1 3-pound round steak
1 tablespoon salt
½ teaspoon pepper
2 onions, sliced
1 carrot, sliced
1 stalk celery, chopped
4 cloves
4 peppercorns
1 teaspoon paprika

1 clove garlic (optional)
1 cup red wine vinegar
2 bay leaves
2 tablespoons kidney fat
  (bacon grease may be substituted)
6 tablespoons butter
3 tablespoons flour
1 tablespoon sugar
5 ginger snaps, crushed

Wipe steak with damp cloth. Season with salt and pepper. Place in earthenware bowl. Combine onions, carrot, celery, cloves, peppercorns, paprika, garlic, vinegar, bay leaves and 2½ pints water (or enough to cover meat). Pour over meat, cover and refrigerate for 4 days. Drain meat. Sauté in fat and 1 tablespoon butter in enamelware, glass or earthenware utensil, until seared on all sides. Add marinade and bring to a boil. Cover, reduce heat and simmer 3 hours. Melt remaining butter in a saucepan and stir in flour. Add sugar, blend and let brown to a dark color. Add to meat. Continue cooking until meat is tender, about 1 hour longer. Remove meat to a warm platter. Stir gingersnaps into gravy and cook until thickened. Pour gravy over meat. Serves 6-8.

Easy Sauerbraten

1 3-pound lean boneless chuck
   roast
½ cup red wine vinegar
2 bay leaves, crumbled

1 clove garlic, crushed
dash of pepper
1 envelope dry onion soup mix
ginger snaps, crushed

Line a shallow baking pan with large sheets of heavy duty aluminum foil. Place roast in center. Pour vinegar over roast and sprinkle with bay leaves, garlic and pepper. Bring foil up over meat, sealing in meat and spices. Marinate 30 minutes at room temperature. Open foil and sprinkle soup mix over roast. Close foil and seal edges. Roast at 325° for 3 hours. Remove meat and strain drippings into a pan. Add enough gingersnaps to make gravy smooth and thick. Serves 4-6.

▼ For excellent open-faced sandwiches, toast French or Vienna bread slices topped with Parmesan cheese, and cover with sliced sauerbraten and gravy.

Most stews are improved by standing and reheating, especially those made with wine.

Herbed Mushroom Pot Roast

1 beef roast (3-4 pounds)
3 to 4 tablespoons flour
cooking oil
salt and pepper
1 onion, sliced
½ cup water
¼ cup catsup
⅓ cup cooking sherry
¼ teaspoon dry mustard

¼ teaspoon marjoram
¼ teaspoon rosemary
¼ teaspoon thyme
1 small bay leaf
1 6-ounce can mushrooms
   and liquid
1 tablespoon cornstarch
½ cup cold water

Dredge meat in flour. Brown slowly on all sides in small amount of oil. Season generously with salt and pepper. Add onion. Mix and add water, catsup, sherry and spices. Cover and cook slowly for 2-2½ hours. Add mushrooms and liquid. Heat. Remove meat to platter. Blend cornstarch and water. Add to gravy, stirring until thickened. Serves 6-8.

▼ Try this in a crock pot.

Apalachicola Spaghetti

3 pounds round or rump roast,
    cut in 1-inch cubes
garlic cloves
¼ pound butter or margarine
6 large onions, chopped
2 6-ounce cans tomato paste
water

2 16-ounce cans tomatoes
1 tablespoon Worcestershire
1 tablespoon sugar
1 tablespoon salt
black pepper to taste
1 bay leaf
thin spaghetti, cooked

Cut a small pocket in each chunk of beef and stud with a very small piece of garlic. Brown meat in half of butter and set aside. Brown onions in remaining butter. Combine beef, onions and tomato paste. Wash paste cans out with water and add water to beef mixture. Add remaining ingredients, except spaghetti. Cook very slowly for 3-4 hours, covered. Add more water if necessary. Serve over spaghetti. Serves 8-10.

French Stew

1 cup dry red wine (burgundy)
1 1⅜-ounce package onion soup
    mix
1 10¾-ounce can cream of
    mushroom soup, undiluted
2 pounds stew beef
⅓ cup pimiento-stuffed olives

1 16-ounce can tiny whole
    carrots
1 4-ounce can tiny button
    mushrooms
1 bell pepper, diced
1 16-ounce jar or can of small
    whole onions

Mix wine, soup mix and soup in Dutch oven. Add beef. Cover and cook at 250° for 4 hours. Check after 2 hours and add more wine if necessary. After 4 hours, add remaining ingredients and cook an additional hour. Add more wine or a little water during this hour if necessary. The stew should be soupy. Serves 6-8.

▼ Better if cooked a day ahead and allowed to season. Reheat to serve.

Spiced Corned Beef

1 4-pound corned beef brisket
3 large onions, sliced
1 bell pepper, sliced
8 cloves

3 garlic cloves, sliced
2 tablespoons peppercorns
2-3 bay leaves
1 teaspoon salt

Remove fat from meat. Cover with water and add remaining ingredients. Bring to a boil. Cover and simmer over low heat about 3 hours or until tender. Serves 6-8.

Pimiento-sauced Short Ribs

12 beef short ribs
flour
4 tablespoons vegetable oil
4 tablespoons plain flour
1½ teaspoons salt
⅛ teaspoon pepper
2 cups beef broth

1 teaspoon dill weed
2 teaspoons prepared mustard
2 tablespoons lemon juice
1 4-ounce jar chopped pimientos
1 8-ounce package wide egg
   noodles, cooked and drained

Dredge ribs in flour and brown on all sides in oil. Transfer to baking pan with rack. Cook at 350° for 45 minutes or until tender. To the drippings in the skillet, add 4 tablespoons flour, salt and pepper. Blend well. Add broth and cook over medium heat until thickened, stirring constantly. Add dill, mustard, lemon juice and pimiento. Bring to a boil. Remove from heat. Place ribs in center of a baking dish, arrange noodles around ribs and pour sauce over all. Bake at 350° for 15 minutes or until thoroughly heated. Serves 4.

Steak Mozzarella

½ cup plain flour
¾ cup Cheddar cheese, grated
1-1½ pounds cube steak, cut
   into serving pieces
1 egg, beaten
⅓ cup salad oil
1 large onion, chopped

1 6-ounce can tomato paste
1 clove garlic, minced
salt and pepper to taste
2 cups hot water
1 8-ounce package Mozzarella
   cheese, sliced
hot cooked noodles

Combine flour and Cheddar cheese. Dip steak in egg and coat with flour mixture. Press into steak. Brown in oil. Transfer steak to a shallow baking dish. In same pan, sauté onion. Stir in tomato paste, garlic, salt, pepper and water. Simmer 10 minutes. Pour over steak and top with Mozzarella cheese. Bake covered at 350° for 1 hour. Serve over noodles. Serves 4-6.
A favorite family dish.

Calzoné

1 medium white onion, chopped
1 clove garlic, minced
¾ pound ground beef
salt and pepper to taste
½ teaspoon oregano
½ teaspoon Italian seasoning
1 15-ounce can tomato sauce

1 8-ounce package refrigerator
   crescent rolls
flour
8 ounces Mozzarella cheese, grated
sliced pepperoni
1 6-ounce jar marinated artichoke
   hearts, sliced
1 4-ounce can sliced mushrooms

Sauté onion, garlic and ground beef for 10 minutes. Season with salt, pepper, half the oregano and half the Italian seasoning. Heat tomato sauce with remaining oregano and Italian seasoning. Place 2 triangles of crescent dough together to form a square. Press edges together to seal. Roll lightly in flour. In center of square, place 2 tablespoons beef mixture. Top with grated cheese, pepperoni, artichokes, mushrooms and about 2 tablespoons sauce. Fold one edge of dough over and seal edges together. Repeat procedure for remaining dough. Place in ovenproof serving dish. Pour about 2 tablespoons sauce over each. If any of beef mixture remains, sprinkle it on top of sauce. Bake at 350° for 20 minutes. Serves 4.

Lasagne
Mrs. Hubert Green

1 pound sweet or hot Italian sausage, skinned and chopped
¾ pound ground beef
½ cup onion, minced
2 garlic cloves, crushed
1-2 tablespoons sugar
1½ teaspoons basil
½ teaspoon fennel seed
1 teaspoon Italian seasoning
1 tablespoon salt
¼ teaspoon pepper
1 35-ounce can Italian style plum tomatoes, mashed
2 tablespoons parsley, chopped
2 6-ounce cans tomato paste
2 8-ounce cans seasoned tomato sauce
½ cup water
12 lasagne noodles
1 16-ounce carton Ricotta or cottage cheese
1 egg
2 tablespoons parsley, chopped
½ teaspoon salt
¾ pound Mozzarella cheese, sliced
¾ cup grated Parmesan cheese

Sauté sausage, beef, onion and garlic until well browned. Add next 11 ingredients and simmer covered about 1½ hours, stirring occasionally. Cook noodles according to directions. Drain and rinse with cold water. Combine Ricotta cheese with egg, parsley and ½ teaspoon salt. To assemble, spoon 1½ cups meat sauce on the bottom of a 13x9x2-inch baking dish. Arrange 6 noodles lengthwise over meat sauce. Spread with half the Ricotta cheese mixture. Top with a third of Mozzarella cheese slices. Spoon 1½ cups meat sauce over Mozzarella and sprinkle with ¼ cup Parmesan cheese. Add in layers, remaining noodles, Ricotta cheese mixture, half the remaining Mozzarella and all the meat sauce. Top with Mozzarella and sprinkle with Parmesan cheese. Cover with foil and bake 25 minutes at 375°. Remove foil and bake 25 minutes more. Cool 15 minutes before serving. Serves 6-8.

Cantonese Beef and Rice

1½ pounds ground beef
3 tablespoons butter
3 medium onions, chopped
1½ cups celery, chopped
1 garlic clove, minced
1 cup raw rice
1 10¾-ounce can cream of
  mushroom soup, undiluted
1 10½-ounce can consommé

2 cups sour cream
3 tablespoons soy sauce
2 teaspoons Worcestershire
1 6-ounce can mushrooms, or
  ½ pound fresh mushrooms
  browned in butter
1 cup salted almonds, or 1 cup
  sliced water chestnuts

In a skillet, brown meat in 1 tablespoon butter. Place meat in large (3 quart) lightly-buttered casserole. Add 1 tablespoon butter to skillet and sauté onion, celery and garlic. Add to casserole. Melt remaining butter in skillet and brown rice. Add rice and remaining ingredients, except almonds. Bake covered at 325° for 1½ to 2 hours, stirring every half hour. More consommé or sour cream may be added during cooking if needed. Add almonds or water chestnuts the last 30 minutes. Serves 6-8.
Great for a late "Masters" supper.

Rissoles
Mrs. Bruce Crampton

1 pound ground beef
1 onion, chopped
1 tablespoon ketchup

¼ teaspoon thyme
¼ teaspoon oregano
1 tablespoon Worcestershire

Mix all ingredients and shape into thick patties. Cook as desired on grill or in fry pan. Serves 3-4.

Bul-kogi

4 tablespoons sugar
4 tablespoons vegetable oil
1 pound beef steak, thinly
  sliced
6 tablespoons soy sauce
dash of pepper
1 green onion, finely chopped

1 clove garlic, minced
4 tablespoons sesame seeds,
  toasted and ground in a mortar
1 tablespoon plain flour
water
cooked rice

In a bowl, mix sugar and 2 tablespoons oil. Stir in beef strips. Mix well. Combine soy sauce, pepper, onion, garlic, sesame seeds and flour. Pour over beef and marinate 15-30 minutes. Heat remaining oil in skillet. Add meat and cook 3-5 minutes. Add small amount of water and the strained marinade. Cover and cook 3-5 minutes more or until tender. Serve over rice. Serves 4-6.
Something different for oriental food buffs to try. The sesame seeds add a great flavor.

Sukiyaki

½ to ¾ cup soy sauce
3 tablespoons sugar
2 chicken bouillon cubes
   dissolved in ½ cup water
2 tablespoons vegetable oil
½-¾ head Chinese cabbage, cut
   into bite-size pieces
12 scallions or green onions,
   cut into 2-inch lengths
1 large onion, sliced lengthwise

½ pound mushrooms, sliced
1 16-ounce can bean sprouts,
   drained
1 8-ounce can water chestnuts
   drained and sliced
1-1½ pounds beef steak, thinly
   sliced
12 ounces spinach, broken into
   bite-size pieces
cooked rice

Add soy sauce and sugar to bouillon. Set aside. Heat oil in a large skillet on medium high. Add cabbage, onion, mushrooms, bean sprouts and water chestnuts. Pour bouillon mixture over vegetables. Cover and cook 12 minutes. Add meat and spinach. Cook 2 minutes. Push down into sauce. Cook 3 minutes. Serve immediately over rice. Serves 4.

Ground Beef with Wine Sauce

1 carrot, diced
1 medium onion, chopped
2 cloves garlic, minced
2 ounces ground beef
3 tablespoons parsley, chopped
3-4 tablespoons butter
7 ounces dry red wine

5 ounces beef stock or bouillon
1 tablespoon tomato paste
1 tablespoon cornstarch
4 4-ounce patties ground round
   beef
4 slices French bread, sautéed
   in butter

Sauté first 5 ingredients in butter over low heat for 10 minutes. Add wine, stock and tomato paste. Simmer for 10 minutes. Dissolve cornstarch in 2 tablespoons water and add to above mixture to thicken. Place beef patties which have been cooked to desired doneness on the French bread. Pour sauce over beef patties. Serves 4.

▼ Sauce may be made ahead and reheated.
Makes a special Sunday night supper!

Moussaka

2 tablespoons butter
1 large onion, chopped
1 green pepper, chopped
1½ pounds ground meat
    (beef, lamb or veal)
3 tomatoes, chopped
3 tablespoons parsley, chopped
salt and pepper to taste

¼ to ½ cup dry white wine
1 medium eggplant
salad oil
6 tablespoons cracker crumbs
2 egg whites, beaten
2 egg yolks
1 cup milk
1 cup Cheddar cheese, grated

In a large frying pan, melt butter. Sauté onion and green pepper. Add meat and brown. Add tomatoes, parsley, salt, pepper and wine. Cover skillet and cook 30 minutes or until liquid is absorbed. While meat is cooking, peel eggplant and cut into ½-inch slices. Season eggplant with salt and drain on paper towels. Sauté in salad oil until brown on both sides. Sprinkle half of cracker crumbs on bottom and sides of a buttered casserole. Add remaining crumbs and egg whites to meat mixture. Mix well. Layer eggplant and meat mixture in casserole, ending with eggplant. Beat egg yolks, milk and grated cheese. Pour over casserole. Bake at 350° for 1 hour. Serves 6-8.

Zucchini Moussaka

3 small zucchini, cut in ¼-
    inch slices
1 large onion, sliced
2 tablespoons vegetable oil
1 pound lean ground beef
1 8-ounce can tomato sauce

1 clove garlic, minced
½ teaspoon salt
¼ teaspoon cinnamon
1 cup cottage cheese
1 egg, slightly beaten
¼ cup grated Parmesan cheese

In large skillet, brown zucchini and onion in oil. Place in shallow 2-quart baking dish. In same skillet, brown beef. Drain. Stir in tomato sauce, garlic, salt and cinnamon. Simmer 10 to 15 minutes. Spread over zucchini and onion. Blend cottage cheese and egg. Spread over meat. Sprinkle Parmesan cheese over all. Bake at 350° for 30 minutes. Serves 4-6.

Halpuchis (Ukrainian Cabbage Rolls)

8 large cabbage leaves
1 pound ground beef
¼ cup onion, chopped
½ cup celery, chopped
1 cup cooked rice

1 teaspoon horseradish
1 tablespoon prepared mustard
1 egg, beaten
2 cups tomato juice

Steam cabbage until barely tender. Set aside. Brown ground beef and onion. Stir in celery, rice, horseradish and mustard. Cook until celery begins to soften. Stir in egg. Spoon mixture into cabbage leaves. Roll and fasten with toothpicks. Place in shallow baking dish, one layer deep. Cover with tomato juice. Bake at 350° for 30 minutes. Serves 8.

▼ Freezes nicely.

Scandinavian Meatballs

1 pound ground round steak
¾ cup rye bread crumbs
   with seeds
1 cup cream (or evaporated milk)
salt and pepper to taste
1 teaspoon MSG
flour

2 tablespoons butter
4 tablespooons olive oil
1 cup sour cream
½ cup dry white wine
3 boiled potatoes, sliced
garnish: caraway seeds and butter

Combine first 5 ingredients and shape into meatballs the size of large marbles. Roll in flour. Quickly brown meatballs in butter and olive oil in a skillet. Drain off some of the grease and add sour cream and wine. Stir until sauce is blended. DO NOT BOIL. Place in serving dish and put potatoes sprinkled with caraway seeds and melted butter around the edge. Serves 4-6.

Hungarian Style Meat Loaf or Meatballs
Mrs. Julius Boros

1 pound ground round steak
2 eggs
½ teaspoon salt
1 medium onion, grated

¼ teaspoon black pepper
4 slices dried bread,
   soaked and drained

Sauce:
1 8-ounce can tomato sauce
1½ cups water
1 tablespoon sugar

1 tablespoon flour
1 cup sour cream

Combine meat ingredients and shape for meat loaf or form balls to fry. For sauce, dilute tomato sauce with water. Add sugar. Bring to a boil. Add flour to sour cream, stirring until smooth. Add to tomato sauce. Stir slowly and bring to a boil. Use as gravy over meat loaf or meat balls. Serves 4.

B's Chili

1 cup bell pepper, chopped
1 cup onion, chopped
1 cup celery, chopped
2 cloves garlic, minced
2 tablespoons butter
1 pound ground beef
1 15-ounce can tomato paste
1 16-ounce can peeled tomatoes

1 15-ounce can kidney beans,
   drained
½ cup water
1 tablespoon chili powder
1½ teaspoons salt
½ teaspoon crushed oregano
¼ teaspoon pepper

Cook bell pepper, onion, celery and garlic in butter until tender. Add meat and brown. Stir in remaining ingredients. Simmer covered for 1 hour. Serves 6.
▼ Can be frozen.

Liver Supreme

1 pound calf liver, cut into
   ½-inch strips
flour, seasoned with salt,
   pepper and paprika
1 garlic clove, minced
2 tablespoons butter

2 tablespoons vegetable oil
½ cup dry white wine
2 tablespoons parsley, snipped
¾ cup sour cream
cooked noodles or rice

Dredge liver in flour. Quickly fry liver and garlic in butter and oil, turning so all strips brown, 2-4 minutes. Transfer to hot dish. Drain most of fat from pan. Add wine and parsley, scraping loose all drippings. Add sour cream. Heat but do not boil. Adjust seasoning. Stir in liver. Heat. Serve over noodles or rice. Serves 4.

Lemon Veal

1 2-pound boneless veal roast
   cut in ½-inch slices
butter
garlic salt
½ cup white wine
1 10¾-ounce can cream of
   celery soup, undiluted

grated rind of 1 lemon
juice of 1 lemon
1 cup mushrooms, sliced, or
   1 4-ounce can mushrooms
1 8-ounce package fettuccini or
   medium egg noodles, cooked
garnish: chopped parsley

Brown veal in butter. Sprinkle with garlic salt. Add wine, soup, rind and juice. Bring to a boil, stirring until smooth. Add mushrooms, lower heat and simmer until veal is tender, about 30 minutes. Serve with buttered noodles. Garnish. Serves 6.
▼ May be cooked in a crockpot.

Scallopini of Veal "A La Crème"

Albert Schnarwyler, Executive Chef at The Homestead, Hot Springs, Virginia

1½-2 pounds veal cutlets,
    pounded thin (scallopinis)
salt and pepper
flour
shortening
¼ stick butter
1 cup fresh mushrooms, sliced

lemon juice
6 medium shallots, minced, or
    1 onion, minced
1 cup white wine
1 cup veal sauce (see below)
1 cup heavy cream

Season veal with salt and pepper. Sprinkle lightly with flour. Sauté quickly on each side in shortening in a hot skillet. Set aside. When all cutlets have been sautéed, drain off shortening. Add butter to skillet and sauté mushrooms with a few drops of lemon juice. When partially cooked, add shallots. Sauté a few minutes without browning the shallots. Add wine and simmer slowly until reduced by half. Add veal sauce (see below) and cream. Simmer to desired thickness. Adjust seasoning. Serves 4-6.

Veal Sauce:

1½-2 pounds veal bones,
    cut into small pieces
1 onion, quartered
½ carrot, quartered
1/6 stalk celery, chopped

¼ bay leaf
pinch of thyme
1/8 cup flour
1/6 bottle dry white wine
1½ quarts water or broth

Brown veal bones in iron skillet in 400° oven. Add vegetables and herbs that have been mixed with flour. Continue baking until flour turns blond in color. Add wine and simmer for 5 minutes. Remove from skillet to large saucepan. Add water and simmer slowly on range for 2 hours. Strain. The excess veal sauce may be used for other sauces and soups.

To make a roux, take equal amounts of flour and fat (butter, margarine or drippings). Stir constantly over low heat until desired color is obtained; light or blonde color for light sauces and a dark or chocolate color for dark sauces. To this basic roux, add seasonings and stock to make various sauces and gravies.

Marinated Veal Shoulder Roast

2 cups full-bodied red wine
1 clove garlic, diced
½-1 tablespoon salt
pepper to taste
2 tablespoons Worcestershire
1 bay leaf
1 tablespoon dried parsley
1 tablespoon celery flakes

3 large onions, quartered
1 3-5 pound veal shoulder roast
3 large pieces salt pork or bacon
flour
2 cups hot water
4 beef bouillon cubes
carrots and potatoes (optional)
2 tablespoons flour (optional)

Combine first 9 ingredients and marinate roast in mixture for at least 6 hours. In Dutch oven, render salt pork until there is enough fat to brown roast. Remove meat from marinade and lightly dredge in flour. Brown on all sides. Remove onions from marinade and add to roast. Stir fry gently. Discard bay leaf. Add marinade, water and bouillon cubes to roast. Cover and simmer about 3 hours. If desired, add vegetables 1 hour before cooking is completed. Gravy may be thickened with 2 tablespoons flour if desired. Serves 4-6, depending on size of roast.

To slice meat very thin, have meat partially frozen.

Veal in Cream Sauce

2 pounds veal steak, ½-inch thick
1 teaspoon salt
ground black pepper
3 tablespoons butter or
  margarine

¼ cup dry white wine
1½ cups whipping cream
1 4-ounce can sliced mushrooms,
  drained
2 tablespoons brandy

Cut veal into large julienne strips. Dry thoroughly. Season to taste with salt and pepper. Heat skillet (electric frypan to 350°). Add 2 tablespoons butter. When butter has foamed and foam begins to subside, add veal. Sauté about 8 minutes, browning well on all sides. Remove meat and keep warm. Add wine and cook until slightly reduced. Add cream and turn heat to simmer. Add mushrooms and cook 5 minutes, until slightly thickened. Taste and correct seasoning. Add meat, remaining butter and brandy. Mix well and simmer until meat is thoroughly heated. Serve on toast points. Serves 4-6.

Curry of Lamb with Rice

6¼ pounds leg or shoulder of lamb,
  or 4 pounds trimmed
8-10 tablespoons vegetable oil
4 cups boiling water
2 teaspoons salt
1 teaspoon pepper
5 or more teaspoons curry powder
4 tablespoons onion, chopped

1 cup celery, chopped
½ cup parsley, snipped
½ cup raisins
6-8 tablespoons flour
cooked rice
garnish: chutney, slivered almonds,
  coconut, crumbled bacon

Trim gristle and fat from lamb. Cut into 1-inch cubes. Brown in oil. Drain. Add water, seasonings, onion, celery, parsley and raisins. Cover and simmer 20 minutes or until done. Stir often. Thicken stock with flour blended with small amount of water. Cook and stir several minutes longer. Serve over rice. Garnish. Serves 12.

Grilled Lamb

1 5-7 pound leg of lamb
baking soda
⅓ cup vinegar
meat tenderizer
1 teaspoon MSG

½ cup prepared mustard
2 teaspoons Worcestershire
1 teaspoon seasoned salt
½ cup soy sauce

Sauce:
¼ cup soy sauce
¼ cup Worcestershire
¾ cup prepared mustard
⅓ cup vinegar

salt and pepper to taste
½ cup salad oil
water (to thin sauce)

Cover lamb with baking soda. Let stand 1 minute, then pour vinegar over lamb. Wash off with water. Sprinkle all sides with tenderizer. Make a paste of MSG, mustard, Worcestershire, seasoned salt and soy sauce. Cover lamb with paste and let stand 1 hour. Combine sauce ingredients. Place lamb on outdoor grill and cook until internal temperature reaches 175+° on meat thermometer. Baste frequently using all of sauce. Serves 8-10.

▼ Best cooked on rotary spit but may be cooked in the oven at 325° allowing 30 minutes per pound.

Colorado Leg of Spring Lamb Rancheros

Edmond Charles Johnsen, Executif Chef-Steward, Broadmoor Hotel South, Colorado Springs, Colorado

1 leg of young spring lamb (6½ to 7 pounds)
6 cloves garlic, halved
salt and pepper

1 medium onion, chopped
4 stalks celery, chopped
4 cloves garlic, crushed
1 medium carrot, chopped

Jus:
⅛ cup plain flour
1 quart lamb stock or water

⅛ cup parsley, chopped
salt and pepper to taste

Sauce Rancheros:
1½ medium onions, diced
2 green peppers, diced
⅛ cup vegetable oil
2 tomatoes, cut in eighths
¼ teaspoon chili powder

⅛ teaspoon cumin seeds
⅛ teaspoon Tabasco
¼ cup chili relish (not too hot), or ¼ cup plain relish with a few drops of Tabasco

Remove excess fat and skin (fell) from lamb. With a small pointed knife, prick 12 holes about 1-inch deep in meat and stud with garlic. Season with salt and pepper. Place in roasting pan. Roast at 325° until it reaches an internal temperature of 175° to 180° for well done or 160° to 165° for slightly rare. After 1 hour, add vegetables to lamb and continue roasting. Remove lamb and keep warm while making Jus. Place pan on top of stove and add flour. Mix well. Add stock or water and beat with a wire whip until smooth. Add parsley. Season to taste. Transfer to 2-quart saucepan and cook to reduce to 1 pint or less. Correct seasoning. Strain and keep warm. For Sauce Rancheros, sauté onion and pepper in vegetable oil until limp. Add remaining ingredients. Simmer for 15 minutes. Keep warm. Carve lamb and serve with Jus and Ranchero Sauce. Serves 10-12.

Roast Leg of Lamb

6-7 pound leg of lamb
1 garlic clove, split
salt and pepper to taste
2 tablespoons dry mustard

4 slices salt pork
2 cups hot coffee
½ pint half-and-half

Rub roast with garlic. Season well with salt, pepper and dry mustard. Place slices of salt pork over lamb and fasten with toothpicks. Roast at 450° for 30 minutes. Remove toothpicks and pork slices. Pour coffee and cream over lamb and turn oven to 300°. Roast for 3 hours, basting every 15 minutes with the pan drippings. Strain and remove grease from the delicious gravy. Serves 8-10.

Devonshire Lamb Pie

¼ cup butter
2½ pounds boneless lamb,
   cut in 1-inch pieces
salt and pepper to taste
5-6 large tart apples, peeled,
   cored and chopped

2 tablespoons brown sugar mixed
   with ½ teaspoon cinnamon
2 large onions, thinly sliced
2 cups brown sauce
   (see below)

Brown Sauce:
2 tablespoons butter
2 tablespoons plain flour
2 cups beef broth

1 tablespoon tomato paste
salt and pepper to taste
2 tablespoons vermouth

Pastry:
2½ cups sifted plain flour
1 teaspoon salt
½ cup butter

¼ cup Crisco
2-5 tablespoons ice water,
     as needed

In heavy skillet, heat butter and brown meat. Season with salt and pepper. Remove meat; drain on paper towel. Set skillet aside to be used for brown sauce. Place layer of meat in 2-quart casserole and cover with layer of apples. Sprinkle with a little of the sugar and cinnamon mixture. Next layer half of onions. Repeat layers, ending with apples. Sprinkle with sugar and cinnamon mixture. Pour brown sauce over mixture. Cover with pastry and prick with a fork. Cover with foil to prevent burning. Bake at 425° for 10 minutes. Lower to 350° and bake 1 hour and 20 minutes. Remove foil for last 10-15 minutes.

Brown Sauce: Measure 2 tablespoons of drippings and return to skillet. Add butter and heat until bubbling. Add flour, stirring until smooth. Cook slowly until mixture turns brown. Stir in broth and bring to a boil. Reduce heat and simmer 20-25 minutes or until thickened. Add tomato paste, salt, pepper and vermouth.

Pastry: Mix ingredients, except water, cutting with pastry blender or 2 knives until mixture is blended. Add ice water if necessary. Knead and roll out pastry large enough to cover pie.

▼ Have butcher prepare lamb cubes to save time and prevent waste. Frozen pie crust may be used.

To prevent sauces from tasting "starchy," cook and stir butter and flour for at least 3 minutes before adding liquid to the roux.

101

Crown Roast of Pork

Amelia Cartledge, Adult Homemaking Division, Richmond County Schools, Augusta, Georgia

1 crown roast of pork (allow 2 ribs per person)	¼ teaspoon dried sweet marjoram
1 pound ground pork	4 tablespoons dried bread crumbs
¼ pound ground veal	1 tablespoon chopped chives
1 garlic clove, split	3 tablespoons milk
salt and freshly ground pepper	salt pork, thinly sliced
1 tablespoon olive oil	1 cup boiling water
1 tablespoon lemon juice	1 10¾-ounce can chicken broth
1 tablespoon onion, minced	1 cup sour cream
5 tablespoons parsley, snipped	2 tablespoons catsup
1 teaspoon fresh basil, chopped, or ¼ teaspoon dried sweet basil	2 tablespoons flour
	1 teaspoon MSG

Ask butcher to trim roast and grind the lean pork scraps (1 pound) with ¼ pound veal. The day before roast is to be cooked, rub inside and outside with garlic, salt and pepper. Make marinade by combining oil, lemon juice, onion, 2 tablespoons parsley, basil and marjoram. With a sharp pointed knife, make about 10 incisions on inside of crown. Rub a little marinade into each incision. Rub remaining marinade on outside of roast. Fill crown with a mixture of ground pork, ground veal, salt, pepper, bread crumbs, 3 tablespoons parsley, chives and milk. Crisscross salt pork over stuffing. Wrap roast tightly with waxed paper. Refrigerate. Before cooking, wipe roast to remove marinade. Bake at 300°, 35 minutes per pound or until meat thermometer reads 185°. After 1 hour, add the boiling water. Scrape pan to blend water with cooking juices. Add more water as pan gets dry. Remove roast and keep warm. To make gravy, skim fat from cooking juices. Place pan over burner. Add broth. Scrape and stir until mixture boils. Stir in sour cream, catsup and enough water to make desired amount of gravy. Thicken with flour blended with water. Add MSG. Adjust seasoning. Serve with roast.

Barbecued Fresh Pork Ham

1 10-12 pound fresh pork ham	2 cups cider vinegar
salt	2 tablespoons black pepper
1 stick butter, melted	1 tablespoon salt

Rub ham heavily with salt. Combine butter, vinegar, pepper and 1 tablespoon salt and bring to a boil. Bake ham at 350°. After 1 hour, remove skin and baste with sauce. Continue baking, basting frequently, for 4 more hours or until meat thermometer registers 185°. Pass remaining sauce when serving. Serves 12-14. *Delicious cooked on the grill.*

Kalua Pork

1 5-pound center-cut pork
   loin roast
¼ cup soy sauce
3 tablespoons sherry
1 large clove garlic, crushed
½ teaspoon ground cinnamon
½ teaspoon thyme

⅔ cup peach preserves
¼ cup chili sauce
1 cup water
1 8-ounce can water chestnuts,
   drained and sliced
garnish: parsley

Marinate roast in sauce made from soy sauce, sherry, garlic, cinnamon and thyme for 2-3 hours, turning often. Place on rack in a shallow roasting pan and roast at 325° for 30-35 minutes per pound or until internal temperature reaches 180° on meat thermometer. In a small saucepan, combine reserved marinade, peach preserves, chili sauce and ½ cup water. Bring to a boil, stirring constantly. Baste pork and cook 10 more minutes. Add remaining ½ cup water to pan to scrape up brown bits. Add pan juices and water chestnuts to sauce and heat through. To serve, place carved roast on platter and spoon sauce and water chestnuts around roast. Garnish. Pass remaining sauce. Serves 8-10.

Roast Boneless Loin of Pork

1 3½-pound boneless loin of pork
salt and white pepper to taste
flour
1 carrot, coarsely chopped
1 stalk celery, coarsely chopped
1 medium onion, coarsely chopped

1 garlic clove, sliced
¼ teaspoon thyme
¼ teaspoon marjoram
¼ teaspoon sage
½ cup water

Sauce:
2 tablespoons flour
2 cups rich beef broth
   (may use bouillon)

2 tablespoons tomato paste
salt and white pepper to taste

Season pork with salt and pepper. Lightly dredge in flour. Place fat side up in roasting pan. Add vegetables, seasonings and water. Cook at 425° for 30 minutes or until meat is well browned. Reduce heat to 325° and cook 30 minutes more, basting frequently. Add more water if necessary. Continue cooking and basting 45 minutes or until internal temperature reaches 180° on the meat thermometer. Remove roast to serving platter and keep warm. For sauce, blend flour into drippings. Heat broth and tomato paste and gradually add to drippings, stirring constantly so that sauce will be smooth. Cook over low heat 10 minutes. Strain if desired. Correct seasonings. Pass sauce when serving. Serves 6.

Accordion Roast Pork with Apples

1 5-pound pork loin roast
4 teaspoons salt
1 teaspoon ground sage
½ teaspoon pepper

1 medium baking apple, cored
  and cut into ½-inch rings
½ cup apple jelly, melted

Cut roast between ribs about ¾ way through. Combine seasonings and rub into roast, including slits. Place roast, fat side up, on rack in shallow pan. Roast about 3 hours at 325° or until meat thermometer registers 180°. About 30 minutes before roast is done, insert half of an apple ring, peeling side up, into slits. Brush generously with jelly. Return to oven, basting frequently with jelly. Let stand 30 minutes before carving. Serves 8.

Bourbon-glazed Ham

1 10-12 pound ham, fully cooked
1 cup bourbon
1 cup light brown sugar, packed

1 teaspoon orange peel, grated
¼ teaspoon ground cloves
whole cloves

Bake ham at 325° for 2 hours. Meanwhile, combine bourbon, sugar, orange peel and ground cloves. Let stand for 30 minutes. Stir often to dissolve sugar. Remove skin from ham, score fat into 1-inch diamonds and insert a clove in each diamond point. Brush with half the bourbon mixture. Bake, basting frequently with remaining mixture, for 1 hour longer. Serves 24.

Tennessee Country Ham

country ham
2 cups molasses
vinegar

dry mustard
brown sugar
whole cloves

Have butcher remove the hock. Scrub ham thoroughly, leaving rind. Soak in cold water overnight. Drain and cover again with cold water. Heat to boiling point. Boil hard for a few minutes. Drain again; cover ham with fresh boiling water immediately. Add molasses. Cover. Replenish water so that ham is immersed at all times. Allow 20 minutes cooking time per pound for hams of 10 pounds or more. Check for doneness by placing ham on plate and piercing the thick end with a sharp fork. If juice is pink it is done; if it is still red it is not. Return to pot and allow to cool in its liquor, uncovered. Skin ham and pat with vinegar. Sprinkle with dry mustard and apply a thick coating of brown sugar. Score (crisscross) fat side with sharp knife in 1-inch diamonds. Place a clove at each point. Bake at 400° until evenly browned.

Pork Chop Quickie
Frank Beard

6 pork chops, trimmed
garlic salt to taste

6 slices butter
buttered pancake syrup

Place chops in greased casserole. Sprinkle generously with garlic salt. Top each chop with butter and cover with syrup. Add small amount of water to prevent burning. Bake at 325° until golden brown and tender, about 1 hour. Serves 4-6.
▼ The garlic salt cuts the sweetness of the syrup.

Spanish Pork Chops
Byron Nelson – 1937 and 1942 Masters' Champion

6 pork chops, extra thick
1 large onion, sliced
1 bell pepper, sliced
2 ribs celery, sliced
3 carrots, sliced lengthwise
6 small potatoes, sliced

1 10¾-ounce can condensed tomato
    soup
1 soup can water
few slivers hot pepper or
    dash of Tabasco
salt and pepper to taste

Brown chops. Place in a large casserole. Top with remaining ingredients. Cover and bake at 350° for 1-2 hours or until tender. Serves 4-6.
Mr. Nelson says, "All is done for a favorite meal of ours. I usually serve with a green salad."

Curry-glazed Pork Chops

salt
8 rib or loin pork chops
    (½-inch thick)
1-2 tablespoons bacon drippings
    or cooking oil
1 large onion, chopped
2 tablespoons plain flour
2 tablespoons brown sugar
1 tablespoon curry powder

1 teaspoon salt
1 teaspoon cinnamon
1 beef bouillon cube, crushed
1 cup water
2 tablespoons catsup
1 4-ounce jar baby applesauce
    and apricots or ½ cup
    applesauce
¼ cup flaked coconut (optional)

Salt chops lightly and brown in hot fat in skillet. Place in single layer in 9x13-inch baking dish. Sauté onion in same skillet. Blend in flour, sugar, curry, salt and cinnamon. Cook until bubbling, stirring constantly. Add remaining ingredients and bring to a boil. Simmer 5 minutes or until thick. Spoon half of sauce over chops and bake at 350° for 20 minutes. Add remaining sauce and bake 20 minutes until glazed. Be careful not to burn. Serves 6-8.

Deviled Pork Chops

4 thick loin pork chops
6 tablespoons chili sauce
3 tablespoons lemon juice
2 tablespoons onion, grated
½ teaspoon dry mustard

4 teaspoons Worcestershire
¼ teaspoon curry powder
1 teaspoon salt
½ teaspoon paprika
½ cup water

Marinate pork chops 1 hour in marinade of remaining ingredients, except water. Drain chops, reserving marinade. Wipe dry and brown chops in a hot, greased skillet. Heat marinade with water and pour around chops in baking dish. Cover and bake at 350° for 1 hour. Serves 4.

▼ May be prepared a day ahead and baked just before serving.

Orange Pork Chop Skillet

6 pork chops, ½ inch thick
6 tablespoons butter or margarine
1 acorn squash
1 6-ounce can frozen orange juice concentrate, thawed

2 tablespoons brown sugar
1½ teaspoons ground ginger
½ teaspoon ground allspice
¼ teaspoon hot pepper sauce
2 oranges, sliced ¼ inch thick

Trim chops. Brown in butter. Pour off fat. Cut squash into ¾ inch rings. Remove seeds. Cut rings in half. Add to chops. Combine orange juice, sugar and spices. Pour over chops. Cover and simmer 45 minutes or until tender. Baste occasionally. Place orange slices over chops last 5 minutes of cooking. Serves 6.
If squash is out of season, try without it.

Chinese Pork and Cabbage with Hot Sauce

1 pound lean pork
1 spring onion, cut into 2-inch lengths
2 garlic cloves, sliced
4 tablespoons vegetable oil
cabbage, cut into 40 2-inch squares

1½ bell peppers, cut into wedges
3 tablespoons soy sauce
2 teaspoons sugar
1 teaspoon hot pepper sauce
1 teaspoon cornstarch, dissolved in 1 tablespoon water

In a large pan, cook pork and onion in enough water to cover for 15 minutes. Drain. Slice pork. Sauté garlic in oil. Add pork, onion, cabbage and bell pepper. Cook 1-2 minutes over high heat. Add soy sauce, sugar and pepper sauce. Cook 1-2 minutes over medium heat. Stir in dissolved cornstarch until thickened. Serves 4.
Try this in your Wok.

Ham Steaks Stuffed with Sweet Potatoes

1 16-ounce can sweet potatoes
4 tablespoons butter, melted
½ lemon rind, grated
½ orange rind, grated
¼ teaspoon ground cinnamon
salt to taste

2-4 tablespoons bourbon or rum
freshly ground pepper to taste
4 ½-pound thick ham steaks
3 tablespoons brown sugar
garnish: orange slices

Mash sweet potatoes with butter. Add lemon and orange rind, cinnamon, salt, bourbon or rum and pepper. Spread mixture thickly on 2 ham steaks and top with remaining steaks. Sprinkle with brown sugar and pepper to taste. Wrap loosely in foil. Bake at 325° for 1 hour. Garnish. Serves 4-6.

Ham Tetrazzini

1 cup ham, diced
2 tablespoons onion, chopped
1 tablespoon butter or margarine
1 10¾-ounce can condensed cream
   of mushroom soup
½ soup can water
1 tablespoon cooking sherry

1 cup Cheddar cheese, grated
1 tablespoon parsley flakes
1 tablespoon Worcestershire
dash Tabasco
1 2-ounce jar pimientos, sliced
1 8-ounce package spaghetti,
   cooked

Sauté ham and onion in margarine. Add soup, water, sherry and cheese. Simmer until cheese is melted. Add parsley, Worcestershire, Tabasco and pimientos. Pour over spaghetti in 1½-quart casserole. Heat at 350° until thoroughly heated. Serves 4.

Lindsey's Barbequed Spareribs

2 pounds spareribs, cut into
   serving pieces
½ tablespoon salt
2 tablespoons vinegar
1 cup white vinegar
2 tablespoons sugar
2 tablespoons Worcestershire

½ cup catsup
1 garlic clove, minced
1 teaspoon salt
1 teaspoon dry mustard
1 teaspoon paprika
⅛ teaspoon pepper

Cover ribs with water. Add ½ tablespoon salt and 2 tablespoons vinegar. Simmer 45 minutes. To make sauce, combine remaining ingredients and heat. Dip ribs in sauce. Grill over charcoal 20-30 minutes or bake at 375° for 30 minutes. Dip several times during cooking until sauce is used. Serves 2-4.

Chinese Sweet and Sour Spareribs

2 pounds spareribs, cut in
  2-inch pieces
8 teaspoons soy sauce
4 tablespoons cornstarch
vegetable oil
1 small onion, sliced
1 large green pepper,
  coarsely chopped

1 15¼-ounce can pineapple
  chunks
1 tomato, cut in eighths
¾ cup sugar
¼ cup soy sauce
2 tablespoons cornstarch
1 cup cider vinegar

Cook spareribs in salted water until tender. Drain. Coat with mixture of 8 teaspoons soy sauce and 4 tablespoons cornstarch. Let stand 1 hour. Brown ribs in oil. Stir while browning. Drain and set aside. To pan, add a little oil and sauté onion and pepper for 1 minute. Add pineapple and tomato and cook for 2 minutes. Add remaining ingredients and bring to a boil. Add spareribs and stir a few minutes. Serve immediately. IMPORTANT: Cook ingredients for exact times specified. Serves 6.

Ham and Asparagus Casserole

½ cup butter
½ cup plain flour
3 cups half-and-half
1½ cups milk
½ cup chicken broth
¾ cup sharp Cheddar cheese,
  grated
½ cup grated Parmesan cheese
juice of 1 lemon

1½ tablespoons onion, grated
1 tablespoon parsley, minced
1 tablespoon prepared mustard
2½ teaspoons salt
pepper to taste
1 cup mayonnaise
¾ pound thin spaghetti
4 cups baked ham, cubed
2 15-ounce cans asparagus

For sauce, melt butter and blend in flour. Slowly add cream, milk and broth. Cook until thickened, stirring constantly. Add cheeses and lemon juice. Season with onion, parsley, mustard, salt and pepper. Remove from heat and add mayonnaise. Cook spaghetti and drain well. Combine sauce, spaghetti and ham. Mix well. In two 2-quart shallow casseroles, arrange layers of ham mixture and asparagus, ending with ham mixture. Bake uncovered at 350° for 30 minutes or until thoroughly heated. Serves 10-12.

Spaghetti Alla Carbonara

1 pound bacon, chopped
4 large onions, chopped
2 cups dry white wine
12-14 eggs, well beaten
2 cups grated Parmesan cheese

1 tablespoon parsley flakes
1 teaspoon pepper
2 pounds spaghetti
   (add 2-3 tablespoons oil and
   salt to taste)

As water is boiling for spaghetti, fry bacon until lightly brown. Remove bacon and sauté onions in same pan until transparent. Return bacon to skillet and add wine. Simmer to sauce consistency. In LARGE bowl, beat eggs and add cheese, parsley and pepper. Cook spaghetti until just done. Pour HOT drained spaghetti into egg mixture. Mix thoroughly and quickly. (Hot spaghetti cooks eggs.) Pour bacon sauce over spaghetti. Mix thoroughly and serve immediately. If too dry, add a little more wine. Serves 12-14.

▼ Bacon sauce may be prepared ahead and reheated.

Sausage-stuffed Eggplant

2 eggplants, ½-¾ pound each
½ pound pork sausage
1 medium onion, chopped
1 large garlic clove, minced
1 16-ounce can tomatoes, drained
   and chopped
½ cup seasoned bread crumbs

1 cup sour cream
salt and pepper to taste
1 tablespoon fresh basil, or
   1 teaspoon dried basil
2 tablespoons fresh parsley,
   snipped
grated Parmesan cheese

Halve eggplants and parboil 10-15 minutes. Remove and cool. Scoop out seeded area, leaving shells, cube and reserve. Cook sausage in a large frying pan 10 or more minutes. Add onion and garlic. Cook 5 minutes more. Drain off excess grease. Add cubed eggplant and cook 5 minutes. Add remaining ingredients, except cheese. Stuff shells; sprinkle with cheese. Place in pan with ¼ inch water. Bake at 350° for 45 minutes or until lightly browned. Serves 4.

Poultry

7

Chicken Crêpes
Nathalie Dupree, Rich's Cooking School, Atlanta, Georgia

Crêpes:
1 cup plain flour, sifted
1 egg
1 cup milk

1 egg yolk
1 tablespoon oil or butter
¼ teaspoon salt

Filling:
4 tablespoons butter
2 onions, chopped
2 cups mushrooms, thinly sliced
¼ cup cooked spinach, drained
   and chopped
4 tablespoons sour cream

2 cups cooked chicken,
   coarsely chopped
2 tablespoons sherry
½ teaspoon salt
dash cayenne pepper

Sauce:
5 tablespoons butter
5 tablespoons plain flour
2 cups chicken broth
1 cup milk
½ cup Swiss or Gruyère cheese,
   grated

½ cup grated Parmesan cheese
salt to taste
dash cayenne pepper
⅛ teaspoon saffron (optional)
½ cup sherry

Crêpes: Put flour in a bowl as broad at the bottom as the top. Add egg and half the milk. Whisk. Mix in egg yolk, oil, salt and remaining milk. Refrigerate 30 minutes to 24 hours. When ready to use batter, if necessary, thin with water or more milk. Ladle approximately 2 tablespoons batter onto the edge of a hot, well oiled crêpe pan. Roll around edges and over bottom only once, pouring off excess batter. Put over heat until crêpe reaches desired color. Cook one side, then turn with round-tipped spatula. The second side does not need to be done, just give it a good "finish." Turn crêpe out on a tea towel, ugly side up or fill immediately.*

Filling: Heat butter in large skillet. Sauté onions until soft and golden. Add mushrooms. Cook for 4 minutes, stirring occasionally. Stir in remaining ingredients. Remove from heat. Refrigerate until needed.
Sauce: Make a cream sauce of butter, flour, broth and milk. Stir in cheeses and seasonings. Remove from heat. Add sherry.

To assemble crêpes: Put 2 tablespoons filling in the center of each crêpe. Flap one side of crêpe over, fold ends in and roll up. Place filled crêpes on a shallow, greased baking dish, seam side down. Pour sauce on top of each crêpe. Bake at 375° for 15 minutes or until lightly browned.
*To freeze crêpes, layer with waxed paper and wrap tightly in foil.

Dinner Party Chicken

8 half-breasts of chicken, boned
1 cup (or more) vermouth
1 tablespoon fresh tarragon, snipped
1 tablespoon lemon juice
salt and white pepper to taste

⅔ stick butter
½ cup flour
1 stick butter, melted
2 teaspoons mild curry powder
chicken broth
1 cup whipping cream

Cover breasts with vermouth. Add tarragon and marinate at least 3 hours. Remove and pat dry. Reserve marinade. Rub breasts with lemon juice, salt and pepper. In a large, heavy skillet, heat ⅔ stick butter until it foams. Cook 4 breasts at a time, turning until their surfaces become white. Place in a baking dish, cover and bake at 400° for 8 minutes. To make sauce, stir flour into melted butter. Cook 3 minutes. Stir in curry. Add enough broth to marinade to make 4 cups. Blend into sauce, stirring until thickened. Stir in cream. Sauce should be quite thick. Just before serving, spoon sauce over breasts and return to oven for about 5 minutes. Serves 8.

One teaspoon of fresh herbs is equivalent to ¼ teaspoon of dried herbs.

Chicken with Crab Meat Stuffing

8 half-breasts of chicken, boned
2 tablespoons margarine
1 teaspoon salt
¼ teaspoon pepper
paprika to taste
½ cup margarine
½ cup sherry
1 teaspoon garlic salt
½ cup catsup
2 4-ounce cans sliced mushrooms

3 slices white bread, cubed
5 tablespoons cream
¼ teaspoon thyme
¼ teaspoon cayenne
1 teaspoon salt
1 teaspoon prepared mustard
½ teaspoon poultry seasoning
¼ teaspoon sage
¼ cup margarine, melted
12-16 ounces crab meat

Rub chicken with 2 tablespoons margarine, salt, pepper and paprika. Bake at 350°, skin side up, for 35 minutes. In saucepan, heat ½ cup margarine, sherry, garlic salt, catsup and mushrooms. Spoon 1-2 tablespoons over each breast. Bake 10 minutes longer. Toss bread in cream until it is absorbed. Add remaining seasonings which have been mixed with ¼ cup margarine. Toss with crab meat.* Stuff breast cavity and bake, stuffing side up, for 30-35 minutes. Baste often. Serves 8.
*May prepare ahead to this point.
A delight for the hungry gourmet.

Chicken Rochambeau

8 half-breasts of chicken, skinned
1 cup seasoned flour
⅓ stick butter
½ cup chicken stock
½ cup water
⅓ cup dry white wine
8 Holland rusks

8 slices boiled ham
1 cup Marchand de Vin Sauce
(see index)
1 cup Blender Béarnaise Sauce
(see index)
garnish: paprika, parsley

Dredge breasts in flour. Sauté in butter 5 minutes on each side. Place in baking dish with stock, water and wine. Bake at 325° for 20 minutes, turning once. De-bone.* Arrange rusks on platter. On each rusk add, in order: 1 slice ham, 2 tablespoons Marchand de Vin sauce, 1 chicken breast and 2 tablespoons Béarnaise sauce. Garnish. Serves 6-8.
*Can be prepared ahead to this point.
An outstanding combination with delightful results.

Baked Chicken with Sausage

8 half-breasts of chicken, boned
1 pound sausage
½ pint sour cream

1 10¾-ounce can condensed cream
of mushroom soup

Flatten each breast with mallet. Crumble sausage into skillet. Cook slowly until almost done. Drain. Spread sausage on each piece of chicken. Roll breasts, using toothpicks to secure. Place in a shallow casserole. Combine sour cream and soup. Pour over chicken. Bake, uncovered, in 300° oven for 2-3 hours, until tender. Serves 8.

Chicken Hmmmmmm

4 half-breasts of chicken, boned
4 teaspoons parsley flakes
garlic salt to taste

¼ cup butter or margarine, melted
1 cup herb stuffing mix

Sprinkle breasts with parsley and garlic salt. Roll up and secure with a toothpick. Roll in butter, then dressing mix. Place in a heavily greased baking dish. Sprinkle remaining crumbs over chicken and moisten lightly with water. Bake at 325° for 30-40 minutes.
Simple, but elegant served alone or on a slice of ham.

113

Chicken Kiev

3 tablespoons butter, softened
1 teaspoon tarragon
½ teaspoon salt
¼ teaspoon pepper

6 half-breasts of chicken, boned
1 egg, beaten
1-1½ cups fine cracker crumbs
vegetable oil

Mix first 4 ingredients. Freeze. Flatten chicken between sheets of waxed paper by pounding with a mallet. Place 1/6 of the frozen butter in the center of each breast. Fold opposite sides over the butter. Roll the other two sides over. Secure with toothpicks. Dip chicken into egg, then crumbs. Repeat. Place on waxed paper-lined baking sheet. Cover with paper. Refrigerate for at least ½ hour before cooking. Deep fry in 325° oil. Oil is ready if it sizzles when a cracker crumb is dropped in. Fry until golden on all sides, 7-10 minutes. Turn gently so the butter mixture does not escape. Drain. Serve immediately. Serves 6.

Poulet Jubilee

3 pounds chicken, cut into
   serving pieces
2 tablespoons margarine
2 tablespoons oil
4 tablespoons onion, chopped
4 garlic cloves, chopped
6 ounces chili sauce

¾ cup water
½ cup brown sugar
½ cup raisins
2 tablespoons Worcestershire
½ cup dry sherry
1 8-ounce can dark sweet pitted
   cherries

Brown chicken in margarine and oil. Add onion and garlic. Combine chili sauce, water, sugar, raisins and Worcestershire. Pour over chicken. Bake at 350° for 1 hour. Add sherry and cherries last 15 minutes. Serves 4-6.
An unusually good, spicy flavor.

Jamaican Chicken

6 pineapple slices
6 half-breasts of chicken, boned
1 chicken bouillon cube
⅓ cup boiling water
1 teaspoon dry instant coffee

1 10¾-ounce can condensed
   cream of chicken soup
¼ teaspoon salt
¼ pound sharp Cheddar cheese,
   shredded

Place pineapple slices in baking dish. Top each with a breast. Dissolve bouillon in water. Combine with coffee, soup and salt. Pour over chicken. Bake at 375° for 40 minutes. Sprinkle with cheese. Return to oven until cheese melts. Serves 6.

Chicken Breasts with Dark Cherries

8 half-breasts of chicken, boned
2 teaspoons salt
½ teaspoon pepper
3 tablespoons butter or margarine
¼ cup dry white wine
½ cup chicken stock
¾ teaspoon rosemary, crushed

¼ teaspoon sage
1 tablespoon flour
1 17-ounce can dark pitted
   cherries, drained
3 tablespoons reserved cherry
   juice

Rub breasts with salt and pepper. Brown on all sides in butter. Place in a 2-quart oven-proof dish. Loosen pan drippings by adding wine and stock. Pour over chicken. Sprinkle with rosemary and sage. Bake at 325° for 40 minutes or until tender. Remove chicken. Blend flour with cherry juice. Stir into liquid in baking dish. Cook over low heat until smooth. Add chicken and cherries. Heat about 5 minutes. Serves 8.

Deboning is easier if chicken is poached.

Chicken Veronique

2 tablespoons flour
½ teaspoon salt
½ teaspoon black pepper
1 3-4 pound broiler, cut into
   serving pieces
¼ cup peanut oil
½ cup dry white wine
⅓ cup orange juice

2 tablespoons honey
1 tablespoon parsley, snipped
2 tablespoons orange peel,
   slivered
1 cup seedless white grapes,
   halved
garnish: grapes, orange sections

Combine flour, salt and ¼ teaspoon pepper. Lightly dust chicken. In a large skillet, brown chicken in oil. Add wine, juice, honey, parsley and remaining pepper. Simmer, covered, over low heat for 30 minutes, stirring occasionally. Add orange peel. Continue cooking until tender, about 15 minutes. Remove chicken to serving platter. Add grapes to gravy. Cook and stir 2 minutes. Pour over chicken. Garnish. Serves 4-6.
Lovely to look at with green and orange accents.

Chicken Breasts with Herb-Mushroom Stuffing

12 half-breasts of chicken, boned
1 cup dry sherry
3 cups mushrooms, coarsely
   sliced
½ cup margarine, plus
  2 tablespoons

2 cups soft bread crumbs
¼ cup parsley, snipped
2 tablespoons marjoram
1 teaspoon thyme
½ teaspoon salt
¼ teaspoon pepper

Pound breasts, skin side up, until flattened. Cover breasts with sherry. Let stand at room temperature for 1 hour. Sauté mushrooms in ½ cup margarine until slightly softened. Remove from heat. Add remaining ingredients except the 2 tablespoons margarine, mixing well. Remove breasts and pat dry. Spread about 2 tablespoons mushroom mixture on inside of each breast. Roll, pulling outside skin taut to cover stuffing completely. Secure with toothpicks or string. Brush with sherry. Place in baking dish, seam side down. Melt remaining margarine and brush over breasts. Bake at 375° for 35-40 minutes. Serves 6.

Saucy Chicken Bake

3 large fryers, cut into
   serving pieces
1 cup plain flour
2½ teaspoons paprika
2 teaspoons salt
¼ teaspoon red pepper
¼ teaspoon freshly ground
   black pepper
¼ teaspoon ground ginger
¼ teaspoon sweet basil
dash of nutmeg
¼ cup margarine

¼ cup shortening
2½ cups chicken broth
1 pint sour cream
2 tablespoons Worcestershire
3 tablespoons chili sauce
1 large clove garlic, minced
1 5-ounce can water chestnuts,
   thinly sliced
1 6-ounce can sliced mushrooms
1½ teaspoons salt
pepper to taste

Boil wings and backs in salted water to make 2½ cups broth. Debone other parts, keeping pieces large. Cut breasts into 2 or 3 pieces. Combine flour, paprika, 2 teaspoons salt, red pepper, black pepper, ginger, basil and nutmeg. Roll chicken in this mixture. Brown gently in margarine and shortening. Transfer chicken to 3-quart casserole. In saucepan, heat broth, sour cream and remaining ingredients. Pour over chicken. Cover and bake at 325° until tender, about 1½ hours. After an hour of cooking, skim off fat and adjust seasoning. Casserole should bubble gently. Serves 8-10.

So nice to use for company because it is much better when prepared a day ahead. Just reheat and read a magazine before the guests arrive.

Chicken and Wild Rice Casserole

1 cup onion, chopped
1 cup butter
½ cup plain flour
2 4½-ounce cans sliced mushrooms, drained (reserve juice)
3 cups chicken broth
3 cups half-and-half
6 cups chicken, cooked and diced

1 6-ounce box long-grain and wild rice mix, cooked
1 cup slivered almonds, toasted (optional)
½ cup pimiento, diced
4 tablespoons parsley, chopped
3 teaspoons salt
½ teaspoon pepper

In a large skillet, sauté onion in butter until tender. Stir in flour, cooking 2-3 minutes. Combine mushroom juice with enough broth to make 3 cups. Slowly stir into onion mixture. Stir in cream. Cook until thickened. Add mushrooms, chicken, rice and remaining ingredients. Pour into a large casserole. Bake at 350° for 30-45 minutes. Serves 10-12.

Chicken New Orleans

salt and pepper
1 fryer, cut into serving pieces and skinned
1 stick butter
1 cup celery, chopped
1 cup ripe olives, sliced

½ cup pimiento, sliced
1 cup mushrooms, chopped
1 garlic clove, minced
1 tablespoon plain flour
1 cup sherry
cooked wild and white rice mixture

Salt and pepper chicken. Brown in butter. Remove chicken. Sauté celery, olives, pimiento, mushrooms and garlic. Stir in flour. After 3 minutes, slowly stir in sherry. Add chicken. Cover and simmer until chicken is tender, about 20 minutes. Serve over rice. Serves 6-8.
Pretty, colorful dish.

Hot Chicken Salad
Mrs. Tommy Aaron – Wife of 1973 Masters' Champion

8 half-breasts of chicken, cooked and chopped
1 cup celery, chopped
1 medium onion, chopped
3 hard-boiled eggs, chopped
¼ cup slivered almonds

1 10¾-ounce can condensed cream of chicken soup
½ cup mayonnaise
salt and pepper to taste
1 tablespoon lemon juice (optional)
2 heaping cups potato chips

Mix all but last ingredient. Crumble chips. Add half to salad. Put in a buttered casserole. Top with remaining chips. Bake at 350° until bubbling hot, 20-30 minutes. Do not overcook. Serves 8-10.

Chicken Divan

2 10-ounce packages frozen
   broccoli
¼ cup butter
¼ cup plain flour
2 10¾-ounce cans condensed
   cream of chicken soup
1½ cups half-and-half

½ cup dry sherry
salt and white pepper to taste
6 half-breasts of chicken, cooked
   and thinly sliced
½ cup Cheddar cheese, grated
¾ cup soft bread crumbs, buttered
garnish: pimiento slices

Cook broccoli according to package directions until just tender. Drain. Melt butter. Blend in flour. Add soup and cream, stirring until thickened. Stir in sherry, salt and pepper. Arrange broccoli in a buttered baking dish. Pour over half the sauce. Arrange chicken on top. Blend cheese in remaining sauce. Pour over chicken. Top with crumbs. Bake at 350° for 20 minutes. Broil until golden brown. Garnish. Serves 6.

Chicken Rice Divan

2 10-ounce packages frozen broccoli
½ cup grated Parmesan cheese
2 cups chicken, cooked and sliced
salt and pepper to taste
1 cup cooked rice

2 tablespoons butter
2 tablespoons flour
1 cup milk
2 tablespoons lemon juice
1 cup sour cream

Cook broccoli according to package directions. Drain. Arrange in buttered baking dish. Sprinkle with half the cheese. Add chicken. Season to taste. Top with rice. Make white sauce with butter, flour and milk. Remove from heat. Stir in lemon juice and sour cream. Pour over rice. Sprinkle with remaining cheese. Bake at 400° until lightly browned, 15-20 minutes. Serves 6-8.

Oven-fried Parmesan Chicken

2½ pounds chicken pieces
1 stick butter or margarine,
   melted
2 cups fine dry bread crumbs
¾ cup grated Parmesan cheese
2 tablespoons parsley, snipped

1 garlic clove, minced
2 teaspoons salt
¼ teaspoon pepper
¼ cup sherry (optional)
1 10¾-ounce can condensed cream
   of chicken soup (optional)

Wipe chicken dry. Dip in butter. Roll in mixture of remaining ingredients, except sherry and soup. Press crumbs down. Place chicken in a shallow, foil-lined pan. Do not overlap pieces. Bake at 350° for 1 hour. Do not turn chicken. May vary by spooning sauce made of sherry and soup over chicken the last 15 minutes of baking. Serves 4-6.

▼ May use 8 half-breasts instead of chicken pieces.

Chicken Florentine

salt and pepper to taste
6 half-breasts of chicken, boned
½ stick margarine
2 tablespoons oil
2 10-ounce packages frozen
   chopped spinach
½ cup mayonnaise

1 10¾-ounce can condensed
   cream of chicken soup
1 tablespoon lemon juice
1 teaspoon curry powder
½ cup sharp cheese, grated
½ cup cornflake crumbs

Sauté lightly salted and peppered chicken in margarine and oil for 10 minutes. Cook spinach. Drain or squeeze dry. Spread spinach in bottom of a 2-quart casserole. Top with breasts. Mix mayonnaise, soup, lemon juice and curry. Pour over chicken. Sprinkle with cheese. Top with crumbs. Bake at 350° for 25 minutes. Serves 6.

▼ For variety, substitute asparagus or broccoli for spinach.

Chicken and Artichoke Hearts

¼ pound mushrooms, sliced
¼ cup butter or margarine
2½ pounds chicken pieces
1 teaspoon MSG
1 teaspoon salt
⅛ teaspoon pepper
⅓ cup sherry

1 9-ounce package frozen or 1
   14-ounce can artichoke hearts
⅓ cup water
1 tablespoon flour
1 cup sour cream
¼ teaspoon paprika
¼ cup ripe olives, sliced

In a large skillet, sauté mushrooms in butter. Remove mushrooms. Add chicken which has been seasoned with MSG, salt and pepper. When brown, add sherry, artichoke hearts and water. Cover and simmer 30 minutes or until chicken is tender.* Add mushrooms last 5 minutes of cooking. Transfer chicken, artichokes and mushrooms to a warm serving platter. Blend flour and sour cream. Stir into pan juices. Heat but do not boil. Spoon over chicken. Garnish with paprika and olives. Serves 4-6.

* May be prepared ahead to this point.

Chicken Curry

celery leaves
7 pounds of chicken
6 cups reserved chicken stock
½ cup rendered chicken fat
1 stalk celery, chopped
1 large onion, chopped
1 medium bell pepper, chopped

1 garlic clove, minced
½ teaspoon ground ginger
1½ tablespoons curry powder
3 heaping tablespoons plain
   flour
1 6-ounce can tomato paste
1 6-ounce can mushrooms

In 2½ quarts water to which celery leaves have been added, simmer chicken 3 to 4 hours. Remove and cut into bite-size pieces. Reserve 6 cups stock and ½ cup rendered chicken fat. Sauté celery, onion, bell pepper, garlic and ginger in fat. Blend in curry and flour. Add reserved stock and tomato paste. Cook 1 hour over low heat, stirring occasionally. Add chicken and mushrooms before serving. Serves 12 as an entrée; 60 for hors d'oeuvres.

▼ Serve over rice with these condiments: coconut, raisins, peanuts and chutney. Use small patty shells for appetizers. Freezes well.

Always snip chives and parsley with scissors rather than a knife.

Easy Curried Chicken

1 5-pound hen
reserved chicken stock
1 cup celery, chopped
½ cup onion, chopped
¼ cup bell pepper, chopped
½ stick margarine
1 4-ounce can chopped mushrooms

2 10¾-ounce cans condensed
   cream of mushroom soup
1 10¾-ounce can condensed
   cream of celery soup
Worcestershire to taste
1 tablespoon curry powder

Stew hen in salted water. Cut into bite-size pieces. Reserve stock. Sauté celery, onion and pepper in margarine until tender. Add mushrooms, soups and enough of reserved stock to make preferred consistency. Add Worcestershire and curry. Heat and add chicken. Serves 8.

▼ Serve over rice with an assortment of condiments: chutney, crumbled bacon, grated hard-boiled eggs, shredded coconut and chopped peanuts.

Chicken Sherry

4 large half-breasts of chicken
salt and pepper to taste
flour

1 stick butter, melted
6-10 ounces dry sherry
1 4-ounce can sliced mushrooms

Place chicken which has been seasoned and floured in a 1½ to 2-quart baking dish. Pour butter over chicken. Bake uncovered at 400° for 30 minutes. Add sherry and mushrooms. Bake uncovered at 325° until tender. Serves 4.

Chinese Chicken with Cashews

6 half-breasts of chicken, cut
   into julienne strips
¼ cup butter or salad oil
2 cups celery, sliced
½ pound green beans, Frenched
1 cup water chestnuts, sliced
1 cup bamboo shoots
¼ cup soy sauce

2 cups chicken broth, boiling
2 teaspoons salt
2 teaspoons MSG
1 teaspoon sugar
1 teaspoon pepper
2 tablespoons cornstarch
1 cup cashews
2 tablespoons butter

In large pot, cook chicken slowly in hot butter until meat is white. Remove chicken. Sauté celery and beans for 2 minutes. Add all but the last 3 ingredients. Cover and cook 5 minutes. Adjust seasoning. Mix a little broth with cornstarch. Stir into sauce. Cook until it thickens. Quickly sauté cashews in 2 tablespoons butter. Sprinkle over the finished dish. Serves 6-8.

Sweet and Sour Chicken

salt and pepper to taste
2 fryers, cut into serving pieces
1 18-ounce jar apricot preserves
¼ cup water

1 envelope dry onion soup mix
1 8-ounce bottle Russian or
   creamy French salad dressing

Salt and pepper chicken. Warm preserves. Coat each piece of chicken with preserves. Place in a 2-quart casserole. Combine remaining ingredients. Pour over chicken. Bake at 350° for 1 hour. Baste often. Serves 8.
Surprisingly delicious, yet easy!

121

Paella

1 5-pound baking hen
1 chicken bouillon cube
1 large onion, chopped
1 large garlic clove, pressed
⅓ teaspoon saffron, ground
½ teaspoon oregano
1 teaspoon salt
2 cups raw long-grain rice
⅓ cup oil
½ pound pepperoni, thinly sliced
½ pound scallops
1 4-ounce can mushrooms

3 tablespoons butter
1 bell pepper, thinly sliced
2 pounds raw shrimp, peeled with tails on
12 clams in shell, canned or fresh
1 pimiento, cut into strips
1 10-ounce package frozen green peas, partially cooked
1 9-ounce package frozen artichoke hearts, partially cooked

Bake hen, skin and cut into 1-inch pieces. Make 4½ cups stock by adding bouillon cube and enough water to juices left from baking the hen. Set aside. In a large Dutch oven, cook onion, garlic, saffron, oregano, salt and rice in oil over low heat. Add stock. Stir and cook 10 minutes. Transfer to a 5-6 quart paella pan. Simmer pepperoni in a small amount of water for 5 minutes. Lightly sauté scallops and mushrooms in butter. Simmer bell pepper in a small amount of water for 3 minutes. Arrange chicken, pepperoni, scallops, shrimp, clams, pimiento, bell pepper, mushrooms, peas and artichoke hearts on top of rice mixture. DO NOT STIR.* Place pan on middle rack of oven. Bake at 375° for 20-30 minutes or until rice is done. Let stand 5 minutes before serving. Serves 10-12.
*Everything can be done ahead except the final baking.
A national favorite in Spain. Serve with sangria.

Spanish Chicken

1½ cups uncooked rice
8 strips bacon
2 ribs celery, chopped
1 medium onion, chopped
½ large bell pepper, chopped
½ pound fresh mushrooms, sliced
1½ tablespoons plain flour

1 16-ounce can tomatoes
1 chicken, cooked, boned and cut into bite-size pieces
salt and pepper to taste
dash Tabasco, Worcestershire
½ cup sharp Cheddar cheese, grated

Cook rice in 3 cups water. Set aside. In large skillet, cook bacon. Remove and crumble. Pour off all but 3 tablespoons bacon fat. Sauté celery, onion, bell pepper and mushrooms in fat. Stir in flour, then tomatoes. When bubbling, add rice and all ingredients except cheese. Pour into a 3-quart casserole. Top with cheese. Bake covered at 350° for 30 minutes. Serves 6-8.

Roquefort Chicken

6 half-breasts of chicken
¾ cup flour
1 teaspoon salt
½ teaspoon pepper, freshly ground
½ teaspoon rosemary, crushed
4 tablespoons butter
1 cup sour cream

½ teaspoon salt
2 teaspoons chives, snipped
1 3-ounce package Roquefort cheese, crumbled
2 teaspoons lemon rind, grated
2 tablespoons lemon juice
¼ cup blanched almonds

Shake chicken in a bag of flour, 1 teaspoon salt, pepper and rosemary. In a heavy skillet, brown chicken in butter. Remove to a shallow baking dish. Mix sour cream, ½ teaspoon salt, chives, cheese, lemon rind and juice. Spread over chicken. Cover and bake at 350° for 30 minutes. Sprinkle with almonds. Bake uncovered for 15 minutes. Serves 6.

▼ Roquefort cheese is a must!

Cheese Glazed Chicken

6 half-breasts of chicken, skinned
3 tablespoons flour
1 teaspoon paprika
1½ teaspoons salt
2 tablespoons butter
1 tablespoon oil

¼ cup dry sherry
1 teaspoon cornstarch
¾ cup half-and-half
⅓ cup sauterne or chablis
1 tablespoon lemon juice
½ cup Muenster cheese, grated

Place chicken in a paper or plastic bag with flour, paprika and 1 teaspoon salt. Shake until chicken is lightly coated. Brown chicken in heated butter and oil over moderate heat. Add sherry. Cover and simmer until tender, about 25 minutes. Remove chicken and debone at this point if desired. Blend cornstarch with cream and remaining ½ teaspoon salt. Stir into pan drippings. Continue cooking until sauce thickens slightly. Add wine and lemon juice. Heat a few minutes longer. Place chicken in ovenproof serving dish. Spoon sauce over chicken and sprinkle cheese over top. Place under broiler until cheese melts and browns. Serves 6.

▼ Serve with hot, thin spaghetti tossed with pesto, a basil-parsley-garlic purée, available in specialty shops, or make your own by combining ground basil, parsley, garlic, Parmesan and ground pine nuts (optional) with olive oil.

Chicken Saltimbocca with Linguine

6 half-breasts of chicken, boned and skinned
6 thin slices Prosciutto or other ham
1 cup Mozzarella cheese, grated
1 tomato, seeded and chopped
½ teaspoon crushed coriander
½ teaspoon sage
½ teaspoon chervil
½ teaspoon basil
¼ teaspoon tarragon
salt to taste

white pepper to taste
⅓ cup fine dry bread crumbs
2 tablespoons grated Parmesan cheese
2 tablespoons parsley, snipped
½ stick butter, melted
¾ cup dry white wine
1 8-ounce box linguine, cooked
½ cup half-and-half
2 tablespoons grated Parmesan cheese
2 tablespoons butter, melted

Cover chicken breasts, boned side up, with waxed paper. Pound lightly with a mallet to 5 x 5 inches. Layer chicken with ham, Mozzarella, tomato and mixed herbs. Season with salt and pepper. Tuck in sides. Roll up and secure with toothpicks to seal. Combine crumbs, 2 tablespoons Parmesan and parsley. Roll chicken in ½ stick melted butter, then crumb mixture. Place in greased, flat baking dish with the wine. Bake at 350° for 45 minutes. Toss linguine with a warmed combination of cream, Parmesan and 2 tablespoons butter. Serve immediately topped with chicken breasts. Spoon drippings from pan over the top. Serves 6.

Spicy Chicken Spaghetti

1 2½-3 pound stewing chicken or hen, cooked
3 cups reserved chicken stock
1 large onion, thinly sliced
3 tablespoons corn oil or chicken fat
1 28-ounce can tomatoes, drained and crushed (reserve juice)
1 6-ounce can tomato paste
¾ cup celery, thinly sliced

1 teaspoon salt
½ teaspoon black pepper
½ teaspoon seasoning salt
1½ tablespoons hot chili powder
1 teaspoon sugar
2 cloves garlic, minced
1 7-ounce can sliced mushrooms
cooked spaghetti

Cut chicken into bite size pieces. Set chicken and stock aside. Sauté onion in oil until limp and clear. Add tomatoes and tomato paste. Cook 10-15 minutes on low heat, stirring constantly. Remove from heat. Stir in stock, celery, seasonings and reserved tomato juice. Cover and simmer for about 30 minutes or until celery is cooked and sauce is thickened. Add chicken and mushrooms and cook 5-10 minutes longer. Serve over spaghetti. Serves 4-5.

Chicken-Green Noodle Casserole

1 3½-pound chicken
1 cup bell pepper, chopped
1 cup onion, chopped
1 cup celery, chopped
1 stick margarine

1 10¾-ounce can condensed
  cream of mushroom soup
½ pound American cheese, cubed
1 6-ounce can sliced mushrooms
1 8-ounce package green noodles
1 cup cheese crackers, crushed

In a large pot, cover chicken with water. Simmer until done. Reserve stock. Cool chicken, bone, and cut into bite-size pieces. In a large skillet, sauté bell pepper, onion and celery in margarine until tender. Add soup. Stir in cheese until melted. Add mushrooms and chicken. Boil noodles in reserved stock. Drain. Combine with chicken mixture. Pour into 2-quart casserole. Top with crumbs. Bake at 350° for 30 minutes. Serves 8.

▼ Freezes well.

Chicken Sandwich Surprise

2 pounds chicken breasts, cooked
  and diced
1 pound chicken thighs, cooked and
  diced
1½ cups celery, diced
2 cups mayonnaise
½ teaspoon chives or onions,
  chopped
1 teaspoon seasoning salt
1 teaspoon salt
1 teaspoon pepper

juice of 1 lemon
20 thin slices bread
butter or margarine, softened
12 ounces cream cheese
3 egg yolks
1 tablespoon lemon juice
½ teaspoon salt
1 tablespoon (or more) milk
  or cream
1 2¼-ounce package slivered
  almonds

Prepare chicken salad using first 9 ingredients. Adjust seasoning. Line cookie sheet with foil. Butter both sides of bread. Place one slice on foil, bountifully cover with salad and top with second slice of bread. Combine cream cheese, yolks, 1 tablespoon lemon juice, ½ teaspoon salt and enough milk to soften. Ice tops and sides of sandwiches. Cover with foil and seal. Refrigerate 24 hours. Uncover and let stand at room temperature before baking. Bake about 30 minutes at 350° until golden brown. Sprinkle with almonds last 15 minutes of baking. Serves 10.

▼ Must be prepared 1 day ahead.
Recipe for chicken salad is excellent to use alone.

Oven-Broiled Chicken Barbecue

½ cup butter or margarine
¼ cup fresh lemon juice
2 tablespoons horseradish
2 tablespoons vinegar
2 tablespoons catsup

2 teaspoons salt
1½ teaspoons Worcestershire
¾ teaspoon Tabasco
1 2-2½ pound chicken, halved
    or quartered

Combine all ingredients except chicken. Heat to boiling. Place chicken halves skin side down on rack in broiler pan. Brush with sauce. Broil 5-7 inches from heat for 40-45 minutes. Turn chicken and baste with sauce every 10 minutes. Serves 4.

Stuffed Cornish Hens
Mrs. John P. Grace

1 teaspoon salt
½ teaspoon pepper
4 Cornish hens
1 8-ounce package herb-seasoned
    stuffing mix
1 onion, chopped, or 3 tablespoons
    onion flakes

4 stalks celery, finely chopped
1 teaspoon celery seed
½ teaspoon poultry seasoning
1 chicken bouillon cube
1 cup boiling water
4 tablespoons margarine, melted
½ teaspoon seasoned salt

Salt and pepper hen cavity. Mix stuffing, onion, celery, celery seed and poultry seasoning. Dissolve bouillon in water. Add 1 tablespoon margarine. Pour over stuffing and toss until all ingredients are moist. Stuff hens lightly. Baste with margarine. Sprinkle with seasoned salt. Wrap each in foil or baking wrap. Bake at 350° for 1 hour. Serves 4.

Stuffed Cornish Hens Burgundy

1 6-ounce box wild and white
    rice mix
4-6 Cornish hens
salt and pepper to taste
1 cup burgundy wine
1 cup currant jelly

4 tablespoons butter
2 tablespoons lemon juice
4 teaspoons cornstarch
3 teaspoons Worcestershire
1 teaspoon ground allspice
dash of salt and pepper

Cook rice according to package directions and stuff hens. Lightly salt and pepper hens. In a saucepan, combine remaining ingredients. Let bubble until thickened. Place hens in a roasting pan and cover tightly with foil. Bake at 400° for 1-1½ hours, basting often with glaze. Split hens down the middle to serve. Pass remaining sauce. Serves 4-6.
Out of this world and so easy!

126

Chicken or Turkey à la King

━━━━━━━━━━━━━━━━━━━━━━━━━━━━━━━━━━━

1 stick butter
⅔ cup plain flour
3 cups hot stock
2½ cups milk, scalded
1 pint half-and-half, scalded
1 tablespoon salt
3 cups mushrooms, sliced and sautéed

6 heaping cups cooked fowl, diced
1½ cups pimientos, cut into strips
6 egg yolks
1½ sticks butter, softened
¾ cup dry sherry
1 tablespoon lemon juice
cooked rice or patty shells

Make cream sauce with first 6 ingredients. Add mushrooms, fowl and pimiento. When steaming hot, stir in yolks which have been mixed with softened butter. Add sherry and lemon juice. DO NOT BOIL. Serve over rice or patty shells. Serves 18. Freezes well.
Great for left-over chicken or turkey.

Crêpes Niçoise
Martha Fleming, "The Cookery," Augusta, Georgia

━━━━━━━━━━━━━━━━━━━━━━━━━━━━━━━━━━━

1 small turkey breast
rich chicken stock
fresh mushrooms, sliced and sautéed
seasoned salt
thyme
white wine sauce (see Shrimp Crêpes)

hard-boiled eggs, wedged
pimiento strips
asparagus spears
paprika
Swiss cheese, grated
grated Parmesan cheese
garnish: mushroom slices and parsley

Poach turkey breast in chicken stock for 45 minutes. Cut turkey into bite-size pieces. For each crêpe (see index for crêpe recipe), combine ⅓ to ½ cup turkey, mushrooms, salt, pinch of thyme and a few tablespoons of white wine sauce. Fill crêpe with this mixture, adding hard-boiled egg wedges and pimiento strips. Fold crêpe and place in ramekin or ovenproof dish. Place asparagus spears around crêpe and top with white wine sauce, paprika, Swiss cheese and Parmesan cheese. Garnish with mushroom slice. Bake at 450° for 12 minutes. Garnish with parsley when serving.

Curried Turkey Casserole

2 eggs, beaten
2 10¾-ounce cans condensed cream of mushroom soup
¾ cup Hellmann's mayonnaise
1 teaspoon curry powder
salt and pepper to taste
1 16-ounce can French-style green beans, drained

3½-4 cups cooked breast of turkey, diced
1 4-ounce can sliced mushrooms
1 8-ounce can water chestnuts, sliced
⅓ cup grated Parmesan cheese
2 cups herb stuffing mix
½ stick butter, melted

Combine eggs, soup, mayonnaise, curry, salt and pepper. Place beans in a buttered 2-quart casserole. Layer half of turkey, mushrooms, water chestnuts, egg-soup mixture and cheese. Repeat. Top with stuffing which has been tossed in butter. Bake at 350° for 30 minutes. Serves 10-12.

Turkey Almondine

¼ cup butter or margarine
¼ cup plain flour
2 cups milk
¼ teaspoon salt
pinch pepper
2 tablespoons dry white wine
2 egg yolks, beaten

2 cups turkey, cooked and diced
1 cup peas, cooked and drained
⅓ cup slivered almonds, toasted
3 tablespoons bread crumbs
1 tablespoon butter
2 tablespoons grated Parmesan cheese

Make a cream sauce with butter, flour and milk. Add salt, pepper and wine. Add a little sauce to yolks. Rapidly stir back into sauce. Stir in turkey, peas and half the almonds. Pour into a 1½-quart baking dish. Scatter remaining almonds and crumbs on top. Dot with butter. Sprinkle with cheese. Brown under broiler. Serves 4.

Chinese Purple Plum Duck

1 4-pound domestic duck, cut into serving pieces
½ cup soy sauce
½ cup peanut oil
1 cup canned purple plums, skinned and mashed
⅓ cup green onion tops, chopped
1 garlic clove, crushed

6 slivers fresh or crystallized ginger
½ teaspoon salt
2 tablespoons Chinese sweet and sour sauce
1-2 tablespoons cornstarch
2 tablespoons reserved plum syrup

Dip duck in soy sauce. Brown in oil. Remove to a baking dish. Mix remaining soy sauce with plums, onion tops, garlic, ginger and salt. Pour over duck. Cover. Bake at 325° until tender, about 2 hours. Remove duck from pan. Skim fat from juice. Add sweet and sour sauce and the cornstarch which has been dissolved in plum syrup. Cook until smooth and clear. Pour over duck. Serves 4.

Roast Duck with Orange Dressing and Sauce

Orange Dressing:
3 cups dry bread crumbs
½ cup hot water
2 teaspoons orange peel, grated
⅔ cup orange sections, cut-up
2 cups celery, chopped

1 egg, beaten
dash pepper
¼ cup butter, melted
¼ teaspoon poultry seasoning

Duck:
1 4-5 pound duck   salt

Orange Sauce:
2 tablespoons butter, melted
2 tablespoons flour
1 cup water
¼ cup orange juice concentrate

⅛ teaspoon salt
¼ cup sugar
1 orange rind, grated

For dressing, soften bread crumbs in water for 15 minutes. Add remaining ingredients and mix lightly. Rub cavity of duck with salt and stuff with orange dressing. Place duck on rack in shallow roasting pan. Roast uncovered at 325° until browned, 2½-3 hours. To make sauce, blend butter and flour in top of double boiler. Add remaining ingredients, stirring constantly until thickened. Serve hot. Serves 2.

Chicken Liver Ragout

1 pound chicken livers
salt and pepper to taste
¼ cup butter or margarine
¼ cup green onion, minced
½ cup sherry or Madeira

1 8-ounce can tomato sauce
1 10¾-ounce can chicken broth
1 small bay leaf
2 teaspoons parsley, snipped
toast points

Dry livers with paper towel. Season with salt and pepper. Sauté in butter until browned. Remove livers. Add onion to drippings. Sauté 2 minutes. Add wine. Cook 1 minute. Stir in tomato sauce, broth and bay leaf. Simmer 10 minutes. Return livers. Bring to a boil. Adjust seasoning. Pour into a serving dish. Sprinkle with parsley. Arrange toast points around livers. Serves 4.

Game
8

Dove Breasts Stroganoff

12 to 18 dove breasts
1 medium onion, chopped
2 tablespoons butter
1 10¾-ounce can condensed
   cream of celery soup
1 4-ounce can button mushrooms
½ cup sauterne

½ teaspoon oregano
½ teaspoon rosemary
salt and pepper to taste
1 teaspoon bottled brown
   bouquet sauce
1 cup sour cream

Arrange birds in a large baking dish. Do not crowd. Sauté onion in butter. Add remaining ingredients except sour cream. Pour over meat. Cover and bake at 325° for 1¼ hours, turning birds occasionally. Stir in sour cream. Bake, uncovered, 30 minutes. Serves 4-8.

Dove in Wine

20 dove breasts
salt and pepper to taste
½ cup butter
1 cup dry white wine
1 carrot, finely diced
1 medium onion, chopped

½ cup green pepper, chopped
1 cup mushrooms, chopped
2 tablespoons flour
2 cups chicken stock
3 slices orange peel, blanched,
   or 2 tablespoons orange liqueur

Season dove with salt and pepper. Brown slowly in butter. Remove to a buttered casserole. Pour wine over dove. Place in 300° oven while making sauce. In same skillet, sauté vegetables for 5 minutes. Stir in flour. Slowly add stock, stirring constantly. When sauce has thickened, add peel or liqueur. Simmer 5 minutes. Pour sauce over birds. Bake, covered, until tender, about 2 hours. Serves 6.

Junior Mann's Dove Pie

9 dove breasts
½ cup carrots, diced
1 8-ounce can tiny English
   peas

salt to taste
1 8-ounce can refrigerator
   biscuits
2 tablespoons sherry (optional)

Boil doves until tender in just enough salted water to cover. Remove birds and debone. Cook carrots in stock until tender. Add peas and boned birds. Adjust seasoning. Roll 2 biscuits out and cut into strips. Cut remaining biscuits into quarters and drop into stock. Cook until thickened. Add sherry. Spoon into casserole and cover pie with biscuit strips. Brown at 375°. Serves 3-4.

▼ Home-made biscuits are an added treat!

Roasted Dove

20-24 dove breasts
flour seasoned with salt and pepper
1 stick butter
1 medium onion, chopped
1 rib celery, chopped
1 tablespoon parsley, snipped
dash paprika and MSG

¼ teaspoon thyme
2 tablespoons Worcestershire
½ cup red wine
2 beef bouillon cubes
1 chicken bouillon cube
½ cup water
½ pound mushrooms, sliced

Dredge birds in seasoned flour. Brown in butter. Place in a large roaster with onion, celery, parsley, seasonings and bouillon which has been dissolved in water. Cover and bake at 350° for 2 hours, adding mushrooms last 30-45 minutes. Serves 8.

▼ This recipe is also good for quail or combination of dove breasts and whole quail.

Marsh Hen, Dove or Quail

3 slices bacon, halved
¼ cup vegetable oil
6 marsh hens, dove or quail
salt and pepper
flour

1 onion, chopped
1 garlic clove, chopped
1 10½-ounce can beef bouillon
1 bay leaf

In Dutch oven, cook bacon until half-done. Remove and pour off fat. Add oil. Brown birds that have been seasoned with salt and pepper and dredged in flour. Add onion and garlic, cooking a few minutes longer. Cover each bird with bacon. Add bouillon and bay leaf. Bake at 300° until tender, about 1-1½ hours. Serves 2-3.

▼ To remove fishy taste from marsh hens, soak in vinegar-salt water for 1 hour, then in soda water for several hours.

Quail with Sour Cream and Bacon

16 thin slices Canadian bacon
salt and pepper to taste
16 quail
16 slices regular bacon

1 cup sour cream
1 10¾-ounce can condensed
    cream of mushroom soup

Line a buttered 9x14-inch casserole with Canadian bacon. Top with seasoned quail wrapped in breakfast bacon. Combine sour cream and soup. Spoon over birds. Bake, uncovered, at 275° for 3 hours. Serves 12.

Heavenly Quail

8 quail	24 large mushrooms, sliced
1 cup vegetable oil	1 cup sauterne
flour seasoned with salt and pepper	1 cup chicken broth (optional)
1 stick butter	8 pieces toast, hot and buttered

Rub quail with oil. Shake in bag containing seasoned flour. Heat remaining oil in a heavy skillet. Brown birds well; remove to a plate. Pour off oil and add butter to skillet. When melted, add quail, mushrooms and wine. Add broth if desired. Cook, covered, over low heat until tender, about 30-45 minutes. Top toast with quail, then spoon gravy over birds. Serves 4.

To freeze dove and small game birds, pack in milk cartons and fill with water. Seal tightly. They will keep in freezer a year.

Quail in Wine

salt and pepper to taste	2 tablespoons bell pepper,
6-8 quail, split in half	chopped
1 stick butter	1 tablespoon flour
1 carrot, diced	1 cup chicken stock
1 small onion, chopped	½ cup white wine or sherry
½ cup mushrooms, sliced	

Salt and pepper birds. In a skillet, lightly brown birds in butter. Remove to a buttered casserole. In same skillet, sauté vegetables for 5 minutes. Stir in flour. Gradually add stock. Simmer 10 minutes. While sauce is simmering, pour wine over birds. Bake at 350° for 10 minutes. Pour sauce over birds. Cover and bake 45-60 minutes longer. Serves 3-4.

Clairmont Quail

8 quail	2 green apples, cut-up
flour seasoned with salt and pepper	8 strips bacon
½ cup oil	1½ cups dry white wine

Wash birds in salt water and dry. Shake in a sack of seasoned flour until completely covered. Brown in hot oil; remove and stuff birds with one of the apples. Wrap each bird with bacon. Place in roaster. Surround with remaining apple. Pour wine over birds. Bake, covered, at 400° for 1 hour. Add ½ cup water if needed. Cook ½-1 hour more or until tender. Serves 4.

133

Quail with White Grapes

4 quail
salt and white pepper to taste
3 tablespoons flour
⅓ cup butter
⅓ cup dry white wine

⅓ cup chicken broth
1 tablespoon lemon juice
¼ cup seedless grapes
2 tablespoons sliced blanched
   almonds, toasted

Rub quail with a mixture of salt, pepper and flour. In a heavy skillet, sauté birds in butter until golden. Add wine, broth and lemon juice. Cover and cook over low heat for 15-20 minutes. Add grapes and almonds. Cook for 5-10 minutes more or until birds are tender. Serves 2.

To tenderize and bring out flavor of quail, rub with lemon before cooking.

Texas-Style Duck with Pecan Stuffing

4 cups fresh bread crumbs
1 cup celery, chopped
1 cup onion, finely chopped
1 cup seeded raisins
1 cup pecans, chopped
1 teaspoon salt
2 eggs, beaten

½ cup milk
2 (2-2½ pounds each) wild ducks
6 bacon slices
1 cup catsup
½ cup chili sauce
¼ cup Worcestershire
¼ cup steak sauce

garnish: orange slices, watercress and currant jelly

For stuffing, mix first 6 ingredients. Combine eggs and milk. Toss lightly with bread mixture. Lightly fill body cavities of ducks with stuffing; close openings. Cover each breast with 3 slices of bacon. Place on rack in shallow roasting pan. Roast uncovered at 500° for 15 minutes. Reduce heat to 350°.Cook until ducks are tender, about 1½ hours. Combine catsup, chili sauce, Worcestershire and steak sauce. Pour over ducks last ½ hour of roasting. If desired, may skim off fat, thicken pan juices and serve sauce. Garnish. Serves 4.

▼ Serve with Orange Rice (see index).

Wild Duck with Mushrooms

1 duck
1 onion, sliced
½ cup butter
salt and pepper to taste
2 cups water

1 bay leaf
1 cup fresh mushrooms, sliced
3 tablespoons butter
2 tablespoons flour
⅛ teaspoon thyme

Brown duck and onion in ½ cup butter in heavy Dutch oven. Add salt, pepper, water and bay leaf. Cover and cook very SLOWLY for 1½ hours. In another skillet, sauté mushrooms in butter. Stir in flour and thyme. Combine with duck mixture and cook 30 minutes more. Serves 2.
The gravy is delicious to serve with wild rice.

Duck Mandarin Style

1 duck, cut into pieces	2 cups water
½ cup soy sauce	1 cup orange juice
1 tablespoon sugar	2 tablespoons cornstarch
½ teaspoon salt	½ cup water
1 teaspoon ground ginger	2 cups orange or
¼ cup salad oil	tangerine sections
1 clove garlic, minced	

Marinate duck in mixture of soy sauce, sugar, salt and ginger for 2 hours. Heat oil with garlic. Sauté duck in oil until brown. Add 2 cups water and orange juice. Cover and simmer until tender (about 2 hours). Thicken sauce with cornstarch mixed with ½ cup water. Add fruit sections. Cook 5 minutes. Pour sauce over duck. Serves 2.

To freeze duck, pack in water in foil pans or foil wrap.

Foil Roasted Wild Duck with Currant Sauce

1 duck	¼ cup red wine
salt and pepper	½ teaspoon thyme
1 onion	1 tablespoon butter

Currant Sauce:

1 pound butter	1 cup duck broth (not drippings)
2 10-ounce jars currant jelly	or chicken bouillon
1 teaspoon Worcestershire	1 tablespoon flour
1 teaspoon A-1 Sauce	sherry to taste
pinch of salt	

Rub inside and outside of duck with salt and pepper. Put onion in cavity. Place on large piece of heavy foil. Pour wine over duck. Sprinkle thyme and dot butter on top. Wrap tightly. Bake at 325° for 2-3 hours. Serves 1.
Currant Sauce: Melt butter and jelly in saucepan. Add Worcestershire, A-1, salt and broth. Mix well. Add flour and cook slowly until thickened. Add sherry to taste and thin. Serve with duck. Sauce for 8 servings.

Country-Style Venison Steak

4 venison steaks
salt and pepper to taste
flour
vegetable oil

1 envelope dry onion soup mix
1 cup water
1-2 tablespoons Worcestershire

Hack steaks to tenderize. Salt, pepper and flour steaks. Brown in oil. Add soup mix, water and Worcestershire. Simmer 1 hour or until tender, adding water as needed. Serves 4.

Game should be cooked in the heaviest cast iron or enameled cast iron available. Be sure tops fit tightly for steaming game to tenderize without drying.

Deer Steak Marinade

½ cup dry red wine
½ teaspoon ground cardamom
⅛ teaspoon garlic powder

⅓ cup vegetable oil
3 tablespoons soy sauce
2-4 deer steaks

Combine first 5 ingredients and pour over steaks. Marinate at room temperature 1-3 hours, turning occasionally. Drain steaks. Broil over charcoal or under oven broiler. Baste frequently if steaks are not well-marbled with fat. Serves 2-4.

Marinade for Venison

meat tenderizer
1 gallon salad oil
8 tablespoons vinegar

8 tablespoons Worcestershire
juice of 8 lemons
     (or 16 tablespoons Realemon)

Sprinkle venison liberally with meat tenderizer before placing in marinade. Use enough marinade to cover meat. For roasts, marinate 18-24 hours minimum. For steaks, marinate 4-6 hours minimum. Drain meat 30 minutes before placing on grill over low fire. Let marinade settle after removing meat. Pour off clear oil and baste meat often with dregs of marinade. Refrigerate clear oil for reuse (will keep up to 1 year). A ham of 10-12 pounds will cook on grill in about 3 hours. Turn every 10 minutes the first hour. Yields about 1 gallon marinade.

Venison Pot Roast

½ cup plain flour
1 venison roast, 2-inches thick
2 tablespoons vegetable oil
¼ cup celery, chopped
1 carrot, chopped

2 tablespoons onion, chopped
½ teaspoon salt
¼ teaspoon pepper
1 cup boiling water
1 cup red wine

Pound flour into meat. In a large skillet, brown meat in oil. Add vegetables, salt, pepper and ½ cup each of water and wine. Simmer, covered for 1 hour. Add remaining liquid and simmer until tender. Serves 4.

Venison Roast

1 6-pound venison roast
salt and pepper
garlic cloves

Worcestershire
1 pound butter
orange and lemon slices

Wash meat thoroughly and dry. Add salt and pepper to all surfaces. Make gashes on all sides and insert a thin slice of garlic in each. Douse with Worcestershire. Place in roasting pan with butter and enough water to assure adequate steam to tenderize. Place citrus slices on top. Cover and cook at 350°, 25 minutes per pound. When done, cut into thin slices. Pour pan gravy liberally over venison slices. Serves 6-8.

Venison Sauerbraten

4 pounds venison roast
1 cup vinegar
1 cup water
4 bay leaves
12 peppercorns
16 cloves
5 tablespoons flour
1 teaspoon salt

½ teaspoon pepper
⅛ teaspoon allspice
fat for browning roast
5 cups onion, sliced
1¾ cups beef bouillon
12 ginger snaps
½ cup hot water
1 tablespoon sugar

Place meat in a close fitting bowl with vinegar, water, bay leaves, peppercorns, cloves and additional water to cover roast. Cover and refrigerate 3-4 days, turning twice daily. Strain liquid, reserving ¼ cup. Sprinkle roast with flour, salt, pepper and allspice. Brown in hot fat. Add onion, bouillon and reserved liquid. Simmer until meat is tender, at least several hours. Remove to a warm plate. For gravy, mash ginger snaps in a small bowl with hot water until dissolved. Add this and sugar to the cooking juices. Heat for 10 minutes. Serves 6-8.
This has a rich, spicy gravy.

137

Cheese, Eggs
9

Eggs Mornay

Mornay Sauce:

2 tablespoons onion, chopped
4 tablespoons butter
4 tablespoons flour
2 cups milk
3 egg yolks, beaten
1 tablespoon whipping cream

2 tablespoons grated
   Parmesan cheese
2 tablespoons Gruyère
   cheese, grated
2 tablespoons butter
salt to taste

6 thin slices of ham
3 English muffins (split),
   toasted, or 6 Holland Rusk, heated

6 eggs, poached
garnish: red pepper and
   parsley

To make sauce, sauté onion until soft in 4 tablespoons butter. Place in double boiler over boiling water. Add flour and milk. Stir constantly until thick (15 minutes). Add egg yolks and cream. Cook over hot (not boiling) water for 10 minutes. Stir in cheeses and remaining butter. Add salt to taste. (Yields 2 cups.) To assemble, place a piece of ham on each muffin. Top with egg. Pour Mornay sauce over egg. Garnish. Serves 6.

▼ Always remember when adding egg yolks to a hot mixture, add a little of the hot mixture to the egg yolks first.

Cheese, like eggs, should be cooked at low temperatures to prevent toughening.

Teased Eggs

6 hard-boiled eggs
½ teaspoon salt
¼ teaspoon pepper
2 teaspoons onion, finely grated
1 pound cooked shrimp, chopped
   (reserve a few for garnish)
2 tablespoons butter

2 tablespoons flour
1 cup milk
¾ teaspoon salt
dash pepper
2 teaspoons bottled horseradish
1 cup sour cream

Shell eggs and halve lengthwise. Mash yolks with salt, pepper, onion and shrimp. Make a white sauce with butter, flour, milk, salt and pepper. When thickened, remove from heat. Stir in horseradish and sour cream. Mix ¼ cup sauce with yolk mixture and stuff eggs. Place in shallow baking dish and cover with remaining sauce. Bake at 350° for about 10 minutes. Garnish with reserved shrimp. Serves 6.

Eggs Hussarde

4 slices Canadian bacon, warmed
4 Holland Rusk or 2 English
  muffins (split), toasted
Marchand de Vin Sauce (see index)

4 eggs, poached
Blender Hollandaise Sauce
  (see index)
garnish: paprika, parsley

Place 1 slice bacon on each muffin. Pour 2 tablespoons Marchand de Vin Sauce over bacon. Top with egg. Pour 2 tablespoons Hollandaise Sauce over egg. Garnish. Serve at once. Serves 2-4.

Eggs Sardou Florentine

2 10-ounce packages frozen
  creamed spinach, cooked
8 artichoke bottoms
anchovy paste
8 eggs, poached

salt and pepper to taste
grated Parmesan cheese
2 cups Hollandaise Sauce
  (see index)

Place spinach in 1½-quart casserole. Place artichokes on spinach. Spread lightly with anchovy paste. Arrange eggs over artichokes. Season with salt and pepper. Sprinkle with cheese. Cover with Hollandaise Sauce. Bake at 350° for 20 minutes. Serves 8.

▼ 1 6-ounce package frozen Alaskan king crab may be added after eggs for a rich luncheon dish.

Egg Casserole

¼ cup butter
¼ cup flour
1 cup half-and-half
1 cup milk
1 pound sharp Cheddar cheese,
  grated
½ teaspoon salt
pepper to taste

1 clove garlic, crushed
¼ teaspoon thyme
¼ teaspoon basil
¼ cup parsley, chopped
18 hard-boiled eggs, sliced
½ pound bacon, fried and crumbled
1½-2 cups bread crumbs, buttered

Make cream sauce with butter, flour, cream and milk. Add cheese and stir until melted. Add seasonings. Pour some of sauce in a greased 3-quart baking dish. Add layer of eggs, bacon, more sauce, repeating process until all ingredients are used up, ending with sauce. Sprinkle with crumbs. Bake at 350° for 20 minutes or until bubbly and crumbs are browned. Serves 10-12.

Brunch Casserole

6 hard-boiled eggs, sliced
salt and pepper
1 pound hot bulk sausage

1½ cups sour cream
½ cup dry bread crumbs
1½ cups Cheddar cheese, grated

Place eggs in buttered casserole and season to taste. Cook sausage, drain and sprinkle over eggs. Pour sour cream over sausage. Combine crumbs and cheese. Sprinkle over casserole. Place in oven to heat thoroughly and brown top under broiler. Serves 6.
A favorite with everyone who tries it.

Mushroom Rarebit

2 tablespoons margarine
2 tablespoons flour
1⅓ cups milk
1 10¾-ounce can condensed
  cream of mushroom soup
1 teaspoon Worcestershire
Tabasco to taste
1 teaspoon salt

1½ cups mushrooms, sliced
8 ounces Cheddar cheese, grated
2 tablespoons dry sherry
6 English muffins or hamburger
  buns, split and toasted
12 slices baked ham
12 slices cooked chicken
garnish: parsley

In heavy saucepan, make a cream sauce with margarine, flour and milk. Add soup, Worcestershire, Tabasco, salt and mushrooms. Heat until bubbly. Add cheese and stir until melted. Remove from heat. Add sherry. Top each muffin with a slice of ham and chicken. Pour rarebit over each. Garnish. Serves 6.

Scotch Eggs

1 pound hot bulk sausage
1 teaspoon sage
salt to taste

6 medium hard-boiled eggs, peeled
8 tablespoons Wesson oil

Combine sausage and sage. Salt outside of eggs. Using 2 tablespoons sausage per egg, completely wrap eggs. Chill in refrigerator to allow sausage to set.* Fry eggs in hot oil until brown. Drain well. Serves 6.
*Can prepare 1 to 2 days in advance. May be fried 2 hours before serving and kept warm.
▼ Eggs may be halved and passed as an appetizer at brunch.

Cheese Fondue

1 pound sharp Cheddar cheese, grated	1 teaspoon dry mustard
1 pound Norwegian Swiss cheese, grated	½ teaspoon garlic, chopped
	dash Tabasco and Worcestershire
3 tablespoons flour	dash of nutmeg
1 cup dry white wine	1 ounce kirsch
	French bread, cubed

Mix cheeses with flour. In a saucepan, combine cheese mixture with all ingredients except kirsch and bread. Stir until smooth over low heat. Add kirsch just before serving. Pour in fondue pot. Dip bread cubes into fondue. Serves 4-6 as a main dish or 12 for hors d'oeuvres.

▼ Gruyère may be substituted for Cheddar cheese.
Good on a cold winter night.

For greater volume, beat egg whites at room temperature.

Cheese Soufflé

4 tablespoons butter	4 egg yolks, well beaten
4 tablespoons flour	1 cup sharp Cheddar cheese, grated
½ teaspoon salt	4 tablespoons grated
⅛ teaspoon pepper	Parmesan cheese
¼ teaspoon dry mustard	4 egg whites, room temperature
⅛ teaspoon nutmeg	¼ teaspoon cream of tartar
1 cup milk	

Part I

In medium size pan, melt butter. Add flour, salt, pepper, dry mustard and nutmeg. Cook over medium heat, stirring constantly, until mixture bubbles. Remove from heat. Add milk slowly. Cook until mixture bubbles and is quite thick. Remove from heat. Slowly beat in egg yolks. Beat in cheeses and set aside to cool.

Part II

Preheat oven to 350°. In a large bowl, beat whites with cream of tartar until stiff but not dry. Gently fold cheese mixture into egg whites. Pour in greased 1½-quart baking dish. Run spoon around top 1 inch from edge to force top hat effect. Bake 40-45 minutes or until soufflé is puffed and golden brown and fairly firm to touch. Serve at once. Serves 8.

Recipe may be doubled.
▼ Part I may be done several hours before serving. Add Part II just before baking.

142

Blender Cheese Soufflé

8 ounces sharp Cheddar cheese, broken
10 slices bread, crusts removed, buttered and torn
4 eggs
2 cups milk
1 teaspoon salt
½ teaspoon dry mustard
pinch of nutmeg

Put half of cheese and bread and 2 eggs in blender. Blend on high until thoroughly mixed. Add remaining cheese, bread, eggs and other ingredients. Blend well.* Bake in greased 1½-quart casserole at 350° for 1 hour, uncovered. Serves 6-8.
*Can be prepared a day ahead, refrigerated and baked before serving.

Sandwich Soufflé

8 slices bread, crusts removed
4 slices ham, preferably Smithfield
4 slices Cheddar cheese
butter
2 cups milk
1 egg
salt and pepper to taste

Make 4 sandwiches with ham and cheese, buttering bread on both sides. Beat remaining ingredients together. Place sandwiches in 8-inch square pan, cover with milk mixture, and soak at least 1 hour. Bake at 400° for 40-50 minutes. Serves 4.

Yvonne's Tomato Quiche

1 9-inch pie shell (may use frozen)
2 large tomatoes, cut in wedges
3 tablespoons flour, seasoned with salt and pepper
2 teaspoons vegetable oil
½ cup ripe olives, sliced
1 cup green onions, minced (reserve 2 tablespoons)
3 slices Provolone cheese
2 eggs, slightly beaten
1 cup whipping cream
1 cup Cheddar cheese, grated

Bake pie shell for 8 minutes at 425°. Cool. Dip tomatoes in flour and sauté in oil. Put olives and onions in pie shell. Add Provolone cheese and tomatoes. Stir eggs into cream. Add Cheddar and pour into pie. Bake at 375° for 45 minutes or until filling sets. Sprinkle with reserved onions. Cool 5 minutes before cutting. Serves 4-6.

Cheesy Ham Quiche

½ cup onion, thinly sliced
⅓ cup green pepper, chopped
1 tablespoon butter
1½ cups sharp Cheddar cheese, grated
1 tablespoon flour
1½ cups cooked ham, cubed

1 deep-dish pie shell, unbaked
2 eggs, beaten
1 cup milk
1 tablespoon parsley flakes
¾ teaspoon seasoned salt
¼ teaspoon garlic salt
¼ teaspoon pepper

Sauté onion and green pepper in butter. Mix cheese and flour. Add ham, onion and green pepper to cheese mixture. Spread in pie shell. Combine remaining ingredients and pour in pie. Bake on a cookie sheet 35-40 minutes at 375°. Serves 6.

A half pound of Cheddar cheese yields approximately 2 cups shredded.

Crab and Shrimp Quiche

Parmesan Pastry:
1¼ cups plain flour
¼ cup yellow cornmeal
¼ cup grated Parmesan cheese
¾ teaspoon salt

dash cayenne
½ cup margarine
3-4 tablespoons cold water

Custard Mixture:
4 eggs
¾ teaspoon salt
⅛ teaspoon pepper
2 cups half-and-half

1½ cups crabmeat and/or cooked shrimp
¼ cup grated Parmesan cheese

To prepare pastry, combine flour, cornmeal, cheese, salt and cayenne. Cut in margarine until particles are size of peas. Sprinkle with cold water using just enough to make a stiff dough. Shape dough into a ball. Chill thoroughly. Roll out a 12-inch circle on a floured board. Fill a 10-inch quiche pan with pastry. Bake at 350° for 5 minutes.

To prepare custard, beat eggs with salt and pepper. Stir in remaining ingredients. Pour into the partially baked crust. Bake at 350° for 40 minutes. Let stand 10 minutes before cutting. Serves 6-8.

Quiche Lorraine

pastry for 9-inch pie shell
8 slices bacon, diced
½ cup green onions with tops, chopped
6 eggs, beaten

1 teaspoon onion salt
1 cup Swiss cheese, grated
2 cups half-and-half
¼ teaspoon nutmeg

Line pie pan with pastry, trim edges and flute. Brown bacon lightly. Drain excess grease. Add onions. Cook until bacon is golden brown. Cool slightly. Combine eggs, onion salt and cheese. Stir in bacon mixture. Add cream. Blend well. Pour into pie shell. Sprinkle with nutmeg. Bake at 375° for 30-35 minutes. Serves 6.

Quiche Lorraine II

The Greenbrier, White Sulphur Springs, West Virginia

3 eggs, whipped
1 pint light cream
½ cup Swiss cheese, grated
salt, pepper, cayenne to taste
½ cup onion, chopped
½ cup ham, diced

¼ cup butter, melted
½ cup bacon, fried crisp and crumbled
½ cup Swiss cheese, diced
pastry shell for 9-inch quiche dish or 10-inch pie plate

Mix eggs, cream, grated cheese and seasonings. Sauté onion and ham in butter; add bacon and diced cheese and spread evenly in bottom of pastry shell. Pour egg mixture over ham mixture and fill to rim of shell. Bake at 400° for approximately 45 minutes or until set. Serves 8.

▼ This may be done in individual quiche or tart shells.

Shrimp Quiche

1½ cups shrimp, boiled and cleaned
8 ounces Swiss cheese, grated
⅓ cup green onions, chopped
2 tablespoons flour

1 deep-dish pie shell, unbaked
1 cup real mayonnaise
2 eggs, beaten
½ cup milk

Put shrimp, cheese, onions and flour in paper bag. Shake. Pour into pie shell. Mix remaining ingredients together. Pour over shrimp mixture. Bake at 350° for 1 hour. Serves 6.

▼ Ham may be substituted for shrimp.

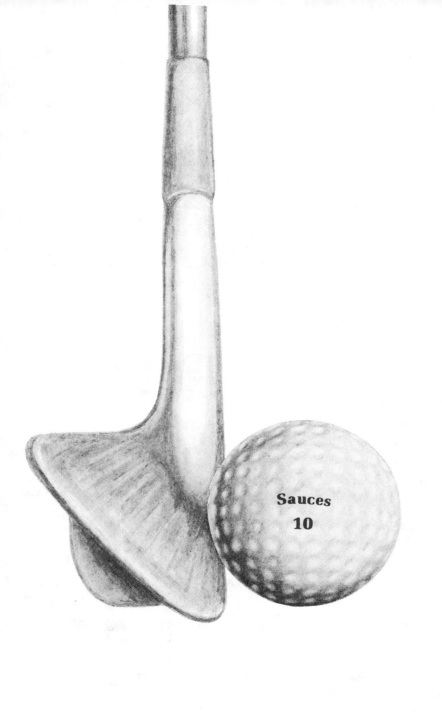

Sauces
10

Blender Mayonnaise

2 tablespoons lemon juice   ½ teaspoon dry mustard
   (1 lemon)   ¼ teaspoon paprika
1 egg   dash Tabasco
¾ teaspoon salt   1 cup oil

Place 1 tablespoon of lemon juice in blender with all ingredients except oil. Turn blender on low. SLOWLY add ½ cup of oil. Add remaining tablespoon of lemon juice and the remaining ½ cup oil. Yields about 1 cup.

Blender Hollandaise Sauce

3 egg yolks   pinch of red pepper
2 tablespoons lemon juice   1 stick butter, melted
¼ teaspoon salt

Put first 4 ingredients in blender and cover. Turn on low, immediately remove cover. SLOWLY pour hot butter in steady stream until all butter is used. Turn blender off. Serve immediately or place in pan that is in 2 inches hot water. Can be reheated in this manner also. Yields ¾ cup.

▼ To serve 6, use 4 egg yolks, 2 sticks butter and 2½ tablespoons lemon juice.

Easy Hollandaise Sauce

¼ cup butter   4 egg yolks
1 teaspoon salt   ¼ cup half-and-half
¼ cup lemon juice

Heat butter in top of double boiler until just melted. Add salt and lemon juice to egg yolks and mix well. Turn down heat so water is just simmering. Stir egg yolks into butter and beat with rotary beater until thick. Add cream and beat 2 minutes more. Yields 1⅓ cups.

▼ This can be made several hours before time to serve. Place top on mixture and remove from bottom part of double boiler. Just before serving, beat a few more times.

Blender Béarnaise

2 tablespoons white wine
1 tablespoon tarragon vinegar
½ teaspoon dried tarragon
¼ teaspoon black pepper,
  freshly ground

2 teaspoons green onion,
  chopped
¾ cup Blender Hollandaise Sauce
  (see index)
1 tablespoon capers

Combine first 5 ingredients in a saucepan. Bring to a boil and cook rapidly until almost all liquid evaporates. Put mixture and hollandaise sauce into blender. Cover and blend on high for 6 seconds. Stir in capers before serving. Yields 1 cup.
▼ Serve on broiled meats or fish.

Hot Curry Mayonnaise Sauce

2 tablespoons butter, melted
¼ teaspoon garlic, minced
  (or garlic salt)

½ teaspoon curry powder
½ cup mayonnaise
1 tablespoon lemon juice

Mix first 3 ingredients in small bowl. Add mayonnaise and lemon juice slowly, stirring well. Set in pan of hot water. Simmer water until sauce is heated. Yields about ⅔ cup sauce.
▼ Serve over broccoli or asparagus.

Dill-Cheese Sauce

1 11-ounce can Cheddar cheese
  soup, undiluted
½ cup plain yogurt

2 teaspoons dried dill weed
¼ teaspoon aromatic bitters

Combine all ingredients in saucepan. Cook and stir over medium heat until heated through but not boiling. Yields about 2 cups.
▼ Serve over broccoli, asparagus, cauliflower or baked potatoes.

Jezebel Sauce

1 12-ounce jar apple jelly
1 12-ounce jar pineapple
   preserves

2½ ounces horseradish
½ ounce dry mustard (½
   small can)

Melt all ingredients in a double boiler. Serve warm on ham or venison. Yields 2 pints.

▼ Will keep indefinitely in refrigerator. Reheat in double boiler, never on direct heat.

Gribiche Sauce

1 cup salad oil
⅓ cup wine vinegar
1 teaspoon fresh black pepper
1 teaspoon salt
1 teaspoon Creole mustard

2 tablespoons parsley, chopped
1 tablespoon pimiento, chopped
1 tablespoon capers
2 hard-boiled eggs, chopped

In blender, combine oil, vinegar, pepper, salt and mustard. Blend until creamy. Stir in remaining ingredients. Serve over shrimp mold, cold meat or as a sauce for beef fondue.

Remoulade Sauce

1 cup mayonnaise
1 tablespoon onion, finely
   chopped
1 tablespoon parsley, finely
   chopped
2 tablespoons Dijon mustard
1 tablespoon celery, finely
   chopped

1 tablespoon prepared
   horseradish
1 teaspoon paprika
½ teaspoon salt
dash Tabasco
¼ cup salad oil
1 tablespoon vinegar
½ teaspoon Worcestershire

Combine all ingredients in bowl and mix until well blended. Chill several hours. Yields 1½ cups.

▼ Serve with boiled shrimp, crab meat, lobster or tomatoes.

Barbeque Sauce

1 quart cider vinegar
1 cup Worcestershire
1 6-ounce jar French's prepared
   mustard
1¼ pounds margarine

2 teaspoons Tabasco
1 teaspoon salt
¾ pound dark brown sugar
2 14-ounce bottles ketchup

Combine all ingredients in saucepan and simmer about 3 hours. Yields enough sauce for 6 chickens.

▼ Keeps in refrigerator indefinitely.

Lemon Barbeque Sauce for Chicken

1 cup salad oil
½ cup lemon juice
1 tablespoon salt
1 teaspoon paprika

2 teaspoons basil, crushed
2 teaspoons onion powder
½ teaspoon thyme
1 clove garlic, crushed

Combine ingredients in a jar and shake well. Pour sauce over chicken and cover tightly. Marinate at least 6 hours in refrigerator. Turn chicken occasionally. Remove from refrigerator 1 hour before cooking. Baste chicken frequently with sauce while cooking. Yields enough sauce for two 2½-3 pound chickens.

Sweet and Sour Sauce

1 cup sugar
½ cup white vinegar
½ cup water
2 tablespoons bell pepper,
   chopped
2 tablespoons onion, chopped

1 teaspoon salt
2 dashes Tabasco
2 teaspoons cornstarch
1 tablespoon cold water
1 tablespoon pimientos, chopped
1 tablespoon parsley, chopped

Mix first 7 ingredients and boil 5 minutes. Strain. Thicken liquid that remains with mixture of cornstarch and water. Simmer until thick. Add pimientos and parsley for color. May be served hot or at room temperature. Yields 1 pint.

▼ Good dip for chicken "drumettes."

Sherry Supreme Sauce

2 tablespoons butter
2 tablespoons plain flour
½ cup half-and-half
½ cup chicken broth

¼ cup Swiss cheese, grated
2 tablespoons sherry
salt to taste

Melt butter. Add flour. Gradually add cream and chicken broth, stirring constantly. Add cheese and stir until thoroughly blended. Add sherry and season to taste. Yields 1½ cups.

❧ Delicious with chicken, seafood or vegetables.

Kebob Marinade

1½ cups salad oil
2 tablespoons dry mustard
2¼ teaspoons salt
1½ teaspoons dried parsley
2 cloves garlic, minced

¼ cup Worcestershire
½ cup vinegar
1 tablespoon black pepper
⅓ cup lemon juice
3 tablespoons soy sauce

Combine all ingredients. Mix well. Marinate 1½-inch chunks of beef for 4-24 hours. Baste kebob with marinade while cooking. Yields 2½ cups.

❧ Can be drained and used a second time. Store in tightly covered container for 1 week in refrigerator or in freezer indefinitely.

Beef Sauce

¼ pound mushrooms, thinly
    sliced
3 tablespoons butter
1 scant tablespoon cornstarch
½ cup water
¼ cup red wine

1 beef bouillon cube
1 teaspoon tomato paste
1 teaspoon Kitchen Bouquet
dash Worcestershire
salt and pepper to taste

Brown mushrooms in butter. Dissolve cornstarch in water and add to mushrooms along with remaining ingredients. Simmer until mixture thickens. Yields 1 cup.

❧ Delicious on steak, roast beef or London Broil.

SAUCES

Marchand de Vin Sauce

½ pound fresh mushrooms, minced
4 tablespoons butter
1½ cups beef broth, hot
½ cup green onions, minced
1 large clove garlic, crushed
½ cup dry red wine
⅓ cup beef broth

2 tablespoons flour
  (browned in oven)
2 dashes Tabasco
⅓ cup ham, minced
juice of ½ lemon
salt, freshly ground pepper
  to taste

Sauté mushrooms in 2 tablespoons butter. Add ½ cup beef broth. Simmer covered, for 10 minutes. In another pan, sauté green onions in 2 tablespoons butter until transparent. Add garlic, 1 cup broth and wine. Cover and simmer 20 minutes. Combine ⅓ cup broth and flour. Stir into onion mixture. Add Tabasco. Bring to a boil. Remove from heat and add mushroom mixture. Add ham, lemon juice, salt and pepper. Serve warm. Yields 1½ cups.

Sauce is delicious served on tenderloin, tournedos, poached eggs and broiled chicken.

Keep brown flour on hand for thickening sauces, gravies or soups. To make brown flour, heat in 325° oven for 30 minutes or until lightly browned, stirring occasionally. Store in airtight container for future use.

Thin Marchand de Vin Sauce

2 garlic cloves, finely chopped
3 green onions, chopped
¼ teaspoon black pepper,
  freshly ground
pinch of marjoram
½ stick butter
½ cup red wine

1 tablespoon plain flour
3 cups beef stock
½ pound mushrooms, sliced and
  broiled in butter
2 tablespoons sherry
2 tablespoons brandy
salt to taste

Braise garlic, onions, pepper and marjoram in butter. Add wine, then flour, and cook to a paste. Add beef stock and simmer 45-60 minutes. Add mushrooms, sherry, brandy and salt. Yields 4 cups.

Delicious over steak or roast or makes a good sauce for "steak bites" served from a chafing dish at a cocktail party.

152

Vegetables and Meat Accompaniments

11

Hot Artichoke Hearts

2 14-ounce cans artichoke hearts, drained
½ cup onion, minced
1 clove garlic, crushed
2 tablespoons butter

¾ cup canned chicken broth
2 tablespoons fresh lemon juice
1½ teaspoons salt
½ teaspoon oregano
¼ teaspoon lemon rind, grated

Combine all ingredients in small saucepan. Simmer for 10 minutes. Serves 6-8. *Unusual tart flavor. Good to serve when you need a "light" vegetable.*

Asparagus Casserole

3 15-ounce cans asparagus spears, drained
1½ cups sour cream
1 small onion, minced
¾ teaspoon salt

½ teaspoon pepper
¼ teaspoon dry mustard
1 clove garlic, minced
1 cup fresh bread crumbs
3 tablespoons butter, melted

Place asparagus in 1½-quart buttered casserole. Combine sour cream, onion, salt, pepper, dry mustard and garlic. Pour over asparagus. Toss crumbs with butter and sprinkle over casserole. Bake at 350° for 30 minutes. Serves 8. *Quick and easy.*

B's Asparagus Bake

2½ pounds fresh asparagus
1 4-ounce jar pimientos, sliced
½ cup milk
1 3-ounce package cream cheese

¼ cup blue cheese, crumbled
1 tablespoon butter or margarine, melted
3 tablespoons bread crumbs

Cook asparagus until almost tender. Drain and place in greased shallow baking dish. Sprinkle pimientos over asparagus. In a small saucepan, heat milk and cheeses, stirring until smooth. Pour over asparagus. Combine butter and bread crumbs. Sprinkle over asparagus. Bake at 325° for 30 minutes or until crumbs are nicely browned. Serves 4-6.

▼ For a short cut, use 2-3 tall cans of asparagus spears instead of fresh asparagus.

154

Barley Casserole

½ pound canned or fresh
   mushrooms, sliced
1 large onion, finely chopped
4 tablespoons butter

1 cup barley
salt and pepper to taste
2-3 cups beef broth
slivered almonds, toasted

Sauté mushrooms and onion in butter. Do not let onion brown. Mix in barley, salt and pepper. Pour into buttered 1½-quart casserole. Cover with broth to ½ inch above barley. Cover and bake at 350° for 45 minutes or until liquid is absorbed and barley is tender. Garnish with almonds. Serves 6.

▼ Excellent used as a stuffing for broiled tomatoes.
Delicious with roast beef.

Steaming vegetables preserves the nutrients better than boiling. Use a rack in a pan with tight fitting cover. Do not let water touch the rack. Approximate times for steaming are: asparagus, broccoli, brussels sprouts, sliced carrots, green peas, 10-20 minutes; cauliflower flowerets, 9-10 minutes; eggplant, 10-12 minutes; onions, 15-30 minutes; potatoes (white or sweet), 30-40 minutes; squash or zucchini, 10-15 minutes.

Dilled Beans

2 16-ounce cans French-style green
   beans and juice, or 2 9-ounce
   packages frozen beans
1½ teaspoons dill weed or dill
   seed
3 tablespoons bacon grease
6 tablespoons butter
6 tablespoons flour
½ cup milk

1 cup bean juice from cooked beans
1 teaspoon pepper
dash Tabasco
3 tablespoons onion, grated
2½ teaspoons MSG
1½ teaspoons salt
1½ cups buttered bread cubes
   for topping

In saucepan, place beans and juice, dill weed or seed, and bacon grease. Boil at least 10 minutes. Let sit at least 4 hours or overnight. Make a sauce by melting butter, adding flour, then milk and bean juice slowly. Stir; add other seasonings and cook until thick. Drain beans; place in a 2-quart baking dish, alternating layers of beans and sauce.* Top with buttered bread cubes. Bake at 325° until it bubbles and bread cubes are brown. Serves 8.
*May be prepared ahead to this point and frozen.

Green Beans with Sour Cream Sauce

2½ pounds fresh green beans or
　　3 9-ounce packages frozen
　　whole green beans

salt and pepper to taste
3 tablespoons butter

Sauce:

¼ cup onion, minced
2½ tablespoons butter
3 tablespoons flour
1½ cups hot milk

¾ cup sour cream
salt and pepper to taste
few drops of lemon juice
garnish: chopped chives or parsley

Cook beans in salted water. Drain. Season with salt, pepper and butter. Keep warm. In a saucepan, sauté onion in butter over low heat until soft but not colored. Add flour and cook the roux, stirring, for 2 minutes. Remove pan from heat and stir in hot milk. Return pan to heat and cook sauce, stirring, until it thickens and comes to a boil. Remove from heat. Cover sauce with buttered round of wax paper until serving time. Remove paper and reheat sauce. Add sour cream and stir until hot. DO NOT BOIL. Season with salt, pepper and lemon juice. Pour over beans in a heated serving dish. Garnish. Serves 8.

▼ For variety, add ½ cup grated Swiss cheese, 2 tablespoons grated onion, and 1 tablespoon bacon grease to sauce.

Sauce is delicious over other fresh vegetables.

Connoisseur's Casserole

1 12-ounce can white shoe peg
　　corn, drained
1 16-ounce can French cut string
　　beans, drained
½ cup celery, chopped
½ cup onion, chopped
1 2-ounce jar pimientos, chopped

½ cup sour cream
½ cup sharp Cheddar cheese,
　　grated
1 10¾-ounce can cream of
　　celery soup
½ teaspoon salt
½ teaspoon pepper

Topping:

1 cup Ritz cracker crumbs
½ stick butter, melted

½ cup slivered almonds

Mix all ingredients except topping. Place in 1½-quart casserole. Sprinkle topping over casserole. Bake at 350° for 45 minutes. Serves 8.

▼ May be frozen.

Delicious! Give it a try.

VEGETABLES AND MEAT ACCOMPANIMENTS

Three-Bean Casserole

Mrs. Tommy Aaron – wife of 1973 Masters' Champion

1 9-ounce package frozen French beans
1 10-ounce package frozen lima beans
1 10-ounce package frozen peas
1 5.33-ounce can evaporated milk

1 cup mayonnaise
1½ tablespoons Worcestershire
1 medium onion, finely chopped
1 8-ounce can water chestnuts, drained and sliced
buttered bread crumbs

Cook beans and peas according to package directions. Drain. Add remaining ingredients except crumbs and mix together. Place in a buttered 2-quart casserole. Top with crumbs. Bake at 350° for 30 minutes. Serves 8-10.

▼ For variety, substitute ½ cup sliced celery and 2 ounces chopped pimiento for water chestnuts. May also add chopped pecans or slivered almonds for crunch. May use herb seasoned stuffing mix for topping.

Orange Beets

2 16-ounce cans sliced beets
¼ cup cider vinegar
¾ cup sugar
¼ teaspoon salt

1 tablespoon butter
3 tablespoons cornstarch
juice of 1 orange
rind of 1 orange, grated

Drain beets reserving ¾ cup juice. In saucepan, combine beet juice with all ingredients except beets. Cook until thickened. Add beets and heat well. Let stand at least 2 hours before serving. May be served warm or at room temperature. Serves 8.

▼ Will keep for 2 weeks in refrigerator.

Stuffed Beets

1 16-ounce can whole small beets (reserve juice)
½ cup cider vinegar
1 teaspoon salt
2 teaspoons sugar

1 3-ounce package cream cheese
cream or milk
1 large clove garlic, pressed
parsley

Scoop a small segment from the top of each beet. Place beets in a glass jar. Mix half of beet juice with vinegar, salt and sugar. Pour over beets. Chill 8-10 hours. Before serving, soften cream cheese with cream or milk as needed. Add garlic. Drain beets. Stuff with cheese mixture, heaping slightly. Chill. Top each beet with sprig of parsley. Yields enough to garnish a medium platter.

Broccoli Casserole

2 10-ounce packages frozen
   chopped broccoli
1 10¾-ounce can condensed
   cream of mushroom soup
1 cup mayonnaise

2 tablespoons onion, grated
1 cup sharp cheese, grated
2 eggs, beaten
cheese cracker crumbs

Cook broccoli for 5 minutes. Drain. Steam in colander 10 minutes. Combine soup, mayonnaise, onion, cheese and eggs. Add broccoli. Put in greased 1½-quart casserole.* Top with crumbs. Bake at 400° for 30 minutes. Serves 6-8.
*Better if made a day ahead but baked just before serving. Do not add crumbs until ready to bake.
▼ For variety, add 1 8½-ounce can drained green peas.

Broccoli Orientale

1 onion, chopped
3 tablespoons oil
1 10-ounce package frozen
   chopped broccoli, thawed
2 tablespoons soy sauce

1 teaspoon sugar
⅛ teaspoon MSG
1 tablespoon cornstarch
½ cup chicken broth

Sauté onion in oil. Add broccoli and lower heat. Add soy sauce, sugar and MSG. Stir and cook 2-3 minutes. Combine cornstarch with broth. Add to broccoli and stir well. Cook 5 minutes. Serves 3-4.
▼ Substitute ½ pound fresh asparagus (cut in 1-inch pieces) for broccoli.

Broccoli Rice Casserole

1 onion, chopped
1 rib celery, chopped
½ stick butter
1 10-ounce package frozen
   chopped broccoli, cooked
   and DRAINED WELL

2½ cups cooked rice
1 10¾-ounce can condensed
   cream of chicken soup
4 ounces Cheese Whiz
dash Tabasco
pepper to taste (no salt)

Sauté onion and celery in butter until tender. Combine onion and celery with remaining ingredients. Pour into greased 1½-quart baking dish.* Bake at 350° for 45 minutes or until hot and bubbly. Serves 6.
*Better if prepared a day ahead. Freezes well.

Broccoli or Spinach Surprise

1 14-ounce can artichoke
  hearts, quartered
½ cup butter, melted
8 ounces cream cheese, softened

1½ teaspoons lemon juice
2 10-ounce packages frozen
  chopped broccoli or spinach
saltine cracker crumbs

Grease 1½-quart casserole. Place artichokes on bottom. Combine butter, cream cheese and lemon juice. Add broccoli or spinach which has been cooked and DRAINED WELL. Pour mixture over artichokes. Top with crumbs. Bake uncovered at 350° for 25 minutes. Serves 6.

▼ For added zip, add Worcestershire, garlic salt and Tabasco (to taste) to cream cheese mixture.

Quick and easy.

Carrot Soufflé
Callaway Gardens

3 tablespoons butter
3 tablespoons flour
1 cup hot milk
¼ teaspoon salt
3 eggs

2 cups cooked carrots,
  mashed
1 teaspoon vanilla
3 tablespoons sugar
½ teaspoon nutmeg

In mixing bowl, blend melted butter and flour. Add milk and mix until smooth. Add remaining ingredients. Pour mixture into a greased casserole. Bake at 350° for 40 minutes. Serves 6.

Aunt Mary's Carrot Pudding

2 cups cooked carrots, mashed
1 teaspoon salt
¾ cup sugar
½ stick butter, melted
2 heaping tablespoons plain flour

pinch of cinnamon
1 cup milk
3 eggs, well beaten
1 teaspoon baking powder
½ cup pecans, chopped

Combine carrots with salt, sugar and butter. Add remaining ingredients and mix. Bake at 350° for 1 hour in 1-quart baking dish. Serves 6.

Very sweet.

Carrots Lyonnaise

2 chicken bouillon cubes
1 cup boiling water
12 carrots, cut in strips
4 tablespoons butter
4 medium onions, thinly sliced

2 tablespoons plain flour
1 cup water
½ teaspoon salt
½ teaspoon pepper
1 tablespoon lemon juice

In a saucepan, dissolve bouillon in boiling water. Add carrots, cover and cook 15 minutes. Melt butter in skillet. Add onions. Cover and cook 15 minutes. Combine flour, water, salt and pepper. Add to onions. Stir and bring to a quick boil. Pour carrots and liquid into 1½-quart baking dish. Pour onion mixture over carrots. Sprinkle with lemon juice. May sprinkle with small amount of sugar if desired. Bake at 350° for 10 minutes. Serves 8.
Colorful and inexpensive. Quick and easy.

Cauliflower Casserole

1 large head cauliflower or
   2 10-ounce packages frozen
   cauliflower
1½ tablespoons lemon juice
1 4-ounce can mushrooms, drained
1 green pepper, chopped
3 tablespoons butter

3 cups thick white sauce
1 8½-ounce can tiny green
   peas, drained
dash red pepper, Worcestershire
1 8-ounce package processed
   pimiento cheese, grated
paprika

Cook cauliflower in salted water with lemon juice until tender. Drain. Sauté mushrooms and green pepper in butter. Combine white sauce, peas, red pepper, Worcestershire and half of cheese. Add cauliflower, mushrooms and green pepper. Pour into 1½-quart casserole. Top with remaining cheese and sprinkle with paprika. Bake at 350° for 25 minutes or until lightly browned. Serves 10.
Serve with ham, turkey or roast beef.

Celery Casserole

3 cups celery, diced
¼ cup almonds, slivered
½ cup water chestnuts, sliced
5 tablespoons butter
3 tablespoons plain flour
1 cup chicken broth

¾ cup half-and-half
½ cup mushrooms, halved
salt and pepper to taste
dash Worcestershire
½ cup Parmesan cheese
½ cup Ritz cracker crumbs

Parboil celery until almost tender. Drain and put in a 1½-quart casserole with almonds and water chestnuts. Melt butter in saucepan, add flour and stir until smooth. Slowly stir in broth and half-and-half. Stir over low heat until thickened. Add mushrooms, salt, pepper and Worcestershire. Pour over celery. Sprinkle with cheese and crumbs. Bake at 350° until hot and bubbly. Serves 6.

▼ Green or lima beans can be substituted for celery.

Corn Fritters

½ cup milk	1½ teaspoons salt
2 cups boiled corn, cut from cob	3 teaspoons baking powder
	2 eggs, well beaten
2 cups plain flour	1 tablespoon butter, melted

Add milk to corn. Sift dry ingredients together. Add to corn mixture. Add eggs and butter. Mix well. Drop by spoonfuls into fat heated to 375°. When brown, drain on paper towels. Serve immediately. Yields 1½ dozen.

▼ Canned whole kernel corn can be substituted for fresh corn.
Children love these!

Eggplant should be soaked in salted water 20-30 minutes prior to cooking to remove bitter taste.

Eggplant and Clam Casserole

1 large or 2 medium eggplants, peeled and sliced	¼ cup green pepper, chopped
2 tablespoons butter	1 small onion, chopped
2 tablespoons flour	1 tablespoon pimiento, chopped
1 8-ounce can minced clams, drained (reserve juice)	1 egg, well beaten
	salt and pepper to taste
clam juice and milk to make 1 cup	Cheddar cheese, grated, and/or bread or cracker crumbs

Cook eggplant in boiling salted water until tender. Drain and put in 1¾-quart casserole. Melt butter. Stir in flour. Gradually add clam juice and milk stirring constantly until mixture comes to a boil. Add clams, green pepper, onion, pimiento, egg, salt and pepper. Simmer a few minutes. Pour over eggplant. Stir lightly. Top with cheese and/or crumbs. Bake uncovered at 325° for 20 minutes or until browned. Serves 6.

Eggplant Parmesan

1 medium to large eggplant	1 15-ounce can tomato sauce
1 egg	2 cloves garlic, finely chopped
¼ cup white wine	½ teaspoon basil
bread or cracker crumbs	½ pound Mozzarella cheese, sliced
olive oil (or olive and corn oil, mixed)	½ cup grated Parmesan cheese

Peel and slice eggplant ⅜-inch thick. Beat egg and wine together. Dip eggplant slices in egg mixture, then in bread crumbs and brown in oil. Drain on paper towels. Simmer tomato sauce, garlic and basil together in saucepan 10-15 minutes. Layer half the eggplant, Mozzarella, Parmesan and sauce in baking dish, then repeat layers. Bake at 350° for 30 minutes. Serves 6.

Eggplant Casserole

1 large eggplant, peeled and sliced into 1-inch rounds	1 large onion, sliced and separated into rings
3 medium tomatoes, peeled and sliced	salt and pepper to taste
1 large bell pepper, diced	1½ cups bread crumbs
	bacon strips

Cook eggplant in salted water until tender. Drain and mash (may keep slices whole if desired). In a 2½-quart casserole, layer the eggplant, tomato slices, bell pepper, onion rings, salt, pepper and bread crumbs. Repeat layers ending with bread crumbs. Place strips of bacon on top. Bake at 350° for 1 hour. Serves 6-8.

This goes beautifully with any meat.

Marion's Baked Apricots

1 4-ounce stack Ritz crackers	⅔ cup light brown sugar
5 17-ounce cans apricot halves	1 stick butter, melted

Roll crackers into crumbs. In a 3-quart casserole, alternate layers of apricots, crumbs and brown sugar. Pour butter over top. Bake at 300° for 30-45 minutes. Serves 12.

▼Good with chicken or quail.

162

VEGETABLES AND MEAT ACCOMPANIMENTS

Hot Curried Fruit

1 29-ounce can peach halves
1 29-ounce can pear halves
1 16-ounce can apricot halves
1 8½-ounce can pineapple chunks

about 20 maraschino cherries
½ cup butter, melted
¾ cup light brown sugar, packed
3½-4 teaspoons curry powder

Drain all fruits. In 3-quart baking dish, place peaches and pears hollow side up. Place apricots on top. Sprinkle pineapple and cherries over fruit. Combine butter, sugar and curry powder. Sprinkle over fruit. Bake at 325° for 1 hour, basting 3 or 4 times. Cool and refrigerate at least 1 day. Heat before serving. Serves 10-12.
Good with ham or pork.

Glazed Pickled Peaches

1 29-ounce can pickled peaches
½ cup reserved peach juice

1 cup brown sugar
¼ cup butter

Drain peaches, reserving ½ cup peach juice. Place all ingredients in large skillet. Simmer slowly, turning peaches often until glazed all over. Drain peaches. Use to garnish poultry or pork.

To preserve the color of fresh vegetables, add a small pinch of baking soda to the water, or leave the pan top off for the first few minutes of cooking.

Mushroom Casserole

1 pound fresh mushrooms, whole
1 8-ounce can pitted black olives, halved
4 ounces Cheddar cheese, grated
1½ tablespoons flour

½ cup half-and-half
1½ tablespoons butter
½ teaspoon salt
½ teaspoon pepper

Layer mushrooms, olives and cheese in a 1-quart casserole. Fill dish to top because it cooks down. Blend remaining ingredients and pour over mixture. Bake uncovered at 350° for 30 minutes. Serves 4-6.
Quick and easy.

Mushroom Newburg

1 pound fresh mushrooms, sliced
3 tablespoons butter
salt and pepper to taste
1 tablespoon cognac

3 tablespoons dry sherry
1 cup half-and-half
¼ cup whipping cream
2 egg yolks, beaten

Sauté mushrooms in butter. Add salt and pepper. Stir in cognac and sherry. Simmer a few minutes. Add half-and-half and cook gently 5 minutes. Blend whipping cream into egg yolks and pour into mushroom mixture. Stir until sauce thickens slightly. Serve in patty shells or on toast points. Serves 6.
▼ Easy but cannot be prepared ahead.

Mushrooms and Sour Cream

1 medium onion, sliced
¼ cup margarine
1 pound fresh mushrooms,
   washed and halved if large

1 cup sour cream
1 tablespoon sherry
1 teaspoon salt
pepper to taste

Sauté onion in margarine until limp. Add mushrooms. Cover and cook slowly 5 minutes. Add remaining ingredients. Simmer until thoroughly heated and mushrooms are tender. Serves 6-8.
Easy, delicious and rich. Serve as a side dish with steak or roast beef.

Mushroom Soufflé

6 slices bread, buttered
   with crusts removed
12 ounces sharp Cheddar cheese
1 pound fresh mushrooms, sliced
   and sautéed

4 eggs, well beaten
2 cups milk
½ teaspoon dry mustard
½-1 teaspoon salt

In a 1½-quart casserole, alternate layers of bread, grated cheese and mushrooms. Combine remaining ingredients, pour over layers and let stand at least 1 hour. Bake at 325° for 1 hour or until knife inserted in center comes out clean. Serves 6 to 8.

Sautéed Mushrooms

1 pound mushroom caps
¼ cup butter or margarine
½ cup white wine
3 tablespoons Worcestershire
3 tablespoons soy sauce

2 tablespoons onion, minced
½ teaspoon oregano
few sprinkles each garlic salt,
  rosemary and chopped parsley

Wipe mushrooms with damp paper towel. Sauté 3 minutes in butter or margarine. Add remaining ingredients. Simmer gently about 15 minutes. Serves 6.

Onion Pie

2 pounds Spanish onions.
  thinly sliced
1 stick butter
3 eggs, well beaten
1 cup sour cream

¼ teaspoon salt
½ teaspoon white pepper
dash Tabasco
1 pastry shell, unbaked
grated Parmesan cheese

Sauté onions in butter. Combine eggs and sour cream. Add to onion mixture. Season mixture and pour in pastry shell. Top with cheese. Bake at 450° for 20 minutes, then at 325° for 20 more minutes. Serves 6.
Good with steak or roast beef.

French-Fried Onion Rings

3-4 large Spanish or Bermuda
  onions
3 cups buttermilk
1 egg, beaten
1 teaspoon salt
1½ teaspoons baking powder

⅔ cup water
1 cup plain flour
1 tablespoon vegetable oil
1 teaspoon lemon juice
¼ teaspoon cayenne pepper
vegetable oil for frying

Peel and slice onions into ⅜ inch slices. Separate into rings. Soak in buttermilk for 30 minutes. Combine egg, salt, baking powder, water, flour, 1 tablespoon vegetable oil, lemon juice and cayenne pepper. Stir until smooth. Heat oil to 375°. Remove rings from buttermilk, one at a time. Dip into batter. Fry in oil until golden brown. Drain on absorbent paper. Serve immediately. Serves 6-8.
Messy to cook, but worth it.

Green Pea Casserole

2 6-ounce cans sliced mushrooms (reserve juice)
2 sticks butter
½ teaspoon MSG
dashes of Tabasco, Worcestershire
4 medium onions, chopped
2 stalks celery, chopped

1 tablespoon flour
2 10-ounce packages frozen early green peas, thawed
2 8½-ounce cans water chestnuts, thinly sliced
salt and pepper to taste
4 ounces herb stuffing mix

Sauté mushrooms in ½ stick butter with MSG, Tabasco and Worcestershire. Set aside. In same skillet, melt 1½ sticks butter. Add onions and celery. Sauté until soft. Add mushroom juice and flour. Stir a few minutes. Add all ingredients except stuffing, mix and season with salt and pepper. Pour into greased 2-quart casserole and cover with stuffing. Bake at 325° for 30 minutes. Serves 10-12.

Caraway Cheese Potatoes

4 large potatoes, peeled and thinly sliced
8 ounces Mozzarella cheese, shredded
½ small onion, grated
1 13-ounce can evaporated milk

2 eggs, beaten
1 teaspoon caraway seed
1 teaspoon salt
¼ teaspoon pepper
2 tablespoons butter or margarine

Cook potatoes in small amount boiling salted water for about 10 minutes. Drain, reserving ½ cup cooking water. In a 2-quart casserole, alternate layers of potatoes and cheese, sprinkling onion between layers and ending with cheese. Combine ½ cup cooking water, milk, eggs, caraway seed, salt and pepper. Pour over potatoes. Dot with butter. Bake at 350° for 30 minutes. Serves 6.

Potato Casserole

6 large boiled Idaho potatoes, peeled and sliced
1 10¾-ounce can condensed cream of chicken soup
2 cups sour cream

2 cups sharp Cheddar cheese, grated
¼-½ cup onion, chopped
crushed corn flakes
butter

Combine first 5 ingredients and put in greased 3-quart baking dish. Top with corn flakes. Dot with butter. Bake at 325° for 30 minutes or until hot and bubbly. Serves 10-12.

Potatoes Au Gratin

3 cups cold cooked new potatoes, diced
6 tablespoons butter
3 tablespoons plain flour
¼ cup celery, diced
¼ cup onion, minced

1½ cups milk
1 cup sharp Cheddar cheese, grated
salt and pepper to taste
¾ cup packaged cornbread stuffing

Put potatoes in shallow baking dish. In a saucepan, over medium heat, melt 3 tablespoons of butter. Blend in flour. Add celery and onions. Gradually add milk, stirring until smooth and thick. Add ½ cup cheese, reserving ½ cup, and stir until melted. Season to taste. Pour mixture over potatoes and mix lightly with fork. Melt remaining butter and mix with stuffing. Sprinkle remaining cheese on potatoes, then top with crumbs. Keep in warm oven (about 30 minutes), then broil until golden brown. Serves 5-6.

To prevent potatoes from turning dark when peeled, put them in salted water until ready to use.

Mashed Potato Surprise

Mrs. Amelia Cartledge – Adult Homemaking Division, Richmond County Schools

6 large baking potatoes
1 stick butter
1 cup onion, finely chopped
36 medium fresh white mushrooms, stemmed and thinly sliced
salt and pepper to taste

2 tablespoons parsley, chopped
¾ cup hot milk
3 tablespoons butter, melted
1 teaspoon salt
1 tablespoon butter

Peel and cut each potato into 8 pieces. Cook in boiling water 30 minutes. Meanwhile, melt stick of butter in a frying pan. Add onion and cook without browning for 3 minutes. Add mushrooms and cook, stirring, until they form their juice. Cook 5 minutes longer. Season with salt and pepper. Add parsley and cook ½ minute longer. Drain potatoes well. Mash potatoes, preferably with an electric beater. Gradually add hot milk and melted butter. Season to taste with salt and pepper. Cover bottom and sides of well-greased, 2-quart baking dish with part of the potatoes, making a hollow in the center. Fill hollow with the mushrooms. Cover with remainder of potatoes. Decorate top with prongs of a fork. Dot with butter. Bake at 500° until lightly browned, about 15 minutes. Serves 6.

Hot Potato Salad Casserole

¼ cup green pepper, chopped
¼ cup green onions, chopped
2 cups cooked ham, diced
1 tablespoon bacon drippings
3-4 medium potatoes, cooked
   and diced

¼ teaspoon salt
dash pepper
¼ cup Hellmann's mayonnaise
8 ounces sharp American cheese,
   diced

Sauté green pepper, onions and ham in drippings, stirring until ham is lightly browned. Add potatoes, salt, pepper and mayonnaise. Heat, mixing lightly. Stir in cheese. Pour into 1½-quart casserole. Bake at 350° until cheese melts (10 minutes maximum). Serves 4.

▼ If using country ham, omit the salt. This could be a main dish.

Potato Soufflé

½ cup cream
2 cups mashed potatoes
1 teaspoon salt
dash nutmeg

3 tablespoons grated Parmesan
   cheese
3 egg yolks, beaten
4 egg whites, stiffly beaten

Add cream to potatoes. Season with salt and nutmeg. Heat potatoes in top of double boiler until very hot. Remove from heat. Add cheese. Cool. Add egg yolks, one at a time, to mixture, beating well after each addition. Fold in egg whites. Fill a deep buttered 1½-quart casserole ¾ full. Bake at 375° for 30-35 minutes or until puffed and brown. Serve immediately. Serves 6-8.

Green Rice

2 cups cooked rice
2 eggs, beaten
2 cups sharp Cheddar cheese,
   grated
2 cups milk
½ cup vegetable oil

1 cup onion, chopped
1 clove garlic, pressed
¼ teaspoon dry mustard
½ teaspoon salt
1 cup parsley, chopped

Mix all ingredients, and put in a 2-quart casserole. Bake uncovered at 325° for 1 hour or until inserted knife comes out clean. Serves 8.
It is like a custard. Delicious!!

Curry Rice

3 cups cooked rice
½ stick margarine
1 teaspoon curry powder
  (or more to taste)
1½ teaspoons salt

1 4-ounce can mushrooms, drained
¼ cup ripe olives, chopped
½ cup raisins
½ cup almonds, slivered

Combine all ingredients and heat on low. Serves 8-10.

Rice and Spinach Casserole

1 10-ounce package frozen
  chopped spinach, cooked
  and WELL DRAINED
1 10¾-ounce can condensed
  cream of mushroom soup
1 soup can milk
2 eggs, beaten
2 tablespoons vegetable oil

1 medium onion, chopped
½ pound sharp Cheddar cheese,
  grated
2 dashes thyme
juice of 1 lemon
¼-½ teaspoon red pepper
½ teaspoon MSG
2 cups cooked rice

Mix all ingredients adding rice last. Place in 2-quart casserole. Bake at 325° for 1 hour. Serves 8.
▼ For variety, substitute broccoli for spinach. Can be frozen.
Good with roast beef, lamb or ham.

Fried Rice

4 strips bacon, chopped
2 tablespoons onion, chopped
1 tablespoon green pepper,
  chopped (optional)

2 tablespoons celery, chopped
2 cups cooked rice
2 eggs, slightly beaten

Cook bacon until crisp and remove from pan. Sauté onion, pepper and celery in bacon grease until tender. Remove vegetables with a slotted spoon. Add rice to skillet. Cook until rice starts to brown. Add onion, pepper and celery to rice. Add bacon and mix well. Make a hole in the mixture. Put eggs in hole. Stir with fork until the eggs are cooked. Then shred eggs through entire mixture. Serves 4.
▼ For variety, add 1 cup cooked shrimp.

Beefy Rice

1½ cups raw long-grain rice
1 4-ounce can mushrooms, drained
2 10½-ounce cans beef consommé
1 envelope dry onion soup mix
1 cup water

1 cup celery, finely chopped
2 teaspoons parsley flakes
2 tablespoons butter
soy sauce to taste
1 teaspoon salt
½ teaspoon pepper

Mix all ingredients in 2½-quart casserole. Cover. Bake at 350° for 1½ hours. Serves 6-8.

St. Paul's Rice

1 pound pork sausage, crumbled
1 large green pepper, chopped
1 large onion, chopped
3 stalks celery, chopped
½ cup raw rice

2 large envelopes chicken noodle soup mix
4½ cups water
½ cup slivered almonds, toasted
cheese, grated (optional)

In a large skillet, brown sausage, pepper, onion and celery. Drain and set aside. In saucepan, combine rice, soup mix and water. Bring to boil. Cook 7 minutes. Combine sausage mixture, rice mixture and almonds. Put into 2-quart casserole. Top with cheese if desired. Cover tightly. Bake at 350° for 1 hour. Serves 8-10.

▼ Almonds may be reserved for topping.
A different but effective combination.

Orange Rice

⅔ cup celery with leaves, chopped
2 tablespoons onion, finely chopped
¼ cup butter
1½ cups water

2 tablespoons orange rind, grated
1 cup orange juice
1 teaspoon salt
⅛ teaspoon dried thyme
1 cup raw long-grain rice

Sauté celery and onion in butter until tender. Add water, orange rind, juice, salt and thyme. Bring to a boil. Slowly add rice. Reduce heat and cook uncovered for 25 minutes or until rice is tender. Serves 6.
Serve with duck or goose.

Spinach-Stuffed Artichoke Bottoms

8 artichoke bottoms, drained
1 clove garlic, mashed
2 hard-boiled eggs, sliced
2 tablespoons onion, minced
1 tablespoon butter
2 tablespoons mayonnaise

10 ounces frozen chopped spinach, cooked and drained well
2 tablespoons sour cream
¼ teaspoon salt
4 ounces Bonbel or Port Salut cheese

Rub artichoke bottoms with garlic. Place in greased shallow baking dish. Put egg slices on artichokes. Sauté onion in butter until golden. Add mayonnaise, spinach, sour cream and salt. Spoon mixture over eggs. Cut cheese into 8 thin slices. Cut each slice into 4 strips. Arrange strips lattice-like over spinach.* Bake at 325° for 20-25 minutes or until hot and cheese is bubbly. Serves 4.
*Can be prepared a day ahead.
▼ Easy and elegant, but expensive.

Spinach and Artichoke Casserole

5 10-ounce packages frozen chopped spinach
1 14-ounce can artichoke hearts

2 cups sour cream
1 envelope onion soup mix
salt and pepper to taste

Cook spinach. DRAIN WELL. Quarter artichokes. Combine all ingredients. Bake in buttered 2-quart casserole at 350° for 30 minutes. Serves 12-14.
Quick, easy and elegant!

Spinach with Tomatoes

6 green onions, chopped
⅓ cup butter
2 10-ounce packages frozen chopped spinach, cooked and DRAINED
¾ cup bread crumbs
3 eggs, beaten

2 teaspoons MSG
½ teaspoon thyme
1 teaspoon black pepper
½ teaspoon cayenne pepper
salt to taste
8 tomato slices
⅓ cup Parmesan cheese, grated

Sauté onions in butter until tender but not brown. Mix with remaining ingredients except tomatoes and Parmesan. Arrange tomato slices in buttered baking dish and top with mounds of spinach mixture. Sprinkle with Parmesan cheese. Bake at 350° for 15-20 minutes. Serves 8.

Creamer's Spinach Casserole

3 10-ounce packages frozen
chopped spinach
1 medium onion, chopped
6-8 fresh mushrooms, sliced
2 tablespoons butter
1 cup sour cream

herb stuffing mix
2 eggs, beaten
2-3 tablespoons lemon juice
grated Parmesan cheese
salt and pepper to taste
butter

Cook spinach. DRAIN WELL. Sauté onion and mushrooms in butter. Combine onion and mushrooms with sour cream, ½ cup stuffing, eggs, lemon juice, ¼ cup Parmesan, salt and pepper. Add spinach. Pour into greased 2-quart casserole, top with more stuffing and cheese and dot with butter.* Bake at 350° for 20-30 minutes. Serves 6-8.
*May be prepared a day in advance.

▼ One 4-ounce can sliced mushrooms may be substituted for fresh mushrooms. More stuffing and cheese may be used if desired.

Spinach-Stuffed Squash

12 firm medium yellow squash
2 10-ounce packages frozen
chopped spinach
1 cup sour cream
1 tablespoon butter

seasoned salt to taste
1 onion, chopped, or onion salt
black pepper to taste
saltine cracker crumbs
grated Parmesan cheese

Wash squash and cut in half lengthwise. Scoop out seeds and discard. Cook in salted water until barely tender. Drain. Cook spinach. DRAIN WELL. Combine spinach with sour cream, butter, salt, onion and pepper. Stuff squash with spinach mixture. Sprinkle with cracker crumbs and cheese. Bake at 325° for 30 minutes. Serves 12-24.

▼ Zucchini may be substituted for yellow squash.
Colorful company dish.

Spinach Soufflé

3 tablespoons butter
¼ cup plain flour
1 teaspoon salt
¼ teaspoon white pepper
⅛ teaspoon nutmeg

1 cup half-and-half
1 cup Swiss cheese, grated
1 10-ounce package frozen chopped
spinach, thawed and drained
4 eggs, separated

172

Melt butter and blend in flour, salt, pepper and nutmeg. Gradually add cream, stirring until well blended. Cook over low heat, stirring constantly, until thick and smooth. Add cheese and spinach. Cook until cheese is melted. Cool. Beat egg whites until stiff but not dry. Beat yolks with same beater until thick and lemon colored. Add yolks to spinach mixture. Fold in whites. Pour into buttered 1½-quart soufflé dish. Bake at 325° for 45-50 minutes. Serve immediately. Serves 4-6.

Spinach Casserole

2 10-ounce packages frozen
   chopped spinach
1 cup sour cream
½ cup sliced mushrooms,
   drained

½ cup tomato sauce
1 cup sharp Cheddar cheese,
   grated
salt and pepper to taste

Cook spinach. DRAIN WELL. Add remaining ingredients. Place in greased 1½-quart casserole. Bake at 350° for 15-20 minutes. Serves 6-8.

▼ For entertaining, garnish with sliced artichoke hearts and pimiento strips. *Quick and easy.*

Sweet Potato Casserole

3 cups cooked sweet potatoes
   (fresh or canned)
½ cup sugar
2 eggs, beaten

½ teaspoon salt
½ stick margarine, melted
½ cup milk
1½ teaspoons vanilla

Topping:
½ cup brown sugar
⅓ cup plain flour

1 cup pecans, chopped
⅓ stick margarine, melted

Mash sweet potatoes. Add sugar, eggs, salt, margarine, milk and vanilla. Mix well. Put in shallow 1½-quart baking dish. Mix topping. Spread over sweet potatoes. Bake at 325° for 30 minutes. Serves 6.

▼ For variety, substitute corn flakes for flour in topping.

Sweet Potato Pudding

½ cup raisins
¼ cup hot water
5 medium sweet potatoes,
  cooked, peeled and mashed
⅔ cup butter, melted

½ cup white sugar
1 teaspoon cinnamon
½ cup evaporated milk
marshmallows

Soak raisins in hot water. Mix with potatoes. Stir in butter, sugar, cinnamon and milk. Beat well. Pour into greased 1½-quart baking dish. Top with marshmallows. Bake at 400° for 8-10 minutes. Serves 6-8.
Good with turkey or chicken.

Sweet Potato Pone

1 stick butter
3 cups raw sweet potatoes,
  grated
1 cup sugar
½ cup milk
3 eggs, slightly beaten
2 tablespoons dark Karo syrup

juice of 1 orange
peel of 1 orange, grated
1 teaspoon ground ginger
⅛ teaspoon ground nutmeg
⅛ teaspoon ground allspice
⅛ teaspoon cinnamon

Melt butter in shallow 1½-quart casserole. Combine remaining ingredients and pour into dish. Bake at 350° for 1 hour. Serves 8.
Good with turkey or ham.

Yam Puff

4 pounds yams or sweet potatoes
1 cup light brown sugar
2 teaspoons lemon rind
2 teaspoons orange rind

½ cup butter, melted
juice of 1 lemon and 1 orange
slivered almonds and
  marshmallows (optional)

Cook yams in boiling salted water until tender. Peel and mash, or put through a food mill. Add sugar, rinds, butter and juices. Beat until light. Put yams in a greased 2-quart casserole. Bake at 350° for 30 minutes. If desired, top with almonds and marshmallows last 5 minutes of baking. Serves 8.

Colache

Mrs. Amelia Cartledge – Adult Homemaking Division, Richmond County Schools

4 small yellow squash or zucchini, unpeeled
4 tablespoons butter and bacon fat mixed (or 2 tablespoons olive oil instead of bacon fat)
1 large onion, thinly sliced
2 green peppers, cut in strips
4 tomatoes, peeled and wedged
1½ teaspoons salt
½ teaspoon freshly ground pepper
⅛ teaspoon cayenne
corn cut from 3 ears or
  1 10-ounce package frozen corn

Dice squash into ½ inch pieces. Melt butter and bacon fat (or olive oil) and sauté squash in it until partly browned. Remove squash (and juice if too much) from pan. Add onion and green pepper. Sauté until limp. Add tomatoes. Season well with salt, pepper and cayenne. Add corn. Cook, uncovered, for 30 minutes. Return squash to pan. Serves 8.

▼ Be sure to season the colache well. It should be quite hot and peppery. Goes well with chicken dishes.

Try stuffing baked potatoes with: a mixture of cream cheese, sour cream, chives and butter,
  or: butter, cream, vermouth, paprika, parsley and grated sharp cheese,
  or: condensed shrimp soup, seasoned salt, Worcestershire, cayenne and butter
  or: sour cream, ground cumin, garlic powder and milk.

Squash Casserole

1½ pounds squash, sliced, cooked and drained
1 medium onion, chopped
2 carrots, grated
1 2-ounce jar pimientos, diced
1 cup sour cream
1 10¾-ounce can condensed cream of chicken soup
1 stick margarine, melted
salt and pepper to taste
2 cups cornbread stuffing mix

Mix all ingredients together except stuffing. Put 1 cup stuffing in bottom of buttered 2-quart casserole. Add squash mixture. Top with remaining stuffing. Bake at 350° for 30 minutes. Serves 12.
Easy.

Squash Casserole with Cheese

2 pounds yellow squash, sliced
1 small green pepper, diced
1 small onion, sliced
½ stick margarine
3 cups Cheddar cheese, grated

2 eggs, beaten
½ cup evaporated milk
16 saltine crackers, crushed
salt and white pepper to taste

Cook squash, green pepper and onion in water until tender. Drain and mash. Add margarine and 2 cups of cheese, reserving 1 cup cheese to sprinkle on top. Add eggs, milk and crackers. Mix well. Season to taste. Place in shallow 2-quart greased casserole. Top with cheese and bake uncovered at 350° for 30 minutes. Serves 8-10.

Squash and Tomato Casserole

12 small yellow squash, sliced
3 tablespoons corn oil
1 onion, finely minced
pinch sweet basil
dash garlic powder
⅛ teaspoon pepper, freshly ground
1 teaspoon salt

1 8-ounce package Velveeta cheese, cubed
1 16-ounce can peeled tomatoes, drained and mashed, or 1 cup fresh tomatoes, cubed
¼ teaspoon salt
2 tablespoons sugar

Sauté squash in oil with onion, basil, garlic powder and pepper. Stir well, cover and simmer until vegetables start to become limp. Remove from heat. Add 1 teaspoon salt and cheese. Stir until cheese melts. Pour into 8-inch square casserole. In pan used for squash, quickly heat tomatoes, salt and sugar. Pour over squash. Bake at 350° for 30 minutes. Serves 6-8.

▼Better if made 2-3 days ahead and refrigerated. May be frozen.
It's rich; serve with simple entrée.

Zucchini Davis

8 strips bacon
1 large onion, chopped
3 cups zucchini, coarsely chopped
1 medium green pepper, chopped

8 small okra pods, thinly sliced
1 6-ounce can tomato paste
pinch thyme
salt and pepper to taste
Parmesan cheese

VEGETABLES AND MEAT ACCOMPANIMENTS

Cook bacon until crisp, crumble and set aside. Reserve 1 tablespoon bacon fat and sauté onion until golden. Add bacon and remaining ingredients except cheese. Cook until zucchini is tender. Transfer mixture to 1½-quart casserole. Sprinkle with cheese. Bake at 350° until cheese is melted and brown. Serves 6.

Baked Stuffed Zucchini

4 medium zucchini	½ teaspoon black pepper
3 tablespoons green onions	(or more to taste)
(white part only), minced	½ teaspoon oregano
2 tablespoons butter	¼ teaspoon garlic powder
1 tablespoon tomato paste	½ cup fresh bread crumbs
½ teaspoon salt	¼ cup butter, melted

Preheat oven to 350°. Cut zucchini in half lengthwise. Scoop out as much pulp as possible taking care not to puncture skins. Dice pulp and set aside. Put zucchini shells in shallow baking dish. Cover tightly with foil. Bake 15-20 minutes or until shells are tender but not limp. Sauté onion in 2 tablespoons butter until soft but not brown. Add zucchini pulp, tomato paste and seasonings. Cook over low heat until mixture is well blended. Remove from heat. Stir in bread crumbs. Stuff shells. Brush with butter. Bake at 400° for 10-15 minutes or until lightly browned. Serves 8.

Zucchini Casserole

3 medium size zucchini	⅛ teaspoon paprika
¼ cup sour cream	1 egg yolk, beaten
1 tablespoon butter	2 tablespoons chives, chopped
1 tablespoon grated	1 teaspoon basil
Parmesan cheese	⅓ cup bread crumbs, buttered
½ teaspoon salt	Parmesan cheese

Wash squash and cut crosswise in ¼-inch slices. Cook in boiling salted water 6-8 minutes. Meanwhile, in saucepan over low heat, combine sour cream, butter, cheese, salt and paprika. When cheese has melted, remove from heat and stir in egg yolk, chives and basil. Drain zucchini. Place in 1-quart oblong baking dish. Spread sauce evenly over squash. Top with crumbs and more Parmesan cheese. Brown in 375° oven. Serves 4-6.

Stuffed Tomatoes

6 medium tomatoes
1 onion, chopped
1 green pepper, chopped
½ stick butter
herb stuffing mix

salt and pepper to taste
sour cream
grated Parmesan cheese or
  bacon bits

Core tomatoes. Scoop out pulp and reserve. Sauté onion and green pepper in butter. Add to tomato pulp. Add sufficient stuffing to thicken. Season with salt and pepper. Stuff tomatoes. Top each tomato with 1 teaspoon sour cream. Sprinkle with cheese or bacon bits. Broil at 375° for 15-20 minutes. Serves 6.

Tomatoes Stuffed with Sausage

1 pound bulk sausage, crumbled
8 tomatoes
1 cup celery, chopped
½ green pepper, chopped
2 tablespoons mayonnaise

2 tablespoons Durkee's sauce
bread crumbs
1 teaspoon sugar
salt and pepper to taste
buttered cracker crumbs

Cook sausage and drain. Scoop out pulp and reserve. Combine sausage, celery, green pepper, mayonnaise, Durkee's, bread crumbs, sugar, salt and pepper with tomato pulp using sufficient bread crumbs to thicken. Stuff tomatoes. Top with cracker crumbs. Bake at 350° for 30 minutes. Serves 8.

Muffin pans are useful for baking whole tomatoes, peppers, onions or potatoes.

Broiled Tomatoes with Dill-Sour Cream Sauce

½ cup sour cream
¼ cup mayonnaise
2 tablespoons onion, chopped
¼ teaspoon dried dill weed

¼ teaspoon salt
4 large, firm, ripe tomatoes
salt and pepper to taste
butter

Mix first 5 ingredients and chill.* Core tomatoes and cut in half crosswise. Season cut surface and dot with butter. Broil 3 inches from heat for 5 minutes. Spoon sauce over broiled tomatoes and serve at once. Serves 8.
*Sauce may be prepared several days ahead.

Stuffed Tomatoes Supreme

10 medium tomatoes
Jane's Krazy Mixed-Up Salt
1 cup onions, finely chopped
½ pound fresh mushrooms, chopped
2 tablespoons butter
1 6-ounce box Uncle Ben's long
    grain and wild rice, cooked

5 strips bacon, cooked and crumbled
¼ teaspoon oregano
1 teaspoon thyme
grated Parmesan cheese
butter
parsley, chopped

Hollow out tomatoes. Drain. Sprinkle insides with Krazy Salt. Sauté onion and mushrooms in butter. When tender, mix with rice, bacon and seasonings. Fill tomatoes and place in baking dish. Top with cheese. Put a pat of butter on each tomato. Add a small amount of water to dish. Bake at 350° for 25-30 minutes. Top with parsley. Serves 10.

Baked Tomatoes and Corn

6 large firm tomatoes
flour seasoned with salt
    and pepper
1 clove garlic, halved
⅓ cup olive oil

10 ears corn, cut from cob
1 large sweet onion, thinly sliced
salt and pepper to taste
¾ cup bread crumbs
½ stick butter

Cut tomatoes in ½-inch slices. Dredge in flour. In large skillet, cook garlic in oil until browned. Discard garlic. Sauté tomatoes in oil until they are slightly golden. Remove from skillet. Sauté corn and onions until barely tender. In a large casserole, arrange alternate layers of tomatoes with corn and onions, and season to taste. Sauté bread crumbs in butter until golden. Sprinkle on top. Bake at 350° for 35-40 minutes. Serves 8.

Wild Rice with Mushrooms and Almonds

¼ cup butter
1 cup raw wild rice,
    washed and drained
2 tablespoons chives, snipped,
    or green onions, chopped

½ cup slivered almonds
1 8-ounce can mushroom pieces,
    drained
3 cups chicken broth

Melt butter in large skillet. Add all ingredients except broth. Stir and cook until almonds are golden brown, about 20 minutes. Pour mixture into ungreased 1½-quart casserole. Heat chicken broth to boiling and stir into rice mixture. Cover tightly. Bake at 325° for 1½ hours. Serves 6-8.

179

Wild Rice and Pea Casserole

½ cup raw wild rice
2 cups bouillon
1 large onion, diced
2 tablespoons butter
2 cups tiny green peas, cooked

½ teaspoon Worcestershire
⅔ cup small pearl onions
1 teaspoon marjoram
salt and pepper to taste
1 cup slivered almonds, toasted

Wash and cook wild rice in boiling water five minutes. Drain and rinse. Repeat, boiling rice 5 minutes, drain and rinse. Cook rice in bouillon until tender, about 45 minutes. Meanwhile, sauté diced onion in butter. Combine all ingredients except almonds in a 2-quart casserole. Cover and bake at 325° about 20 minutes. Fold in almonds. Serves 8-10.

▼ Sautéed sliced mushrooms can be substituted for pearl onions.

Mushroom Spaghetti

4 medium onions, thinly sliced
6 tablespoons butter, divided
1 pound fresh mushrooms, sliced
1½ teaspoons salt
pepper to taste

½ teaspoon nutmeg
1 cup whipping cream
8 ounces spaghetti, cooked and warm
grated Parmesan cheese

Sauté onions in 3 tablespoons butter until lightly browned. Cover and cook over very low heat for 1 hour, stirring occasionally. Sauté mushrooms in remaining butter until tender. Season with salt, pepper and nutmeg. Add to onions. Five minutes before serving, add cream and heat. DO NOT BOIL or cream will curdle. Just before serving, add spaghetti to sauce and mix. Sprinkle with cheese. Serves 8.
Good meat accompaniment!

Spaghetti with Tomato Sauce
Mrs. Ray Floyd – Wife of 1976 Masters' Champion

2 cups onion, chopped
1 stick butter
1 28-ounce can whole tomatoes
2 tablespoons olive oil

1 teaspoon salt
1 tablespoon sugar
1 clove garlic, pressed
1 pound spaghetti, cooked

In a large skillet, sauté onion in butter until soft. Add tomatoes, oil, salt, sugar and garlic. Simmer about 30 minutes stirring occasionally. To serve, pour sauce over spaghetti and toss. Serves 4.

Marinara Alla Gambetta
Mrs. Terry Diehl

2 cloves garlic, minced
1 tablespoon olive oil
2 29-ounce cans pear-shaped
  whole tomatoes, drained
1 15-ounce can tomato sauce
1 tablespoon oregano

1 tablespoon basil
1 tablespoon parsley flakes
salt to taste
2 pounds vermicelli, cooked
grated Romano or Parmesan
  cheese

In a small skillet, brown garlic in oil. Combine tomatoes and tomato sauce in a large saucepan, breaking tomatoes into pieces with a fork. Add seasonings, garlic and oil. Simmer about 30 minutes. To serve, pour over cooked vermicelli and sprinkle with cheese. Serves 8-10.

▼ Does not freeze well.

Casserole Marie-Blanche

8 ounces noodles, cooked and
  drained
1 cup cream-style cottage cheese
1 cup sour cream

½ teaspoon salt
⅛ teaspoon pepper
⅓ cup chopped chives
1 tablespoon butter

Combine noodles, cheese, sour cream, salt, pepper and chives. Pour into a buttered 1½-quart casserole and dot top with butter. Bake at 350° for 30 minutes or until noodles begin to brown. Serve immediately. Serves 6.

Easy Curly Noodles

1 small onion, chopped
1 6-ounce can mushrooms,
  drained (reserve juice)
4 tablespoons butter

2 10½-ounce cans beef consommé
1 8-ounce package curly noodles
1 cup almonds, slivered and
  sautéed (optional)

Sauté onion and mushrooms in butter. Add consommé and mushroom juice. Bring to boil, add noodles and cook until liquid is absorbed. Mix in almonds if desired. Serves 8.
Good with beef. Quick and easy.

Cheese-Garlic Grits

1 6-ounce roll Kraft garlic
  cheese, divided
4 cups cooked grits
2 eggs
½ cup milk

1 stick butter, melted
corn flakes, onion rings
  or cracker crumbs for
  topping (optional)

Cut ¾ of cheese into small pieces. Add to hot grits to melt cheese. Beat eggs and milk. Add to grits and cheese, along with butter. Stir well. Pour into a greased 2-quart casserole. Dot top with remaining cheese. Add any topping desired. Bake at 350° for 45 minutes. Serves 6-8.

▼ Good for brunch or as an accompaniment for beef burgundy, stew, grillades or grilled fish.

Baked Grits with Cheese

1 cup grits, uncooked
2 cups Cheddar cheese, grated
2 eggs, beaten

⅛ teaspoon cayenne pepper
paprika

Cook grits according to package directions. Add 1½ cups cheese, reserving enough for top. Add eggs and pepper. Mix well. Pour into greased shallow 1½-quart casserole. Top with remaining cheese. Sprinkle with paprika. Bake at 375° for 20 minutes. Serves 6-8.
Good brunch dish.

Chestnut Stuffing for Turkey

½ cup shallots, minced
3 tablespoons butter
½ pound sausage
turkey liver, minced
1 cup herb seasoned stuffing mix
½ teaspoon thyme
3 tablespoons celery, minced

3 tablespoons parsley, minced
1 teaspoon salt
¼ teaspoon pepper, freshly ground
1 cup canned or fresh, boiled
  chestnuts, chopped
1 apple, peeled and minced
6 tablespoons whipping cream

In a heavy skillet, sauté shallots in 1 tablespoon butter until lightly browned. Add sausage and crumble with a fork. Cook until lightly browned. Turn skillet contents into a fine sieve set over a bowl to drain off excess fat. In same skillet in remaining butter, quickly brown the liver. Stir in drained sausage, stuffing, thyme, celery, parsley, salt and pepper. Mix well. Add chestnuts, apple and cream. Stuff turkey loosely in both cavities. Sew or skewer openings. Yields enough to stuff a 9-12 pound turkey.

Breads
12

Maple Wheat Bread

2½ cups plain flour, sifted
2 packages yeast
1 teaspoon salt
1 teaspoon cinnamon
1¼ cups water
¾ cup maple syrup

⅓ cup vegetable oil
2 eggs
2⅓-3 cups whole wheat flour,
   sifted
1 cup raisins (optional)
2 tablespoons butter, melted

Combine plain flour, yeast, salt and cinnamon in large mixing bowl. Mix water, syrup and oil in pan. Heat until very warm (120°-130°). Add eggs and warm liquid to flour mixture. Blend at low speed until moistened, then beat 2 minutes at medium speed. Stir in wheat flour and raisins (optional) to form a stiff dough. Cover dough and let rise in warm place until light and doubled in size (45-60 minutes). (Can be placed in oven with a pan of hot water.) Punch dough down and toss lightly on floured surface until no longer sticky. Shape into 2 loaves and place in greased 9x5-inch loaf pans (can cut dough into 24 pieces and shape into balls, placing 12 balls in each pan, forming 2 rows). Brush 2 tablespoons melted butter over dough. Cover and let rise again (30-45 minutes). Bake at 375° for 25-30 minutes until well browned.

▼ ¼ cup molasses or honey or ⅓ cup firmly packed brown sugar may be substituted for the syrup. Use 1 cup water and ¾ cup milk instead of 1¼ cups water.

Whole Wheat Bread

2 packages dry yeast
3 cups warm water
¾ cup honey
¼ cup vegetable oil

1 scant tablespoon salt
7-8 cups unsifted whole wheat
   flour, divided

All ingredients except water must be at room temperature. Allow yeast to soften in a bowl with the warm water and honey for 5 minutes or more. Add oil, salt and 5 cups flour. Beat by hand 100 or more strokes (or 7 minutes on low on electric mixer). Stir in 2 or 3 cups more flour or enough to make a stiff dough. Turn dough out onto a well-floured surface. Knead until smooth, adding a little more flour to prevent sticking. Place in oiled bowl; cover and let rise in a warm place until doubled in size (about 1 hour). Punch down and let double again. Knead to original size and divide into 3 equal parts. Place in greased loaf pans. Let rise until dough reaches top of pans. Bake at 350° for 50 minutes or until browned. Yields 3 one-pound loaves.

▼ This is a heavy bread and cuts best if cold (refrigerated).

Sylvester's "Six-Pack" Sour French Bread

4½-5½ cups plain flour, unsifted
¼ cup wheat germ
1 tablespoon sugar
2 teaspoons salt
2 packages yeast
1 12-ounce can malt liquor or beer

¼ cup water
1 tablespoon margarine
corn meal
1 egg white, slightly beaten
sesame or poppy seeds

In a large bowl, thoroughly mix 1½ cups flour, wheat germ, sugar, salt and undis-solved yeast. Combine beer, water and margarine in a saucepan. Heat over low heat until warm (120°-130°). Margarine does not need to melt. Gradually add to dry ingredients. Beat 2 minutes at medium speed, scraping bowl occasionally. Add ½ cup flour or enough to make a thick batter. Beat at high speed 2 minutes, scraping bowl occasionally. Add enough flour to make a soft dough. Use clean hands to work in flour. Turn onto floured board and knead until smooth and elastic (8-10 minutes). Place in greased bowl and turn to grease top. Cover and let rise in warm, draft-free place until doubled (about 1 hour). Punch down and turn onto floured board; divide in half. Form into 2 smooth balls. Place on greased baking sheets that have been sprinkled with corn meal. Cover and let rise until doubled (about 1 hour). Brush with beaten egg white. Sprinkle with sesame or poppy seeds. With sharp knife, slash tops of loaves crosswise and across again about ⅛-inch deep. Bake at 400° for 20-25 minutes or until done. Cool on wire racks.
"Now you may drink the other five cans of malt liquor!"

Test bread when minimum baking time is up. Yeast breads are done when they are golden brown and sound hollow when tapped lightly.

Swiss Cheese French Bread

1 medium onion, finely chopped
½ pound butter
2 heaping tablespoons poppy seed
dash salt

1 long loaf French bread
1 12-ounce package
Swiss cheese slices

Sauté onion in butter. Add poppy seed and salt. Cut French bread in 2-inch slices taking care not to cut all the way through. In each cut, place a slice of Swiss cheese. Spoon onion mixture into each cut. Wrap securely in foil. Bake at 350° for 15-20 minutes. Serves 8.
Gooey, but good!

French Bread

5¾ cups sifted plain flour
 (approximately)
2 tablespoons sugar
2 teaspoons salt

2 packages active dry yeast
2 cups very warm water
¼ cup shortening, melted
1 egg white, unbeaten

In a large bowl, thoroughly mix 2 cups flour, sugar, salt and yeast. Add water and shortening. Beat at medium speed for 2 minutes. Gradually stir in 3½ more cups flour or enough flour to make a soft dough. Sprinkle remaining ¼ cup flour on bread board or pastry cloth. Turn dough out on flour. Knead until smooth and satiny (5-10 minutes). Shape into smooth ball. Place in greased bowl, turning once to grease top. Cover and let rise in a warm place (80°-90°) until doubled (about 1 hour). Punch down. Divide in half. Shape each half into a ball. Cover for 5 minutes. Rub a little shortening on palms of hands. Roll each ball of dough under the hands to form a long, slender loaf about 3 inches in diameter. Start rolling at the center and gently work hands toward end of loaf, repeating until loaf is shaped. Place loaves 4 inches apart on lightly greased baking sheet. With a sharp knife cut diagonally about ¼ inch deep and 1½ inches apart into top of each loaf. Cover and let rise until a little more than doubled (about 1 hour). Bake at 425° for 25-35 minutes. Remove from oven. Brush with egg white. Return to oven for 2 minutes. Remove from baking sheet and cool on racks. Yields 2 loaves.
▼ For crustier loaf, bake bread with a shallow pan of water on lower rack.

Mother Clara's Bread

1 package dry yeast
½ cup warm water
4 rounded tablespoons shortening
5 rounded tablespoons sugar
1 teaspoon salt

1 cup milk, scalded
1 egg, beaten
5 cups sifted plain flour or
 enough to make stiff dough
butter, melted

Dissolve yeast in warm water (105°-115°). Add shortening, sugar and salt to hot milk. When lukewarm, add egg, then yeast mixture. Gradually stir in enough flour to have a stiff batter. Cover and let rise until doubled in bulk. Work in remaining flour so that dough is manageable. (If dough is sticky at this point, sift in additional flour.) Knead 10 minutes. Return to bowl and let rise again. Punch down and knead. Divide dough into two balls. Knead and place in greased loaf pans (4x8). Let rise until doubled in size. Bake at 300° for 1 hour. Brush with butter and let cool on rack. Slice. Yields 2 large loaves or can make 3 small loaves.
▼ Excellent to reheat wrapped in foil.

186

Beer Bread

4 cups Bisquick
3 tablespoons sugar

1 12-ounce can of beer, at room temperature

Mix all ingredients. Pour into 2 small, greased loaf pans. Allow bread to rise for 10 minutes. Bake at 375° for 30 minutes.
Easy yet delicious.

Unbleached flour is best for white bread.

Active dry yeast should be dissolved in warm (105°-115° F.) liquid. Too much heat can kill the action of yeast.

All ingredients, other than yeast, should be at room temperature. This includes utensils.

Sugar and salt should be dissolved in warm liquid before flour is added to mixture.

If the bread seems to brown too quickly, lay a sheet of clean paper over it to finish baking.

Dilly Casserole Bread

1 package yeast
¼ cup warm water
1 cup cottage cheese, heated to lukewarm
2 tablespoons sugar
1 tablespoon instant minced onion

1 tablespoon butter, softened
2 teaspoons dill seed
1 teaspoon salt
¼ teaspoon baking soda
1 egg, unbeaten
2¼-2½ cups plain flour, unsifted

In large mixing bowl, dissolve yeast in water. Combine cottage cheese, sugar, onion, butter, dill seed, salt, soda and egg. Add to yeast. Add flour to form a stiff dough, beating well after each addition. (Can use mixer on low speed for first part.) Cover and let rise in warm place (85°-90°) until light and doubled in size, 50-60 minutes. Punch down dough. Turn into well greased 1½ or 2-quart casserole. Let rise until light, 30-40 minutes. Bake at 350° for 40-50 minutes until golden brown. Brush with softened butter and sprinkle with salt. Yields 1 large round loaf.

Zucchini Bread
Mrs. Arnold Palmer, wife of Masters' Champion 1958, 1960, 1962 and 1964.

4 eggs
1½ cups sugar
1 cup oil
3½ cups plain flour, sifted
1½ teaspoons baking soda
1½ teaspoons salt

1 teaspoon ground cinnamon
¾ teaspoon baking powder
2 cups zucchini, grated
1 teaspoon vanilla
1 cup nuts, chopped
1 cup raisins (optional)

Blend first 3 ingredients thoroughly. Sift dry ingredients together. Add to egg mixture. Add zucchini and remaining ingredients. Fill greased loaf pans half full. Bake at 350° for 45-55 minutes. Makes 2-3 loaves.

Unless otherwise directed, remove loaves from pans as they come from the oven and cool on racks.

Sour Cream Corn Bread

¾ cup yellow corn meal
1 cup plain flour, unsifted
¼ cup sugar
2 teaspoons baking powder
½ teaspoon baking soda

¾ teaspoon salt
1 cup sour cream
¼ cup milk
1 egg, beaten
2 tablespoons Wesson oil

Mix all ingredients just enough to blend well. Pour in a greased 8-inch square pan. Bake at 425° for about 20 minutes. Serves 6-8.
A delicious, sweet corn bread.

Sally Lunn

½ cup butter
½ cup sugar
3 eggs
1 cup milk

2 cups sifted plain flour
2 teaspoons baking powder
¾ teaspoon salt

Cream butter and sugar. Beat and add eggs alternately with milk to sugar mixture. Sift dry ingredients. Add to first mixture, beating gently but thoroughly until smooth. Bake in greased muffin tins or 1 large shallow cake pan. For muffins, bake at 425° for 15 minutes; for cake pan, bake 25 minutes. Sprinkle sugar on top while still hot. Serves 8-10.
▼Recipe may be doubled to use in a bundt pan.

Onion-Cheese Supper Bread

½ cup onion, chopped
1 tablespoon shortening
1 egg, slightly beaten
½ cup milk
1¼ cups Bisquick

1 cup sharp Cheddar cheese,
  grated
1 tablespoon poppy seeds
2 tablespoons butter, melted

Sauté onion in shortening until golden. Mix egg and milk; then blend with Bisquick. Add onion and half of cheese. Spread dough in greased 8x1½-inch round cake pan. Sprinkle top with remaining cheese and poppy seeds. Pour melted butter over all. Bake at 400° for 20-25 minutes. Serve hot with butter. Serves 6-8.
Fancy addition for a spaghetti supper or use as potato substitute with meats.

Daisy's Spoon Bread

2 cups milk
½ cup plain corn meal
1 teaspoon sugar
½ teaspoon baking powder

1 teaspoon salt
3 eggs, separated
½ stick butter, melted

Heat milk until nearly boiling. Gradually add corn meal, stirring vigorously. Cook over low heat until consistency of mush. Cool. Add sugar, baking powder, salt, egg yolks and butter. Fold in stiffly beaten egg whites. Pour into greased 2-quart casserole. Bake at 350° for 35-40 minutes. Serve at once. Serves 6 to 8.
Soufflé consistency, to be eaten with a fork.

Cranberry-Orange Bread

2 cups plain flour, sifted
1 teaspoon salt
1½ teaspoons baking powder
½ teaspoon soda
1 cup sugar
1 orange

2 tablespoons Crisco oil
boiling water
1 egg, beaten
1 cup pecans, chopped
1 cup cranberries, thinly sliced

Sift dry ingredients together. Grate rind of orange into a measuring cup. Add juice from orange and oil. Add enough boiling water to measure ¾ cup (probably only a few teaspoons). Add egg. Mix liquids and dry ingredients. Fold in nuts and cranberries. Pour into greased loaf pan which has been lined with 2 layers of wax paper (on bottom only) and greased again. Bake at 325° for 65-75 minutes. Remove bread carefully from pan.

Apricot Bread

1 cup dried apricots
(1 6-ounce package)
1 cup sugar
2 tablespoons butter or
margarine, softened
1 egg
¼ cup water

½ cup orange juice
2 cups plain flour, sifted
2 teaspoons baking powder
¼ teaspoon baking soda
1 teaspoon salt
½ cup nuts, chopped

Cover apricots with warm water and soak 30 minutes. Drain and cut into ¼-inch pieces. Blend sugar, butter and egg. Add water and orange juice. Sift dry ingredients together and add to liquids. Beat until smooth. Add apricots and nuts. Blend thoroughly. Pour into greased loaf pan which has been lined with waxed paper. Let mixture stand for 20 minutes. Bake at 350° for 55-65 minutes. Cool and remove from pan.

▼ This recipe doubles easily to make 2 loaves.

Bread has a tart taste!

Orange Bread

3 cups plain flour, sifted
3 teaspoons baking powder
¾ teaspoon salt
1 cup sugar
1 egg, slightly beaten

1-2 tablespoons orange rind,
grated
1 cup orange juice
⅓ cup shortening, melted
½ cup pecans, chopped

Sift dry ingredients together. Combine egg, orange rind, juice and shortening. Pour into flour mixture. Add nuts. Stir just enough to moisten. DO NOT BEAT. Pour into greased loaf pan. Bake at 350° for 1 hour or until done.

▼ Better if made a day ahead.

Lemon Bread

½ cup butter or margarine,
softened
1 cup sugar
2 eggs, slightly beaten
1⅔ cups sifted plain flour

½ teaspoon salt
1 teaspoon baking powder
½ cup milk
½ cup nuts, chopped
grated rind of 1 lemon

Glaze:
¼ cup sugar

juice of 1 lemon

190

Cream butter and sugar. Add eggs. Sift flour with salt and baking powder. Alternately add flour mixture and milk to butter mixture, beating constantly. Stir in nuts and lemon rind. Pour into greased 9x5-inch loaf pan. Bake at 350° for 1 hour. *Glaze:* Combine sugar and lemon juice. Prick hot bread with toothpick and pour on glaze. Remove bread from pan. Allow to cool before slicing.

▼ Note: Orange rind and juice may be substituted for lemon.

Delicious toasted with butter and served for breakfast.

Pineapple Pecan Loaf Bread

¾ cup brown sugar
¼ cup shortening
1 egg
2 cups plain flour, sifted
1 teaspoon baking soda
½ teaspoon salt

3 ounces (⅓ cup) frozen orange juice concentrate, thawed
1 8¼-ounce can crushed pineapple, undrained
½ cup pecans, chopped

Cream sugar and shortening. Add egg. Blend. Sift together dry ingredients. Add alternately with orange concentrate to creamed mixture, stirring well after each addition. Stir in pineapple and nuts. Pour into greased and floured loaf pan (8½x4½x2½). Bake at 350° for 50-60 minutes. Remove from pan and cool on rack.

Pumpkin Bread

3 cups sugar
1 cup oil
3 eggs
1 16-ounce can pumpkin
3 cups plain flour, unsifted
½ teaspoon salt
½ teaspoon baking powder

1 teaspoon baking soda
1 teaspoon ground cloves
1 teaspoon ground cinnamon
1 teaspoon ground nutmeg
1 cup pecans, chopped
¾-1 cup dates, chopped (optional)

Mix first 4 ingredients well. Add dry ingredients and spices. Mix thoroughly. Fold in nuts and dates. Divide mixture among 3 one-pound coffee cans which have been greased and floured. Bake at 350° for 65-70 minutes. Makes 3 small loaves.

▼ Better made a day or two ahead. Taste improves with time.

Good served warm or with cream cheese.

Whole Wheat Banana Nut Bread

½ cup butter
¾ cup brown sugar
1 egg
1 cup whole wheat flour, unsifted
½ cup unbleached white flour
1 teaspoon baking soda

¾ teaspoon seasoned salt (or ½ teaspoon plain salt)
1¼ cups ripe bananas, mashed
¼ cup buttermilk or plain yogurt
1 cup pecans, chopped

Cream butter and sugar. Add egg. Sift dry ingredients together. Combine bananas and buttermilk or yogurt, stirring just enough to mix. Add dry ingredients alternately with banana mixture. Stir in nuts. Pour into greased 9"x5" loaf pan. Bake at 350° for 50-60 minutes. Cool 10 minutes. Remove from pan to cooling rack.
Especially good re-heated for breakfast.

Popovers

1 cup sifted plain flour
1 cup milk

2 eggs
½ teaspoon salt

Mix ingredients thoroughly using blender, mixer or whisk. Pour into well-greased glass custard cups or greased and heated popover pans. Fill ⅔ full. Bake at 425° for 20 to 30 minutes or until golden brown. Makes 6-8 popovers.

Envelope Rolls

1 cup milk, scalded
½ cup sugar
½ cup vegetable oil
1 teaspoon salt

1 package dry yeast dissolved in ¼ cup warm water
3 eggs, beaten
4½-5 cups plain flour, unsifted melted butter

Combine first 4 ingredients. Cool to lukewarm (105°-115°). Add yeast mixture. Add eggs. Mix in 4½ cups flour to form smooth dough (beat 50-100 strokes by hand). If dough is too sticky, add more flour (it should not stick to sides). Place in an oiled bowl and turn to grease top. Cover and let rise until doubled in size. Turn out onto well-floured surface. Knead in enough flour to make manageable. Roll out and cut into rolls, folding over like an envelope. Place on greased pans; brush tops with melted butter.* Cover and let rise until doubled in size. Bake at 350° for 20 minutes or until lightly browned. Yields about 100 rolls.
*Can be made the day before and refrigerated after being cut out, but before final rising.

Tom's Rolls

Part I:

1 cup boiling water
½ teaspoon salt
¼ cup sugar

2 tablespoons shortening
1 cup plain flour, sifted

Part II:

½ tablespoon sugar
1 egg, well beaten

1 package dry yeast, dissolved
in 2 tablespoons warm water

Add sugar and egg to yeast mixture. Mix well.

Part III:
2 cups plain flour

Mix Part I and Part II. Beat well. Add Part III. Mix well. Place in refrigerator 24 hours. Roll out, cut with biscuit cutter and fold. Place on lightly greased pan and let rise 3-4 hours. Bake at 425° for 15-20 minutes. Yields 3 dozen.

▼ When hurried, do not refrigerate. Let rise in a warm place until doubled (about 1 hour). Roll out, cut and fold. Let rise again 20-30 minutes and bake as above. Dough can be kept in refrigerator for a week if tightly covered.

Wallace's Whole Wheat Rolls

---

1 package dry yeast
½ cup lukewarm water
1¼ cups boiling water
⅔ cup shortening
½-¾ cup sugar

2½-3 cups plain white flour,
sifted
2 eggs
2 cups whole wheat flour
2 teaspoons salt

Dissolve yeast in lukewarm water. Pour boiling water over shortening. Add sugar. Stir until dissolved. Beat in 2 cups white flour. Add eggs and beat again. When mixture is lukewarm, add dissolved yeast. Mix well. Add 2 cups whole wheat flour containing 2 teaspoons of salt. Finally, add ½ to 1 cup white flour. Let dough rise 2-3 hours. Shape as desired. Place in well greased pan and let rise 2-3 more hours. Bake at 350° for 10-15 minutes or until tops of rolls are lightly browned. Yields 4-5 dozen.

▼ May substitute white flour for whole wheat flour.

193

Grandmother's Refrigerator Rolls

⅔ cup butter
1 cup milk, scalded
½ cup sugar
1 teaspoon salt
2 eggs, well beaten

1 cup mashed potatoes
1 package yeast dissolved in
¼ cup warm water
4 cups (or more) plain flour

Melt butter and add to scalded milk. Add sugar and salt. Let cool to lukewarm. Add remaining ingredients. Almost enough flour has been added when dough is hard to stir. Put dough on a floured surface. Add flour until dough will not stick to surface. Knead until smooth and elastic. May place in a bowl to rise or can be placed in refrigerator for future use. To use at once, let dough rise until double in size. Roll out and shape rolls. Place on baking sheet and let rise again. Bake at 400° for 20 minutes or until nicely browned. Yields 5 dozen small rolls.

Angel Biscuits

5 cups White Lily flour, sifted
1 teaspoon baking soda
3 teaspoons baking powder
1 teaspoon salt
¼ cup sugar

1 cup Crisco
1 package yeast dissolved in
3 tablespoons warm water
2 cups buttermilk
(room temperature)

Sift flour with dry ingredients. Cut in shortening. Add yeast to buttermilk. Stir buttermilk mixture into flour mixture until all flour is damp. Refrigerate before using.* Do not roll out. Simply pinch and roll amount needed. Handle very lightly. Bake at 425° for 10 to 15 minutes or until brown. Yields 4 dozen small biscuits.
* Dough can be kept a week.

Buttermilk Biscuits

2 cups plain flour, sifted
¾ teaspoon salt
2 teaspoons baking powder

½ teaspoon baking soda
3 heaping tablespoons Crisco
1 cup buttermilk

Sift dry ingredients together, and cut in Crisco. Make a well in center of flour mixture, pour in buttermilk, and mix lightly with a fork. Place on a floured cloth, and knead for about 1 minute. Roll dough out to about ½ inch thickness and cut with a small cutter. Place ½ inch apart on ungreased cookie sheet. Bake at 450° for about 10 minutes. Yields 2 dozen.

Baking Powder Biscuits

2 cups sifted plain flour
4 teaspoons baking powder
1 teaspoon salt

4 tablespoons shortening
⅔ cup milk

Sift flour, baking powder and salt. Cut in shortening until mixture has the appearance of corn meal. Add milk, working only enough to combine ingredients. Turn out on well-floured area. Knead until smooth. Pat or roll out ½-inch thick. Cut with biscuit cutter. Place on lightly greased pan. Bake at 450° for 10 to 15 minutes. Yields 8-10 biscuits.

Hot Herb Biscuits

2 cups sifted plain flour
3 teaspoons baking powder
1 teaspoon salt
½ cup shortening
¾ cup milk

2 tablespoons parsley, chopped
1 teaspoon chives, chopped
(or 1 teaspoon onion, grated)
2 teaspoons celery seed

Combine all ingredients. Roll dough out on a floured surface to desired thickness, and cut with a small cutter. Bake at 450° for 10-15 minutes. Yields approximately 2 dozen biscuits.

Quick Corn Biscuits

¾ stick butter
1½ cups Bisquick

1 8½-ounce can cream
style corn

Melt butter on a sided cookie sheet. Mix Bisquick and corn. Drop by teaspoonfuls on cookie sheet. Turn each biscuit so that it is coated with butter. Bake at 400° for 20 minutes or until golden. Yields 1½ dozen.
Crisp and delicious biscuits. Quick and easy.

Wallace's Cheese Biscuits

⅓ cup Crisco
2 cups self-rising flour,
unsifted

1 cup sharp Cheddar cheese,
grated
¾ cup buttermilk or milk

Cut shortening into flour. Add cheese and mix well. (May need to mix with hands to distribute cheese evenly.) Add milk and mix well. Roll out dough on floured surface to ⅛-inch thickness. Cut out and bake at 400°-425° for 8-10 minutes. Yields 2 dozen biscuits.

195

Brown Sugar Muffins

½ cup butter or margarine
1 cup dark brown sugar
1 egg, beaten
1 cup milk
2 scant cups flour, sifted

1 teaspoon soda
1 teaspoon baking powder
salt to taste
½ cup nuts, chopped

Cream butter and sugar. Combine egg and milk. Add dry ingredients to sugar mixture alternately with the egg-milk mixture. Add nuts. Bake in well-greased muffin tins at 350° for 12 minutes or until they begin to shrink from edge of pan. Yields 24-32 muffins.

Cottage Cheese Muffins

⅓ cup sugar
3 tablespoons butter
1 teaspoon lemon peel, grated
(or orange peel)

½ cup cream-style cottage cheese
1 egg
1¾ cups packaged biscuit mix
½ cup milk

Cream butter and sugar. Beat in lemon peel and cottage cheese. Add egg. Beat well. Stir in biscuit mix and milk just until moistened. Spoon into greased small muffin pans. Bake at 400° for 20 minutes or until done. Yields 24 small muffins or 16 regular muffins.

Rice Muffins

2 cups plain flour, unsifted
6 teaspoons baking powder
1 teaspoon salt
2 tablespoons sugar

½ cup cooked rice, cold
1 cup milk
1 egg, beaten
3 tablespoons shortening, melted

Sift first 3 ingredients into a bowl. Add sugar. Combine rice, milk and egg. Add to flour mixture. Stir in shortening. Put in greased muffin pans. Bake at 375° for 15-20 minutes. Yields 1 dozen muffins.

Six Weeks Bran Muffins

2 cups Bran Buds
2 cups boiling water
1 heaping cup Crisco
2 cups sugar
4 eggs

1 quart buttermilk
5 cups sifted plain flour
5 teaspoons baking soda
1 teaspoon salt
4 cups All-Bran cereal

In a bowl, soak Bran Buds in boiling water. Cream Crisco with sugar. Add eggs one at a time. Add buttermilk and Bran Bud mixture. Mix well. Pour into a large mixing bowl. Mix flour, soda and salt. Add to above mixture. Fold in All-Bran. Mix. Store covered in refrigerator for up to 6 weeks. Bake at 375° in greased muffin tins (10 minutes for small muffins, 15 minutes for large muffins).
▼ May add 2 cups seedless raisins and/or chopped nuts.

To substitute sweet milk for buttermilk, add one tablespoon lemon juice or vinegar to 1 cup milk at room temperature. Stir and let stand for 10 minutes.

Sour Cream Muffins

2 cups self-rising flour, sifted
1½ sticks butter, melted

½ pint sour cream

Combine all ingredients, and spoon into small, ungreased muffin tins. Bake at 350° for 20-30 minutes.* Yields 24 small muffins.
* May be frozen.

Aunt Joye's Hush Puppies

1 cup plain corn meal
½ cup plain flour, sifted
1 teaspoon baking powder
1 teaspoon salt

1 teaspoon sugar
½ cup onion, chopped
1 16-ounce can cream-style corn
sweet milk, if needed

Mix dry ingredients. Add onion and corn. Mix well. If more liquid is needed to make desired consistency, add a little sweet milk. Drop heaping teaspoons into deep hot fat. Fry until golden brown. (If cooked in deep fat, they float to the top when done.) Yields 10-12 hush puppies.

Honey Orange Braids

5-6 cups plain flour, sifted
1 cup mashed potato flakes
2 envelopes dry yeast
1 teaspoon salt
1½ cups water
½ cup orange juice
½ cup honey
⅓ cup shortening
1-2 teaspoons orange peel, grated
2 eggs, slightly beaten
1 cup raisins

Combine 1½ cups flour, potato flakes, yeast and salt in a large bowl. Combine water, orange juice, honey, shortening and orange peel in saucepan. Heat until very warm but not hot. Add to flour mixture. Blend at low speed; then beat at medium speed for 2 minutes. Add eggs and 1 cup flour by hand to dough. Beat at high speed for 2 minutes. Stir in raisins and enough of remaining flour to make a stiff dough. Knead on floured surface for 8-10 minutes or until smooth and satiny. Let rise in warm place until doubled in size (40-60 minutes). Divide dough in half and shape into either 2 loaves or 2 braids. Place in well greased pans. Let rise again until doubled in size. Bake at 350° for 35-40 minutes or until a deep golden brown. Yields 2 loaves.

Jan Smuts' Tea Cakes
Mrs. J. Cole, mother of Bobby Cole, South Africa

Bottom Layer:
1 stick butter
1½ cups plain flour, unsifted
½ cup sugar
pinch salt
1 teaspoon baking powder
1 egg, beaten
2-3 tablespoons milk
tart jam

Top Layer:
½ stick butter
¼ cup sugar
1 egg, beaten
2 tablespoons flour
½ teaspoon baking powder

Bottom layer: Cut butter into flour. Add sugar, salt, baking powder and egg. Gradually add milk, just enough to roll out. Roll approximately ¼ inch thick. Cut to fit in bottom of tiny muffin tins. (Easier to handle if refrigerated first.) Place a teaspoon of jam on top of each.
Top layer: Cream butter and sugar. Add egg and beat. Beat in flour and baking powder. Mix well. Drop a teaspoon of mixture on top of jam. Bake at 425° for 12-15 minutes. Let cool slightly before removing from muffin tins. Yields 24.
▼ Best served at room temperature.

Chocolate Chip Coffee Cake

1 cup sugar
½ cup butter
2 cups plain flour
1 cup sour cream
2 eggs

1 teaspoon baking powder
1 teaspoon baking soda
1 teaspoon vanilla
1 6-ounce package semi-sweet
  chocolate pieces, divided

Topping:
½ cup light brown sugar
1½ teaspoons cocoa
½ cup plain flour

¼ cup butter
½ cup almonds, sliced or
  chopped

Cream sugar and butter until fluffy. Add flour, sour cream, eggs, baking powder, soda and vanilla. Beat on low speed until moistened. Beat on medium speed 3 minutes. Stir in ½ cup chocolate chips. Pour batter into greased 9-inch tube pan. *Topping:* Combine brown sugar, cocoa and flour. Cut in butter until mixture resembles coarse crumbs. Stir in nuts and remaining chocolate chips. Crumble mixture evenly over batter. Bake at 350° for 60-65 minutes. Cool completely before removing from pan.

▼ Freezes well.

Sausage Breakfast Bread

1 cup raisins
1 pound pork sausage
1½ cups brown sugar
1½ cups white sugar
2 eggs
3 cups plain flour

1 teaspoon ginger
1 teaspoon baking powder
1 teaspoon pumpkin pie spice
1 teaspoon baking soda
1 cup cold strong coffee
1 cup nuts, chopped

Simmer raisins in a little water for 4 to 5 minutes. Drain well and set aside. Mix uncooked sausage and sugars until well blended. Add eggs. Mix well. Sift together flour, ginger, baking powder and pumpkin pie spice. Stir soda into coffee. Add flour mixture and coffee alternately to meat mixture, beating well after each addition. Stir in raisins and nuts. Mix well. Pour into greased and floured 9-inch tube pan. Bake at 350° for 1½ hours or until toothpick inserted comes out clean. *Keeps indefinitely in refrigerator. Good served warm or cold.*

Sour Cream Coffee Cake

1 cup butter, softened
2 cups sugar
2 eggs
1 cup sour cream

1 teaspoon vanilla
2 cups sifted cake flour
1 teaspoon salt
1 teaspoon baking powder

Topping:
½ cup pecans, chopped
2 teaspoons cinnamon

4 tablespoons brown sugar

In large bowl, cream butter and sugar. Add eggs one at a time beating well after each addition. Fold in sour cream and vanilla. Sift dry ingredients and add to mixture. Put half the batter in a greased and floured 10-inch tube pan. Sprinkle half of topping over batter. Add remaining batter. Add remaining topping. Bake at 350° for 55-60 minutes. Cool thoroughly before removing from pan. Sprinkle with powdered sugar.

Blender Crêpes

1 cup cold water
1 cup cold milk
4 eggs
¼ teaspoon salt

2 cups sifted flour
4 tablespoons butter, melted
1 teaspoon sugar (optional,
     for dessert crêpes only)

Put all ingredients in blender and blend well. Let sit overnight in refrigerator. If too thick, dilute with milk. Place 2 tablespoons batter in hot crêpe pan which has been greased with margarine. Swish batter around pan and cook about 1½ minutes. Turn and cook other side. Put margarine in pan as needed. Cool on rack a few minutes before stacking. Yields 24 crêpes.

Cakes
13

Cake Hints

Always preheat the oven unless otherwise indicated.

All ingredients should be at room temperature (75°).

Flour used in cakes should be sifted once before measuring and as many times afterward as indicated in recipe. Measure accurately.

To substitute all-purpose flour for cake flour, use 2 tablespoons less for each cup.

To prepare pans, grease with a thin film of shortening and sprinkle with flour to cover entire bottom and sides. Turn pans over and thump bottoms to remove excess.

The secret for success in butter cakes is creaming the butter and sugar. Cream butter thoroughly, gradually add sugar and continue creaming until mixture is light, fluffy, and pale ivory in color.

When adding flour and liquid to a cake, always begin and end with flour. Fold in flour; don't beat it in. Don't overmix; it causes failure.

Cakes should be baked on center rack of oven. Never allow pans to touch.

Cakes may vary greatly in cooking time due to the difference in ovens so always test for doneness.
1. *Insert a clean broom straw or cake tester into center of cake after three-fourths of baking time has passed. If it comes out clean, the cake is done.*
2. *Touch the center of the cake lightly with your finger. If it is done, it will spring back easily leaving no impression.*
3. *Do not open oven door until ¾ baking time is complete, or cake will fall.*
DO NOT OVERBAKE.

Never remove a cake from the pan the moment it comes from the oven. Cool in pan 10 minutes, then turn out on cake rack.

Carrot Cake
Mrs. George F. Burns III

Cake:

4 eggs	1 teaspoon baking soda
1½ cups vegetable oil	2 teaspoons cinnamon
2 cups sugar	¼ teaspoon salt
2 cups plain flour	3 cups grated carrots
1 teaspoon baking powder	

Icing:

1 8-ounce package cream cheese, softened	1 16-ounce box 4X powdered sugar
1 stick butter, softened	1½ teaspoons vanilla
	1 cup pecans, chopped

Cake: Blend together eggs and oil. Sift sugar and other dry ingredients together. Add to egg mixture, mixing well. Add carrots. Blend well. Pour mixture into two 9-inch cake pans which have been greased and floured. Bake at 375° for 30-40 minutes. If a 12½x8x2-inch pan is used, bake at 350° for 45 minutes.

Icing: Cream together cream cheese and butter. Add sugar, vanilla and nuts, mixing well. Frost between layers, top and sides.

Banana Cake
Mrs. Henry G. Picard, wife of 1938 Masters' Champion

Cake:

1 stick butter	4 tablespoons buttermilk
1½ cups sugar	2 cups sifted plain flour
2 eggs	½ cup pecans, chopped
3 bananas, mashed	1 teaspoon vanilla
1 teaspoon baking soda	

Icing:

1 tablespoon butter, softened	1 cup pecans, chopped
1-2 ripe bananas, mashed	1 tablespoon lemon juice
1 16-ounce box powdered sugar	

Cake: Cream butter, then blend in sugar. Add eggs, one at a time, beating well after each addition. Add bananas. Dissolve soda in buttermilk and add alternately with flour. Add pecans and vanilla. Pour into two 9-inch or three 8-inch pans which have been greased and lined with waxed paper. Bake at 350° for 15-25 minutes.

Icing: Blend butter and bananas in mixer. Add sugar and mix well. Add pecans and lemon juice. Ice cake. Serves 12.

Fresh Apple Cake

1½ cups vegetable oil
2 cups sugar
4 eggs
2½ cups plain flour
2 teaspoons baking powder

1 teaspoon cinnamon
1 teaspoon salt
3 cups apples, chopped
1 cup pecans, chopped
1 teaspoon vanilla

Topping:
1½ cups brown sugar
1 stick butter

½ cup nuts, chopped
3 teaspoons milk

Blend oil and sugar together. Add eggs one at a time, beating well after each addition. Sift together dry ingredients and add to egg mixture. Stir in apples, pecans and vanilla. Pour into greased and floured 10-inch tube or bundt pan. Bake at 350° for about 1 hour. Remove from pan when slightly cool. To make topping, place all ingredients in saucepan and bring to a boil. Cook until soft ball stage (234°F.). Pour topping over warm cake.

Strawberry Jam Cake

Cake:
3 cups sifted plain flour
1 teaspoon baking soda
½ teaspoon salt
1 teaspoon cinnamon
1 teaspoon allspice
1 teaspoon nutmeg

1 cup butter, softened
1½ cups sugar
4 egg yolks
1 cup buttermilk
1 cup strawberry jam
4 egg whites, stiffly beaten

Filling:
3 cups sugar
½ cup butter

1 cup milk
pinch of salt

Cake: Grease 3 layer cake pans and line with greased waxed paper. Sift first 6 ingredients together. Cream butter and sugar. Add yolks. Alternately add flour, buttermilk and jam. Fold in egg whites. Bake at 300°-325° for 40-60 minutes depending on how many layers your oven will hold.
Filling: Boil ingredients together in 3-quart saucepan over medium heat until syrup forms a ball when dropped in water and flattens when removed, or candy thermometer reads 234°-240°. Stir often to prevent sticking. Remove from heat and beat with spoon until it creams. It should be somewhat runny when you put the layers together as it will harden.*
*Frost a day ahead of time because it will cut better.
This is a good but "different" birthday cake for adults.

204

Orange Cake

Cake:

2 sticks butter
2 cups sugar
4 eggs, separated
1 teaspoon baking soda
1½ cups buttermilk

4 cups plain flour, sifted
2½ tablespoons orange rind, grated
1 cup pecans, chopped

Glaze:

2 cups confectioners sugar
2 teaspoons orange rind, grated

1 cup orange juice

Cake: Cream butter. Gradually add sugar. Add egg yolks one at a time, beating well after each addition. Dissolve soda in buttermilk and add alternately with the flour. Fold in rind and nuts. Fold in stiffly beaten egg whites. Pour mixture into greased and floured tube or bundt pan. Bake at 325° for 1 hour and 15 minutes or until done.

Glaze: Combine glaze ingredients and bring to a boil. Punch lots of holes in cake and slowly pour glaze over hot cake while still in pan. Leave in pan until glaze is absorbed and cake is cool, or cake can be removed from pan onto cake plate and glazed.

▼ This cake is even better several days later.

Grand Marnier Cake

Cake:

2½ cups sifted plain flour
1½ teaspoons baking powder
1 teaspoon baking soda
¼ teaspoon salt
1 cup butter
1¼ cups sugar

3 eggs
1 cup sour cream
2 heaping tablespoons orange rind, grated
½ cup almonds, finely chopped

Glaze:

¼ cup orange juice
½ cup Grand Marnier

½ cup sugar
garnish: orange sections

Cake: Grease and flour tube pan. Preheat oven to 325°. Sift first 4 ingredients together. Cream butter, add sugar, and beat until fluffy. Add eggs one at a time. Add flour in 3 parts, alternating with sour cream in 2 parts. Stir in orange rind and nuts. Bake 50-60 minutes.

Glaze: Warm glaze ingredients and pour over hot cake. Garnish.

Fresh Coconut Cake

Cake:
1 cup butter, softened
1½ cups sugar
1⅔ cups sifted cake flour

5 large eggs
1 teaspoon vanilla

Filling:
1 coconut
1 cup sugar

1 cup milk

Cake: Cream butter with sugar until fluffy. Alternately add flour and eggs, blending well after each addition. Add vanilla. Continue beating on medium speed until batter is smooth. Pour into 3 8-inch greased and floured cake pans. Bake at 350° for 20-30 minutes. Cool on racks.

Filling: Reserve coconut juice. Finely grate coconut meat. Reserve 2 tablespoons for garnish. In a saucepan, mix remaining coconut, coconut juice, sugar and milk. Cook slowly over low heat for 20 minutes. The mixture will be thin. Spread mixture over layers, stacking the layers as each is being covered. Use all the liquid. The cake will absorb the liquid and be very moist. Cover and allow to mellow in refrigerator for 24 to 72 hours. Cake may be frozen at this point and frosted before serving.

▼ 2 cups grated frozen coconut may be substituted for fresh coconut. Decrease sugar to ½ cup and increase milk to 1¼ cups.

Seven-Minute Frosting:
2 unbeaten egg whites
1½ cups sugar
2 teaspoons light corn syrup

⅓ cup cold water
dash of salt
1 teaspoon vanilla

Beat egg whites, sugar, corn syrup, water and salt in top of a double boiler for 1 minute. Place the mixture over, but not touching, boiling water. Beat constantly while cooking until soft peaks form (about 7 minutes). Use a timer. DO NOT OVERCOOK. Remove from heat. Add vanilla. Beat until blended (about 2 minutes). Frost sides and top of cake. Garnish with reserved coconut. Store in refrigerator.

Excellent for special occasions. Time-consuming but well worth it!

Quick Coconut Cake

1 18½-ounce box Duncan Hines Golden Butter cake mix
2 cups sugar
2 cups sour cream

2 9-ounce packages frozen coconut, thawed
1½ cups Cool Whip, thawed

Bake cake as directed using 2 layer pans. Split each layer in half. Combine sugar, sour cream and coconut. Chill. Reserve 1 cup sour cream mixture for frosting. Spread remainder between layers of cake. Combine reserved sour cream mixture with Cool Whip. Blend until smooth. Spread on top and sides of cake. Store in air-tight container in refrigerator for 3 days before serving.
This cake is well worth waiting for!

Nutmeg Delight Cake

Cake:

2 cups plain flour	4 teaspoons nutmeg
1½ cups sugar	1 teaspoon vanilla
1 teaspoon salt	½ cup shortening
1 teaspoon baking powder	1 cup buttermilk
1 teaspoon baking soda	3 eggs

Vanilla Frosting:

¼ to ⅓ cup whipping cream	1 16-ounce package Pillsbury
½ teaspoon vanilla	White Frosting Mix

Place all cake ingredients in large mixing bowl. Mix on low speed until ingredients are moistened, then beat 3 minutes on medium speed. Pour into two 9-inch pans that have been greased and floured. Bake at 350° for 25-30 minutes. Cool for 10 minutes and remove from pans. For frosting, combine frosting ingredients in small mixing bowl. Beat at low speed until moistened, then on medium until thickened. Frost cake. Keep in refrigerator.

Miracle Cake

2 eggs	1 cup sugar
whipping cream (little less than ½ pint)	1 cup self-rising flour
	1 teaspoon almond extract

Break eggs into measuring cup and add whipping cream to make 1 cup. Beat well. Mix with sugar, flour and almond extract. Grease 7x11-inch pan and line with waxed paper. Bake at 350° for about 35 minutes. Serves 6.
Delicious topped with fresh strawberries and whipped cream.

Lane Cake

Cake:

½ pound butter	1 cup milk
2 cups sugar	8 egg whites
3¼ cups sifted plain flour	1 teaspoon vanilla
2 teaspoons baking powder	

Filling:

1 stick butter	1 cup pecans, chopped
1 cup sugar	1 cup white raisins
8 egg yolks, beaten	1 teaspoon vanilla
½ cup brandy	

Cake: Cream butter and sugar together until very light. Sift flour and baking powder 3 times and add alternately with milk to creamed mixture. Fold in well-beaten egg whites and vanilla. Bake in four 8-inch or three 9-inch pans, which are well greased and floured, at 375° for 20-25 minutes.

Filling: Cream butter and sugar together. Add yolks and brandy. Cook in double boiler, stirring constantly, until thick. Add pecans and raisins. Cool and spread between layers. Frost entire cake with a boiled white icing.

Fruit Cake

1 pound candied citron	1 pound pecans, chopped
1 pound candied cherries	1 pound butter
1 pound candied pineapple	2½ cups sugar
whiskey to cover fruit	12 eggs, separated
4 cups sifted cake flour	1 tablespoon nutmeg
1 pound almonds, chopped	1 tablespoon mace

Cut up fruit and soak overnight in whiskey. Sift flour 5 times and set aside. Slightly flour nuts with some of the measured flour. Set aside. Cream butter, gradually adding sugar. Add egg yolks one at a time, beating well after each addition. Flour fruit well with some of the measured flour. Slowly add flour to butter mixture, then spices, fruit and nuts. Fold in stiffly beaten egg whites. Pour mixture into a well-greased and floured tube pan. Loosely cover top of pan with cardboard or foil. Place small pan of water on bottom rack of oven. Bake in a preheated 250° oven for 4 hours. Turn cake out on rack to cool completely. Wrap cake in cheesecloth that has been slightly moistened with whiskey. Wrap in foil and place in cake tin. To keep cake moist after cutting, place a piece of apple in the tin and sprinkle whiskey on cake as needed.

This cake will keep for several months.

Alice's Layer Cake with Caramel Icing

Cake:

2 sticks butter
2 cups sugar
4 eggs, separated
3 cups sifted flour

2 teaspoons baking powder
pinch of baking soda
1 cup buttermilk
1 teaspoon vanilla

Caramel Icing:

3 cups light brown sugar
¾ cup butter
few grains of salt

¾ cup half-and-half
   (or evaporated milk)
1 teaspoon vanilla

Cake: Cream butter until very light in color. Gradually add sugar. Add egg yolks one at a time until well mixed. Sift flour, baking powder and soda together. Add flour alternately with buttermilk to butter mixture. Fold beaten egg whites into mixture with a large spoon. Add vanilla. Pour into three 9-inch greased and floured cake pans. Bake at 375° for about 20 minutes. Let cake cool COMPLETELY before icing.

Caramel Icing: Combine sugar, butter, salt and cream in saucepan. Stir over low heat until dissolved. Let mixture boil, stirring often, until it reaches soft ball stage (238°). Remove from heat. Beat until cool and add vanilla. Spread between layers, on top and sides of cake.

▼This is an excellent basic layer cake recipe.

Brown Sugar Pound Cake

3 sticks butter or margarine
1 16-ounce box plus 1 cup
   light brown sugar
5 eggs
3 cups sifted plain flour
½ teaspoon baking powder

½ teaspoon salt
1 cup milk
½ teaspoon maple flavoring
1 teaspoon vanilla
1 cup nuts, chopped (optional)

Cream butter, gradually add sugar. Add eggs, one at a time, beating well after each addition. Sift dry ingredients together and add alternately with milk. Add flavorings and nuts. Bake in a well greased and floured tube pan at 325° for 1-1½ hours or until done. Remove from pan immediately.

Sour Cream Pound Cake
Augusta National Golf Club, Augusta, Georgia

2 sticks butter (no substitutes)
2⅔ cups sugar
6 eggs
¼ teaspoon baking soda

1 8-ounce carton sour cream
3 cups plain flour
1 teaspoon vanilla

Cream butter and sugar well. Add one egg at a time, mixing well. Stir soda into sour cream. Add flour and sour cream to butter mixture. Add vanilla. Bake at 300° for 1 hour (do not open oven). Continue baking at 325° for 15 minutes longer.
Clifford Roberts' favorite!

Georgia Pound Cake

1 pound butter
2⅔ cups sugar
8 large eggs
8 tablespoons whipping cream

3½ cups plain flour
2 teaspoons vanilla
¼-½ teaspoon mace (optional)

Cream butter. Add sugar gradually. Add eggs one at a time, beating well after each addition. Alternately add cream and flour. Add vanilla and mace. Pour into buttered and floured tube pan. Bake at 350° for 1-1½ hours or until done. Slice very thin.

Chocolate Pound Cake

3 sticks butter
3 cups sugar
5 eggs
3 cups cake flour

¾ cup cocoa
½ teaspoon salt
½ teaspoon baking powder
1 cup milk

Cream butter; gradually add sugar. Add eggs, one at a time, beating well after each addition. Sift dry ingredients together and add mixture alternately with milk. Pour into a greased and floured tube pan. Bake at 325° for 1-1½ hours or until done. DO NOT OVERBAKE or cake will be dry. Powdered sugar may be sprinkled on top of cake.

Soft Gingerbread with Lemon Sauce

Gingerbread:

¼ cup butter	1½ teaspoons baking soda
¼ cup shortening	1 teaspoon cinnamon
½ cup sugar	1 teaspoon ground ginger
2 eggs, beaten	½ teaspoon ground cloves
1 cup molasses	1 teaspoon salt
2½ cups sifted plain flour	1 cup hot water

Lemon Sauce:

2 cups sugar	1 tablespoon cornstarch
1 tablespoon butter	2 eggs
juice and/or rind of 2 lemons	2 cups boiling water

Gingerbread: Cream butter and shortening. Add sugar. Add eggs and molasses. Sift together remaining dry ingredients and add to butter mixture. Add hot water and beat until smooth. Bake in greased shallow pan at 350° for about 35 minutes. Serve with lemon sauce or whipped cream.

Lemon Sauce: Beat together sugar, butter, juice and/or rind, cornstarch and eggs. Add water. Heat to boiling point. Serve over gingerbread.

Secret Cake

Cake:

1 stick margarine	½ cup buttermilk
¼ cup shortening	2 eggs
1 cup water	1 teaspoon vanilla
3½ tablespoons cocoa	1 teaspoon baking soda
2 cups sifted plain flour	½ teaspoon salt
2 cups sugar	

Icing:

1 stick margarine	1 16-ounce box 4X powdered sugar
3½ tablespoons cocoa	1 cup nuts, chopped
⅓ cup buttermilk	(optional)

Bring first 4 ingredients to a boil. Pour over flour and sugar and beat well. Add remaining ingredients. Mix well. Pour into a greased and floured 11x16x2-inch pan (broiler pan). Bake at 400° for about 20 minutes or until done. DO NOT OVERBAKE. To make icing, boil margarine, cocoa and buttermilk until blended. Remove from heat and beat in sugar. Add nuts. Frost cake while hot and still in pan.

▼ Best made day ahead. Keeps well up to a week. Freezes well.

Easy and excellent for children's birthday parties or picnics.

211

Cookie Sheetcake
Mrs. Tom Watson, Wife of 1977 Masters' Champion

Cake:
2 cups plain flour
2 cups sugar
1 teaspoon baking soda
2 sticks butter
4 tablespoons cocoa

1 cup water
2 eggs, beaten
½ cup buttermilk
1 teaspoon vanilla

Icing:
1 stick butter
4 tablespoons cocoa
6 tablespoons buttermilk

1 16-ounce box powdered sugar
1 teaspoon vanilla
nuts, chopped (optional)

Cake: Sift together flour, sugar and soda. Set aside. Combine butter, cocoa and water. Bring to a boil. Add butter mixture to dry ingredients and mix well. Add eggs, buttermilk and vanilla. Beat well. Pour onto greased and floured cookie sheet with sides (jelly roll pan). Bake at 350° for 15-20 minutes. DO NOT OVERBAKE.
Icing: Combine butter, cocoa and buttermilk. Bring to a boil. Beat in sugar, vanilla and nuts. Pour over hot cake and let cool.

Chocolate Lovers' Favorite Cake

Cake:
1 cup plain flour
1 teaspoon baking powder
pinch of salt
1 stick margarine
1 cup sugar

4 eggs
1 16-ounce can Hershey's chocolate syrup
1 teaspoon vanilla extract

Fudge Icing:
1 cup sugar
1 stick butter (not margarine)

½ cup chocolate chips
⅓ cup evaporated milk
½ teaspoon vanilla extract

212

Cake: Sift flour, baking powder and salt together. In a large bowl, cream margarine, adding sugar gradually. Add eggs, one at a time. Alternate adding dry ingredients and chocolate syrup. Beat until well mixed. Add vanilla. Pour into greased and floured 13x9x2½-inch pan. Bake at 350° for 30 minutes.

Fudge Icing: Put all ingredients except vanilla in a heavy saucepan. Blend over medium heat, stirring constantly, until mixture begins to boil. Boil 3 minutes by the clock. Remove from heat and add vanilla. Beat icing with a spoon until it cools and thickens. Placing saucepan in sink with a few inches of cold water will cool it faster. Spread icing quickly on cake. Cut into squares when cool. Yields 24 2-inch squares or may be cut smaller for "party food". Will keep a week or more in an air-tight container — if there is any left to keep!

This is a treat for Masters® guests or a consolation for children who are sad to be left at home.

Chocolate Marble Cake

3 cups plain flour, sifted
2 teaspoons baking powder
½ teaspoon salt
1 cup butter
2 cups sugar
3 eggs

1 cup milk
2 teaspoons vanilla
¾ cup chocolate syrup
¼ teaspoon baking soda
¼ teaspoon peppermint extract

Frosting:
1½ cups sugar
6 tablespoons cornstarch
1½ cups water, boiling
¾ teaspoon salt

3 1-ounce squares semi-sweet chocolate, broken
6 tablespoons butter
1 tablespoon vanilla

Cake: Sift first 3 ingredients together. Set aside. Cream butter. Add sugar gradually. Add eggs one at a time, beating well after each addition. Combine milk and vanilla. Add alternately with dry ingredients to creamed mixture. Blend well after each addition. Turn two-thirds of batter into greased 10-inch tube pan. Add chocolate syrup, soda and peppermint to remaining batter. Mix well and pour over batter. DO NOT MIX. Bake at 350° for 60-70 minutes.

Frosting: Mix sugar and cornstarch thoroughly in a 2-quart saucepan. Stir in boiling water, salt and chocolate. Cook over medium heat, stirring frequently, until mixture thickens (about 5 minutes). Remove from heat. Beat in butter and vanilla. Spread on cake while frosting is hot.

Chocolate Praline Cake with Broiled Icing

Cake:
1 cup buttermilk
1 stick butter
2 cups light brown sugar
2 eggs

2 cups sifted plain flour
1 teaspoon baking soda
3 tablespoons cocoa
1 tablespoon vanilla

Icing:
1 stick butter
1 cup light brown sugar,
  packed

½ cup whipping cream or
  evaporated milk
1 cup pecans, chopped

Cake: In a small saucepan, warm buttermilk and butter (DO NOT SCALD). Pour liquid into a mixing bowl. Add brown sugar and eggs. Beat well. Sift dry ingredients and slowly add to mixture. Stir in vanilla. Pour into a greased and floured 9x13x2-inch pan. Bake at 350° for 25 minutes or until done.
Icing: Combine all ingredients in a saucepan. Gradually bring to a slow boil. Cook for several minutes until mixture begins to thicken. Spread mixture over top of warm cake. Place cake 4 inches below broiler. Broil until icing bubbles and turns golden (1-2 minutes). Serve plain or with whipped cream.
Out of this world!

Mocha Cream Cake

Cake:
2½ cups sifted plain flour
1 teaspoon baking soda
½ teaspoon salt
½ cup boiling water
4 ounces German sweet chocolate,
  broken into small pieces
1 teaspoon dry instant coffee

1 teaspoon vanilla
1 cup butter
2 cups sugar
4 egg yolks
1 cup buttermilk
4 egg whites, stiffly beaten

Frosting:
2 cups whipping cream
3 tablespoons cocoa
½ cup sugar

3 teaspoons dry instant coffee
garnish: chopped nuts or
  pecan halves

Cake: Grease three 9-inch round cake pans. Sift together flour, soda and salt. Set aside. In a small bowl, pour water over chocolate and coffee. Stir to melt, then cool. Add vanilla. Cream butter and sugar. Add egg yolks one at a time. Add buttermilk alternately with the flour mixture. Mix just until blended. Stir in chocolate mixture. Gently fold in egg whites. Bake at 350° for 30-40 minutes.
Frosting: Combine cream, cocoa, sugar and coffee. Mix well. Chill 1 hour. Whip mixture and frost cake. Garnish.

Skillet Pineapple Upside Down Cake

Mrs. Jack Nicklaus, Wife of Masters' Champion, 1963, 1965, 1966, 1972 and 1975

Topping:
1 stick butter
1-1½ cups light brown sugar

1 15¼-ounce can pineapple rings

Cake:
2 eggs, separated
1 cup sugar
¼ teaspoon vanilla
⅜ cup hot water

1 cup sifted plain flour
1½ teaspoons baking powder
pinch of salt
whipped cream (optional)

Topping: In large iron skillet, melt butter and brown sugar together. Arrange pineapple rings on top of sugar mixture and cook until bubbly.
Cake: Beat egg yolks well. Add sugar gradually. Add vanilla. Add hot water and mix well. Slowly add dry ingredients. Fold in beaten egg whites. Pour batter over topping. Bake in skillet at 325° for 50 minutes. Turn out on cake plate to serve. May be topped with whipped cream. Serves 6-8.

Plum Cake with Topping

Cake:
Crisco
flour
2 cups self-rising flour
2 cups sugar
1 cup oil

3 eggs
1 teaspoon cinnamon
1 teaspoon ground cloves
2 4¾-ounce jars plum baby food
1 cup pecans, chopped (optional)

Topping (optional):
1 stick butter, softened
1½ cups powdered sugar

3 tablespoons orange juice or
  2 tablespoons lemon juice

Cake: Grease entire tube pan with Crisco. Flour bottom of pan. Sift flour three times. Add sugar, then oil. In mixer, add eggs one at a time, to flour and sugar mixture. Add spices. Mix thoroughly. Add plums and nuts. Bake at 325° for 1-1¼ hours. Serves 12.
Topping: Stir ingredients until smooth. Ice cake with half the icing when cake is removed from oven. Ice with remainder when cooled.
   ▼Freezes well.

Orange Cranberry Torte

2½ cups sifted plain flour
1 cup sugar
¼ teaspoon salt
1 teaspoon baking powder
1 teaspoon baking soda
1 cup pecans, chopped

1 cup fresh whole cranberries
1 cup dates, diced
grated rind of 2 oranges
2 eggs
1 cup buttermilk
¾ cup salad oil

Topping:
1 cup sugar

1 cup orange juice

Combine flour, sugar, salt, baking powder and soda. Stir in nuts, washed cranberries, dates and orange rind. Combine eggs, buttermilk and salad oil. Add to flour mixture, stirring well. Pour into greased tube pan. Bake at 350° for 1 hour. Let cake cool slightly. Combine topping ingredients and pour over warm cake. Let stand until topping is absorbed. Remove from pan. Wrap in foil and refrigerate.
Keeps for weeks!

Rum Cake

1 cup pecans, chopped
1 18½-ounce box Duncan Hines
   Golden Butter cake mix
1 3¾-ounce package instant
   vanilla pudding mix

4 eggs
½ cup light rum
½ cup water
½ cup Crisco oil

Glaze:
1 stick butter
1 cup sugar

¼ cup light rum
¼ cup water

Grease and flour a bundt or tube pan. Sprinkle nuts on bottom of pan. Mix dry ingredients and add eggs and liquid. Beat 3 minutes. Pour gently into pan. Bake at 325° for 50-60 minutes. Mix glaze ingredients and boil for 3 minutes. Pour hot glaze over cake and leave in pan for 1 hour before removing.
▼ This cake keeps well for 5 days.

Beulah's Poppy Seed Cake

¼ cup poppy seeds
1 cup unsweetened pineapple
  juice
1 18½-ounce box Duncan Hines
  yellow cake mix
1 3¾-ounce package instant
  vanilla pudding mix

5 eggs, slightly beaten
½ cup vegetable oil
1 tablespoon almond extract
  margarine
3 tablespoons white or brown
  sugar

Soak poppy seeds in pineapple juice for 1 hour. Combine poppy seeds, juice, cake mix, pudding mix, eggs, oil and almond extract. Mix well. Grease bundt or tube pan with margarine and sprinkle with sugar. Bake at 350° for 1 hour or until done.

"Sock It To Me" Cake

1 18½-ounce box Duncan Hines
  Golden Butter cake mix
½ cup sugar
¾ cup buttered Wesson oil
4 eggs

1 cup sour cream
1 cup pecans, chopped
1 teaspoon almond extract
2 tablespoons brown sugar
2 teaspoons cinnamon

Mix together cake mix, sugar, oil, eggs and sour cream. Blend well. Stir in nuts and almond extract. Combine brown sugar and cinnamon. Pour half of batter in greased and floured tube or bundt pan. Sprinkle sugar mixture over batter and add remaining batter. Bake at 325° for 1 hour and 10 minutes. Cool 10 minutes before removing from pan.

Vanilla Wafer Cake

2 sticks butter
2 cups sugar
6 eggs, beaten
1 7-ounce package coconut

1 12-ounce box vanilla wafers,
  crushed
½ cup milk
1 cup pecans, chopped

Cream butter, then add sugar. Add remaining ingredients. Mix well and pour into a greased tube or bundt pan. Bake at 325° for 1-1¼ hours. Let cool in pan for at least 2 hours.
▼One teaspoon vanilla extract may be added, if desired.
This is quick and extremely good!

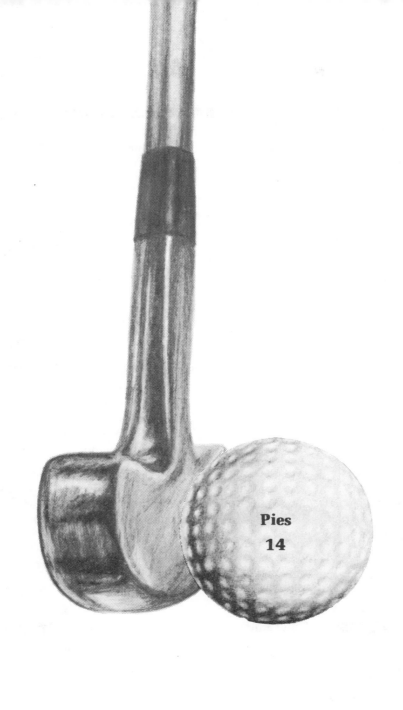

Pies

14

Amelia Island Mud Pie

Shell:
12 Oreo cookies (without filling), finely crushed
2 tablespoons butter, melted

1 tablespoon Sanka coffee grounds, perked

Filling:
2-3 cups chocolate ice cream, softened
1 tablespoon Sanka coffee grounds, perked
2 tablespoons brandy

2 tablespoons Kahlua
2 tablespoons liquid instant Sanka coffee
4 tablespoons whipped cream (or more to taste)

Topping:
Kraft fudge topping
¼ cup pecans, chopped

whipped cream, sweetened to taste

Mix Oreos with butter and coffee grounds. Press in pie plate and freeze. Whip ice cream with coffee grounds, liqueurs and coffee. Fold in whipped cream. Pour in shell. Freeze until hard. Cover with thin layer of fudge topping and nuts. Garnish with whipped cream. Serves 6-8.

▼ The coffee grounds give the pie an interesting texture. The amount of brandy and Kahlua used may be decreased according to taste.

Chocolate Pie

2½ cups milk
2 squares unsweetened chocolate
1 cup sugar
6 level tablespoons plain flour
½ teaspoon salt
2 egg yolks, beaten

1 teaspoon vanilla
2 tablespoons butter
1 9-inch pie shell, baked
1 cup whipping cream, whipped
unsweetened chocolate shavings

In a double boiler, mix milk and chocolate, cooking until chocolate melts. Separately, mix sugar, flour and salt and combine with liquid mixture. Mix thoroughly with hand mixer or blender. Return to stove and cook 15 minutes over hot water. Add a little of hot mixture to egg yolks, then add egg mixture to hot mixture. Stir and cook 2 minutes. Remove from heat. Add vanilla and butter. Cool at room temperature. Pour into pie shell. A couple of hours before serving, ice with whipped cream and shaved chocolate. May serve with a dab of whipped cream on each slice. Serves 6-8.

▼ To keep a skim from forming on top of chocolate mixture while it cools, cover top of mixture with plastic wrap.

Coffee-Toffee Pie

Pie-shell:
5 ounces packaged pie crust mix
¼ cup brown sugar, packed
¾ cup walnuts, finely chopped

1 ounce unsweetened chocolate, melted
1 tablespoon water
1 teaspoon vanilla

Filling:
½ cup butter, softened
¾ cup sugar
2 teaspoons dry instant coffee

1 ounce unsweetened chocolate,
melted and cooled
2 eggs

Topping:
2 cups whipping cream
½ cup 10X powdered sugar

2 tablespoons dry instant coffee
chocolate curls

Combine pie crust mix, sugar, nuts and chocolate. Add water and vanilla. Pat into well greased 9-inch pie plate. Bake at 375° for 15 minutes. Cool. For filling, beat butter and sugar. Add coffee and chocolate. Add 1 egg and beat 5 minutes. Add the other egg and beat 5 more minutes. Put into crust and refrigerate covered overnight. Before serving, combine cream, sugar and coffee. Cover and chill 1 hour. Beat cream mixture until stiff. Spread on pie. Sprinkle with chocolate curls. Chill 2 hours or more before serving. Serves 8.

Toffee Ice Cream Pie

Pie:
12 ¾-ounce Heath bars
1¼ cups chocolate wafer crumbs

¼ cup butter, melted
½ gallon vanilla ice cream

Sauce:
1 stick butter
1 12-ounce package chocolate
chips

2 cups 10-X powdered sugar
1 13-ounce can evaporated milk
2 teaspoons vanilla

Pie: Put Heath bars in freezer to harden. Mix crumbs and butter. Line 9x13-inch pan. Press mixture evenly. Put into refrigerator to harden. Crush Heath bars and mix with softened ice cream. Put in crust and freeze overnight.
Sauce: Melt butter and chocolate chips. Add sugar and milk. Cook about 8 minutes or until thick, stirring constantly. Add vanilla. Serve warm over pie. The sauce can be made early in day and heated at last minute. Serves 8-10.

▼ Oreos may be substituted for chocolate wafers if the filling is scraped off.

Fudge Ribbon Pie

Sauce:

2 tablespoons butter or margarine
2 ounces unsweetened chocolate
1 cup sugar

⅔ cup evaporated milk
 (5.3 ounce can)
1 teaspoon vanilla

Filling:

1 quart pink peppermint
 ice cream

1 9-inch pie shell,
 baked and cooled

Meringue:

3 egg whites
½ teaspoon vanilla
¼ teaspoon cream of tartar

6 tablespoons sugar
4 tablespoons peppermint
 stick candy, crushed

Sauce: In saucepan, mix butter, chocolate, sugar and milk. Cook and stir until mixture is thick and bubbly. Stir in vanilla. Cool.

Filling: Spread half the ice cream in pie shell; cover with half the cooled fudge sauce. Freeze until firm. Repeat layer of ice cream and fudge sauce. Freeze overnight or until firm.*

Meringue: Beat egg whites with vanilla and cream of tartar until soft peaks form. Gradually add sugar, beating until sugar is dissolved. Fold in 3 tablespoons peppermint candy. Just before serving, spread meringue over chocolate layer; seal to edge. Sprinkle 1 tablespoon peppermint candy over top. Place pie on wooden board. Bake at 475° for 5-6 minutes or until meringue is golden. Serves 6-8.

*All but the meringue may be made a day ahead and kept in freezer. Make meringue and bake just before serving.

Frosty Orange Pie

1 cup uncooked oats, quick
 or old-fashioned
¾ cup flaked coconut, divided
⅓ cup brown sugar, firmly
 packed

⅓ cup butter, melted
1 quart vanilla ice cream,
 softened
¼ cup frozen orange juice
 concentrate, thawed

Place oats in shallow baking pan. Toast at 350° about 10 minutes. Combine toasted oats, ½ cup coconut, sugar and butter. Mix until crumbly. Press firmly on bottom and sides of 9-inch pie plate. Chill. Spread half of ice cream in pie shell. Sprinkle with 2 tablespoons orange juice concentrate. Repeat layers. Toast remaining coconut. Sprinkle on pie. Freeze until firm.

▼ Sherbet can be substituted for ice cream and orange juice.

221

Apple Pie

6 to 8 tart apples
½ cup sugar
½ cup brown sugar
2 tablespoons plain flour
¾ teaspoon nutmeg
¾ teaspoon cinnamon

2 tablespoons lemon juice
1 double crust pastry, unbaked
4 tablespoons butter
milk
granulated sugar

Pare and core apples. Cut into eighths. Place in bowl and toss with sugars, flour, spices and lemon juice. Let stand 15 to 20 minutes. Place in pie shell and dot with butter. Cover with pastry. Brush top with milk and sprinkle with sugar. Bake at 400° for 35-45 minutes.

Macaroon Pie

12 dates, finely chopped
½ cup pecans, chopped
12 saltine crackers, crushed
1 cup sugar
¼ teaspoon baking powder

1 teaspoon almond flavoring
3 egg whites, stiffly beaten
whipping cream, whipped
maraschino cherries

Combine dates, nuts and crackers. Add sugar, baking powder and flavoring. Fold in egg whites. Pour into greased and floured pie pan or 9x9-inch square pan. Bake at 350° for 25 minutes. Serve with whipped cream and top with cherries. Serves 6.

Date Nut Pie

½ cup butter, softened
1 cup sugar
2 eggs, separated
¼ cup water
½ cup dates, chopped

½ cup nuts, chopped
2 tablespoons plain flour
½ teaspoon vanilla
1 9-inch pie shell, unbaked
whipping cream

Cream butter and sugar. Add beaten egg yolks and water. Add dates and nuts that have been rolled with flour. Add vanilla. Fold in stiffly beaten egg whites. Pour into pie shell. Bake at 275° for 1 hour and 15 minutes. Serve topped with whipped cream, sweetened to taste, if desired.
Very rich!

No-Crust Coconut Pie

¼ cup margarine
1 cup sugar
2 eggs
1 cup milk

¼ cup self-rising flour
½ of 7-ounce can flaked coconut
1 teaspoon vanilla

Cream margarine, adding sugar gradually. Add eggs, one at a time, beating well after each addition. Add milk and flour, mixing well. Add coconut and vanilla. Pour into lightly greased 9-inch pie pan. Bake at 350° for 45 minutes. Serves 6-8.
▼ This can be easily doubled to make 2 pies.

Old Fashioned Chess Pie

½ cup butter, melted
1 tablespoon vinegar
3 eggs, slightly beaten
1 tablespoon plain corn meal

1½ cups sugar
1 teaspoon vanilla
1 9-inch pie shell, unbaked,
   or 8 individual pie shells

Combine butter and vinegar. Let stand while beating eggs. Sift corn meal and sugar together. Combine butter mixture, eggs and sugar mixture. Mix well. Stir in vanilla. Pour into pie shell. Bake at 350° for 40-50 minutes or until set. Serves 8.

Rum Cream Pie

Crust:
2¼ cups graham cracker crumbs
½ cup butter, melted

2 tablespoons sugar
½ teaspoon ground cinnamon

Filling:
1 envelope unflavored gelatin
½ cup cold water
5 egg yolks
1 cup sugar

⅓ cup dark rum (or to taste)
1½ cups whipping cream,
   whipped
unsweetened chocolate, grated

For crust, combine all ingredients and press into a 9-inch deep-dish pie pan. Chill. For filling, soften gelatin in water. Place over low heat. Bring almost to a boil, stirring to dissolve gelatin. Beat egg yolks and sugar until very light. Stir gelatin into egg mixture. Cool. Gradually add rum, beating constantly. Fold whipped cream into egg mixture. Cool until mixture begins to set, then spoon into crust. Chill until firm. Top with grated chocolate.

Grasshopper Pie

Crust:
1¼ cups chocolate wafers, crushed   ⅓ cup butter, melted

Filling:
24 large marshmallows   1 cup whipping cream, whipped
⅔ cup milk, scalded   slivered almonds (optional)
¼ cup crème de menthe   whipped cream (optional)
2 tablespoons crème de cacao

Combine wafers and butter and press in pie plate. Chill. For filling, slowly add marshmallows to milk in double boiler, stirring constantly. Cool to room temperature. Add liqueurs. Fold whipped cream into above mixture. Pour into crust. Freeze. To serve, top with either almonds or whipped cream. Serves 6-8.

▼ Oreos may be scraped and substituted for chocolate wafers.

Lillian's Lime Tarts

1 cup sugar   rind of 2 limes, grated
½ cup butter   green food coloring
3 eggs, beaten   tart shells, baked
1 egg yolk, beaten   slivered almonds, toasted
½ cup lime juice

Cook sugar and butter in top of double boiler until sugar is dissolved. Slowly add a little of hot mixture to eggs, stirring quickly. Pour egg mixture back into hot mixture, stirring constantly. Add lime juice, stirring almost constantly until thickened. Add rind. Cool. Add 2 drops green food coloring. Chill. To serve, pour into tart shells and sprinkle almonds on top. Yield 8 individual or 24 bite-size tarts.

Dark Pecan Pie

3 eggs, well beaten   1 tablespoon vanilla
1 cup brown sugar   3 tablespoons butter, melted
¾ cup dark Karo syrup   ⅔ cup pecan halves
¼ teaspoon salt   1 9-inch pie shell, unbaked

Combine eggs, sugar, syrup, salt, vanilla, butter and nuts. Mix thoroughly and pour into pie shell. Bake at 400° for 10 minutes. Reduce heat to 325° and bake 35 minutes longer.

Aunt Mary's Lemon Pie

3 egg yolks
1 cup sugar
5 tablespoons cornstarch
juice, grated rind of 2 lemons
2 cups boiling water

¼ teaspoon salt
2 tablespoons butter
1 9-inch pie shell, baked
3 egg whites
6 tablespoons sugar

In top of double boiler, beat egg yolks. Combine 1 cup sugar and cornstarch and add to yolks. Gradually add lemon juice, rind, water and salt. Cook until thick, stirring occasionally. Remove from heat and add butter. Pour cooled filling into cooled pie shell. Beat egg whites. Add 6 tablespoons sugar and beat until stiff. Put on top of filling. Bake at 400° until brown. Serves 8.
This is a very rich pie. Use with a light meal.

Georgia Peanut Pie

3 large eggs, slightly beaten
¼ teaspoon salt
½ teaspoon vanilla
¼ cup brown sugar
1 cup light corn syrup

1 cup raw Georgia peanuts
1 9-inch deep-dish pie shell,
   unbaked
whipping cream, whipped and
   sweetened to taste

Combine eggs, salt, vanilla, sugar, syrup and peanuts. Pour into pie shell. Bake at 450° for 10 minutes, reduce heat to 350° and bake 35 minutes. Chill before serving. Garnish with whipped cream.

Light Pecan Pie

½ cup white sugar
½ cup dark brown sugar
1 cup light Karo syrup
¼ teaspoon salt
3 eggs, well beaten

⅓ cup butter, melted
2 teaspoons vanilla
1 cup pecans, chopped
1 9-inch pastry shell,
   unbaked

Combine filling ingredients. Pour into pie shell. Bake at 325° for 1 hour.

Strawberry Pie

1 8-ounce package cream cheese
milk
1 9-inch deep-dish pie shell
5 cups strawberries

1¼ cups sugar
3 tablespoons cornstarch
1 tablespoon fresh lemon juice
1 cup whipping cream

Combine softened cream cheese with enough milk to spread evenly on bottom of baked and cooled pie shell. Arrange choice berries (about 2 cups) on cream cheese, reserving a few for garnish. Mash remaining berries in blender. In a saucepan, combine mashed berries, sugar and cornstarch. Cook until thick and mixture coats spoon well. Cool. Add lemon juice. Pour over berries in pie shell. Top with cream which has been whipped and sweetened to taste. Garnish with reserved berries. Chill.

To whip cream, chill bowl, beaters and cream before whipping. For best re-sults, cream should be whipped at the last minute. If necessary to do ahead, add a small amount of gelatin. To sweeten, use powdered sugar, not granulated.

Easy Frozen Strawberry Pie

Crust:
1 cup graham cracker crumbs
2 tablespoons sugar

3 tablespoons butter or
   margarine, melted

Filling:
8 ounces cream cheese, softened
1 cup sour cream

2 10-ounce packages frozen
   sliced strawberries, thawed

Crust: Combine all ingredients and press into 9-inch pie plate. Chill until firm (about 45 minutes).
Filling: Blend cream cheese and sour cream. Reserve ½ cup berries and syrup. Add remaining berries to cheese mixture. Pour into pie crust. Freeze until firm.*
Remove from freezer 10 to 15 minutes before serving. Cut, and spoon reserved berries over pie.
*May be prepared a day to a week ahead.
▼ Be sure to use sweetened strawberries.

226

Petite Cherry Cheesecakes

2 8-ounce packages cream cheese
¾ cup sugar
2 eggs
1 tablespoon lemon juice

1 teaspoon vanilla
vanilla wafers
1 21-ounce can cherry pie
   filling

Beat first 5 ingredients together until fluffy. Place paper cupcake liners in muffin tins. Put 1 vanilla wafer in bottom of each cup. Fill ⅔ full with cream cheese mixture. Bake at 375° for 15-20 minutes. Do not let mixture brown on top. When cool, put 1 teaspoon of cherry filling on top of cream cheese mixture in each cup. Yields 3 dozen.

▼ Cakes can be frozen when cool but do not add cherry filling until ready to serve.

Sweet Potato Pie
Mrs. Lee Elder

1 cup cooked mashed sweet
   potatoes
1 cup evaporated milk,
   undiluted
1 cup light brown sugar,
   packed
3 eggs, slightly beaten

¼ cup Courvoisier Cognac
1 teaspoon cinnamon
1 teaspoon nutmeg
¼ teaspoon mace
1 9-inch pie shell, unbaked
whipping cream, whipped

Combine sweet potatoes, milk and sugar. Mix well. Stir in eggs, brandy and spices. Mix well. Pour mixture into pie shell. Bake at 400° for about 50 minutes. Serve while warm with whipped cream or may serve cool. Serves 6-8.

Never-fail Pie Crust

4 cups plain flour
1¾ cups Crisco
1 tablespoon sugar
2 teaspoons salt

1 tablespoon vinegar
1 egg
½ cup water

Mix first 4 ingredients with a fork. In a separate dish, combine vinegar, egg and water. Add to flour mixture. Stir with fork until all ingredients are moistened. Shape into ball. Chill at least 1 hour. Roll out to make crusts. May be divided into five balls, wrapped, and frozen. Yields 5 9-inch crusts.
This is a very pliable, workable dough. It never fails!

Pastry
Mrs. Dwight D. Eisenhower

2 cups sifted flour
¾ teaspoon salt

⅔ cup shortening
cold water

Mix flour and salt, then sift together. Cut shortening into flour mixture with pastry blender or 2 knives until flour and shortening particles are the size of small peas. Sprinkle 1 tablespoon cold water over mixture and mix in lightly with a fork. Continue adding water in this fashion until pastry gathers around fork in a soft ball. Divide pastry in half and roll each half separately on lightly floured board. Handle rolling pin lightly. Yields 2 9-inch pie crusts.

"Tissie" Pastry

1 3-ounce package cream cheese,
  softened

1 stick butter, softened
1 cup plain flour

Combine cream cheese and butter. Blend well. Stir in flour. Chill. Roll out as desired.

Hot Water Pie Crust

2 pounds shortening, softened
2 cups hot water
4 teaspoons salt

4 teaspoons sugar
1 teaspoon baking powder
10 cups sifted flour

Mix shortening and water. Beat in electric mixer for 15 minutes or until creamy white. Combine salt, sugar and baking powder and add to shortening mixture. Beat well. Fold flour into mixture using a big spoon. Dough will be soft. Chill at least 3 hours before using. Yields 6-7 two-crust pies.

▼ Recipe can be cut in half. Pastry will keep in refrigerator 2-3 weeks.

For pastry, do not substitute oil for shortening unless specifically called for.

Cold water aids in producing a tender pastry. Use only enough to hold pastry together. Excess water may cause shrinkage and a soggy, tough pastry.

Do not overmix pastry – overhandling toughens pastry.

If a pastry shell is to be baked unfilled, prick it thoroughly with a fork to prevent buckling.

Desserts
15

Crème Brûlée

---

1 quart whipping cream (4 cups)
4 tablespoons sugar
3 teaspoons vanilla extract

8 egg yolks
pinch of salt
1¼ cups light brown sugar

In a large saucepan, scald cream. Remove from heat. Add sugar. Stir until sugar is completely dissolved. Add vanilla. Stir well. In a large bowl, beat yolks until light lemon color. Then, CAREFULLY, stir hot cream mixture into yolks. Add a pinch of salt. Strain mixture into a 10-inch deep-dish pie plate or eight 4-ounce ramekins. Place dish in a pan of hot water. Bake at 350° for 50-60 minutes; ramekins 35-40 minutes. Custard is cooked when a knife inserted in center comes out clean or almost clean. Cool. Refrigerate until well chilled.

For crust, preheat broiler. Push brown sugar through a sieve. Spread on top of chilled custard, making a layer about ¼ inch thick. It must be as smooth as possible. Broil about 4-6 inches from broiler, turning dish if necessary to broil evenly. Broil until sugar has caramelized (2-5 minutes). Chill or cool before serving. To serve, crack the crust with the back of a spoon and slice custard like pie. Serves 8-10.*

*Custard may be made 2-3 days in advance. Crust may be made several hours in advance. If crust is made in advance, refrigerate before serving.

▼Follow directions precisely!
A fabulous make-ahead dessert.

Caramel Flan

½ cup sugar
2½ tablespoons water
3¾ cups milk
1 vanilla bean or 1½ teaspoons
   vanilla extract

5 large eggs
4 large egg yolks
¾ cup sugar

To caramelize mold: Combine ½ cup sugar and water in a heavy saucepan. Bring to a boil over low heat, STIRRING CONSTANTLY, for at least 10 minutes, until mixture is caramel colored. Immediately pour hot syrup into 6-8 cup mold, turning to coat bottom and sides. Cool.

Flan: Heat milk to simmering. Steep vanilla bean in milk for 10 minutes. Beat eggs and egg yolks with wire whip, gradually adding sugar. When mixture is light and foamy, add milk, in a thin, steady stream. (Beat in vanilla extract if used.) Strain through a fine strainer into mold. Set in pan of boiling water. Bake at 350° in lower third of oven for about 40 minutes or until knife inserted in center of custard comes out clean. Be sure water is simmering. May be served warm or cold. Unmold to serve. Serves 6-8.

Praline Soufflé

1½ cups sugar	2 tablespoons rum
½ teaspoon cream of tartar	4 eggs, separated
½ cup cold water	1 cup milk
1 cup pecans	3 cups whipping cream, whipped
2 envelopes unflavored gelatin	chocolate square, curled
⅔ cup boiling water	green seedless grapes

Prepare praline mixture day before serving. In saucepan, combine sugar, cream of tartar, cold water and pecans. Cook, without stirring, until a dark color, shaking the pan occasionally. Pour mixture on a buttered cookie sheet to cool. Let harden at room temperature. Break some of the praline mixture into blender. Turn on high speed and blend until powdered. Repeat until all the praline mixture is powdered. Place gelatin in large bowl. Add boiling water. Beat with electric mixer until light and frothy. Beat in rum, egg yolks, milk and 3 cups powdered praline mixture. Beat egg whites until stiff. Fold into praline mixture along with the whipped cream. Carefully turn into a 2-quart soufflé dish that has a foil collar tied around it to extend the depth. Refrigerate at least 3 hours. Remove collar and garnish with chocolate curls and green grapes. Serves 12.

Scottish Trifle

Crust:

2 3-ounce packages ladyfingers, split	⅓ cup sherry
	⅓ cup orange juice
6 almond macaroon cookies	

Filling:

4 eggs	6 tablespoons sugar
dash of salt	3 cups milk

Topping:

1 cup whipping cream	1 teaspoon vanilla extract
½ cup powdered sugar	¼ teaspoon almond extract

Crust: Line bottom and sides of dessert bowl with ladyfingers. Sprinkle crumbled macaroons on top. Sprinkle sherry and orange juice over macaroons.
Filling: In top of double boiler, beat eggs, salt, sugar and milk together. Cook over moderate heat, stirring constantly, until mixture coats spoon. Remove from heat and spoon over crust. Chill thoroughly.*
Topping: Before serving, whip cream. Add sugar gradually. Add vanilla and almond extract. Spread over custard. May garnish with raspberries if desired. Serves 10-12.
*May prepare ahead to this point. Keep chilled.
This is a rich dessert guaranteed to please the boss!

Strawberry Bavarian

1 14-ounce can sweetened
   condensed milk
⅓ cup lemon juice
1 tablespoon lemon rind, grated
1 pint fresh strawberries, sliced

1 cup whipping cream
2 tablespoons sugar
2 3-ounce packages ladyfingers,
   split

Combine milk, juice and rind. Stir until thickened. Fold in berries. Whip the cream and add sugar. Fold half of whipped cream into mixture. Line sides and bottom of a 9x5x3-inch loaf pan with ladyfingers. Pour in mixture. Cover top with remaining ladyfingers. Chill until firm (at least 3 hours). Unmold and spread remaining whipped cream on top and sides. Garnish with strawberries. Serves 8.

Strawberry Roll

Sponge Roll:
4 eggs separated
¾ cup sugar, sifted
1 teaspoon vanilla

¾ cup sifted cake flour
¾ teaspoon baking powder
powdered sugar

Filling:
1 pint fresh strawberries
¼ cup sugar
1½ tablespoons cornstarch
1 cup red currant jelly

1 tablespoon rum
1 pint whipping cream, whipped
   and sweetened to taste

Sponge roll: Beat egg yolks until light. Gradually add sugar and beat until creamy. Add vanilla. Sift flour and baking powder together and gradually add it to egg mixture. Beat until smooth. Beat egg whites until stiff but not dry. Fold lightly into batter. Lightly grease a 15½x10½x1-inch jelly roll pan. Line sides and bottom with waxed paper. Pour batter into pan. Bake at 375° for 10-15 minutes or until done. Turn hot cake out on a dish towel which has been sprinkled with powdered sugar, pull waxed paper off and roll cake up in towel. Chill several hours.
Filling: Wash, drain and hull strawberries. Mash enough to make 1 cup mashed. Set remaining strawberries aside. In small saucepan, mix sugar and cornstarch together. Stir in mashed strawberries, jelly and rum. Cook over medium heat, stirring constantly, until jelly is melted and mixture comes to a boil. Reduce heat; boil gently 1 minute. Remove from heat. Pour into bowl. Cool to lukewarm. Carefully unroll cake and spread with filling. Reroll cake and place open end down on serving platter. Chill well. Just before serving, ice cake roll with whipped cream and decorate with remaining strawberries. Serves 8-10.
▼ Make 1 day ahead.

Company Torte

Cake:
½ cup butter	¾ cup sifted plain flour
½ cup sugar	1 teaspoon baking powder
4 egg yolks	1 teaspoon vanilla
4 tablespoons milk	1 cup whipping cream

Meringue:
4 egg whites	½ cup pecans, chopped
1 cup sugar	

Cake: Cream butter and sugar. Add egg yolks and milk. Sift flour and baking powder together. Add to batter. Add vanilla. Beat until well blended. Divide batter evenly into 2 greased and floured 9-inch cake pans.

Meringue: Beat egg whites with sugar until stiff. Spread over cake batter and sprinkle with pecans. Bake at 350° for 20-25 minutes or until done. Watch carefully so pecans do not burn. Turn out on cake rack to cool. Wrap in plastic wrap until ready to assemble. This can be done a day ahead. To assemble, place meringue side of cake on plate and spread sweetened whipped cream on cake. Top with other cake layer, meringue side up. Serves 10-12.

Austrian Lintzer Torte
Roland Mesnier, Pastry Chef, The Homestead, Hot Springs, Virginia

6 ounces butter, softened	6 ounces plain flour
6 ounces sugar	½ teaspoon baking powder
2 ounces almond flour	raspberry preserves
1 teaspoon cinnamon	apricot jam
6 eggs	powdered sugar

Ingredients are by weight and not by measuring cup. Mix butter, sugar, almond flour and cinnamon together. Add eggs one at a time, beating well after each addition, until mixture is very creamy. Then slowly mix in flour and baking powder. Grease a 12-inch mold and line it with paper. Fill mold ⅓ full with mixture. On top of this, put ⅛ inch of raspberry preserves. Put the rest of mixture on this. Pan should not be more than ¾ full. Bake at 300° for 35-45 minutes. Allow to cool. Remove from pan. Glaze top of cake with apricot jam and dust sides with powdered sugar. Serve with vanilla ice cream or vanilla custard sauce. Serves 16.

Lemon Meringue

Meringue Shells:
6 egg whites
dash of salt
1 teaspoon cream of tartar

1 16-ounce box 4X powdered sugar,
sifted

Lemon Filling:
6 egg yolks
¾ cup sugar
juice of 2 lemons

rind of 2 lemons, grated
1 teaspoon vanilla
½ pint whipping cream

Shells: Beat egg whites until very stiff. Add remaining ingredients, adding sugar very slowly. Cut brown paper to fit a cookie sheet. Grease paper and shape mixture on top of paper to form 2 rectangles or circles. Bake at 250° for 50-60 minutes.

Lemon Filling: Cook egg yolks, sugar, lemon juice and rind in double boiler until thickened, stirring constantly. Remove from heat. Add vanilla and let cool. Whip the cream. Fold cream into egg mixture. Layer 1 meringue shell, half of lemon filling, the other meringue shell and the remaining filling.* Serves 8.
*May be made a day ahead.

▼ Do not make meringue shells on a damp or humid day. Top meringue with fresh sugared strawberries and mint leaves, if desired.

Lemon Fluff

7 egg yolks
1¼ cups sugar
juice of 3 lemons (½ cup)
rind of 2 lemons, grated
1 tablespoon unflavored gelatin

¼ cup cold water
7 egg whites
12 ladyfingers, split
whipping cream, whipped and
sweetened

Beat yolks in double boiler with 1 cup sugar until they are light. Add lemon juice and rind. Cook over boiling water, stirring until thickened. Soften gelatin in cold water. Add to hot mixture, stirring to dissolve. Beat egg whites until frothy, adding remaining sugar gradually. Beat until stiff. Fold egg whites into yolk mixture. Line a 2-quart springform pan with ladyfingers. Spoon lemon mixture over ladyfingers. Chill several hours until set, then unmold. Cut into wedges. Garnish with whipped cream. Serves 8-10.
Very light and fluffy so it's nice after a heavy meal.

Lemon Charlotte

<hr>

2 3-ounce packages unfilled
  lady fingers, split
1 envelope unflavored gelatin
4 tablespoons fresh lemon juice
5 eggs, beaten

½ cup sugar
pinch of salt
2 teaspoons lemon rind, grated
½ pint whipping cream

Sauce:
3 tablespoons apricot preserves
3 tablespoons orange marmalade
juice of 1 orange

1 tablespoon fresh lemon juice
2 tablespoons butter
¼ cup slivered almonds

Line bottom and sides of a 7 or 8-inch springform pan or bowl with lady fingers. Soften gelatin in lemon juice. Dissolve over hot water. Place eggs, sugar and salt in top of double boiler over simmering water. Beat with electric beater until mixture is thick and light in color. Add dissolved gelatin mixture and lemon peel, beating a few seconds more. Cool. Whip cream and fold into mixture. Pour into springform pan or bowl. Refrigerate overnight.
Sauce: Melt first 4 ingredients together over low heat. In separate saucepan, melt butter and add almonds. Sauté until lightly browned. Add almonds to sauce. Blend well. Remove from heat. Sauce should be served at room temperature. Top each serving with a spoonful of sauce. Serves 8-12.

Wine Bars and Glaze
Mrs. Jack Nicklaus, wife of Masters' champion, 1963, 1965, 1966, 1972 and 1975

<hr>

Bars:
1 cup butter, softened
1½ cups brown sugar
2 eggs
1 tablespoon vanilla
4 tablespoons milk

4 tablespoons port wine
2 cups walnuts or pecans,
  chopped
12 tablespoons plain flour
1 teaspoon baking powder

Glaze:
2 cups powdered sugar
2 tablespoons butter

4 tablespoons port wine
dash of salt

Bars: Cream butter and sugar. Add eggs and beat well. Add vanilla, milk and wine. Add nuts alternately with dry ingredients which have been sifted together. Put in buttered and floured 9x13-inch pan. Bake at 350° for 20-30 minutes.
Glaze: Combine glaze ingredients. Beat well. When cake is cool, top with glaze. Cut into bars.

Bananas Foster

4 tablespoons butter
4 tablespoons light brown sugar
3 ripe bananas
pinch of cinnamon

1 tablespoon banana liqueur
1½ ounces rum or brandy, warmed
vanilla ice cream

Cook butter and brown sugar over medium heat in flambé pan or large skillet until caramelized. Quarter bananas lengthwise, then cut in halves or thirds. Add bananas to pan. Cook until tender, turning once. Add cinnamon and liqueur. Stir. Pour rum or brandy on top of mixture. DO NOT STIR. Flame. Spoon mixture over vanilla ice cream while flaming. Serves 6.

Crêpes Fitzgerald

4 heaping teaspoons cream
  cheese
4 tablespoons sour cream
1 tablespoon powdered sugar
4 crêpes

3 pats butter
1 10-ounce package frozen
  sliced strawberries, thawed
1½ ounces strawberry liqueur
1½ ounces kirsch

Have cream cheese and sour cream at room temperature. Combine cream cheese, sour cream and sugar. Fill each crêpe with 1 heaping tablespoon cream cheese mixture and roll. Place on dessert plates, 2 for each serving. Melt butter in flambé pan. Add strawberries and simmer. Pour strawberry liqueur over strawberries. Add warmed kirsch. Ignite and flame. When flame burns out, pour over crêpes and serve. Serves 2.

Peach Refrigerator Cake

½ pound marshmallows
½ cup orange juice
3 ounces ginger ale
1 cup whipping cream, whipped

sponge cake or lady fingers
6-8 peaches, sliced
½ cup crystallized ginger,
  chopped

Cut marshmallows in quarters. Combine marshmallows and orange juice. Stir over hot water until marshmallows are almost melted. Cool slightly. Add ginger ale. When slightly thickened, fold in ¾ cup whipped cream. Line a springform pan with waxed paper. Arrange layer of cake or lady fingers on bottom, then a layer of peaches, then layer of filling. Repeat until there are 3 layers of cake, 2 layers of peaches and 2 layers of filling. Chill overnight. Unmold and garnish with remaining peaches and whipped cream. Sprinkle ginger on top. Serves 6-8.

Danish Apple Cake
Mrs. Billy Casper, wife of 1970 Masters' champion

1 cup sugar
2 sticks butter
1 teaspoon cinnamon
1 4-ounce package Holland Rusk

2 pints whipping cream
2 tablespoons sugar (to taste)
1 quart applesauce
sliced almonds

Melt sugar, butter and cinnamon. Add crushed Holland Rusk, stirring until well coated. Stiffly beat cream, adding sugar. In an 11¾x7½x1¾-inch baking dish, layer alternately Rusk mixture, applesauce and cream. Top with cream layer. Sprinkle with almonds. Chill overnight. Serves 12.
Good with pork!

Easy Fresh Peach Cobbler

2 cups peaches, peeled and sliced
½ cup sugar
1 stick butter
1 cup sugar

½ cup milk
1 cup sifted plain flour
1½ teaspoons baking powder
pinch of salt

Mix peaches with ½ cup sugar. Let stand for 30 minutes or until juice forms. Melt butter in 2-quart baking dish. Make batter of remaining ingredients. Pour batter over butter, then pour fruit and juice over batter. DO NOT STIR. Bake at 350° for 30-45 minutes or until brown. Serves 8-10.

▼ Other fruits may be substituted for peaches.

Fresh Peach Cobbler

1 quart fresh peaches, peeled
   and sliced
¾-1 cup sugar
1 stick butter or margarine

1½ cups all-purpose flour
¾ teaspoon salt
½ cup shortening
5-6 tablespoons cold water

Combine peaches, sugar and margarine in 1½-quart saucepan. Cook slowly, stirring often, until peaches are tender and syrup begins to thicken. Transfer to 1½-quart baking dish and set aside. Sift flour and salt together; cut shortening into flour with pastry blender or fork until particles are size of peas. Sprinkle water evenly over flour mixture, using just enough to dampen flour. Stir gently until dough clings lightly together when pressed with fingers. Place on floured board and roll out in a thin layer. Cut into strips 1-1½ inches wide. Cover peaches with some of the pastry strips. Bake at 350° until pastry is lightly browned. Gently punch browned pastry into peach mixture with a spoon. Add another layer of pastry strips and brown. Serves 6.

Poached Pears Chantilly
Augusta Country Club

Sugar Syrup:
3 cups water   4 cups sugar

Poached Pears:
6 firm, ripe pears   red food coloring
1 12-ounce jar red currant jelly   1 tablespoon cornstarch
3 cups sugar syrup   ½ cup Cointreau

Chantilly Cream:
1 cup whipping cream   2 tablespoons brandy
2 tablespoons confectioners   1 egg white, stiffly beaten
  sugar

Prepare sugar syrup by boiling water and sugar for 5 minutes. Set aside. Peel pears, leaving stems intact. Melt jelly in 3 cups sugar syrup in a saucepan over medium heat. Bring to a boil. Add enough food coloring for deep red color. Place pears in baking pan stems up and pour syrup over pears. Bake covered at 275° for 1 hour. Carefully remove pears and place in serving dish. Pour syrup from baking pan into saucepan. Bring to a boil. Combine cornstarch and Cointreau. Stir into syrup and cook until clear and thickened. To make Chantilly cream, whip cream until soft peaks form. Gradually add sugar. Add brandy slowly. Fold in egg white gently but thoroughly. Pour syrup over pears and serve hot or cold with Chantilly cream.

Macaroon Pudding

2 envelopes unflavored gelatin   1 tablespoon vanilla
1 quart milk   4 egg whites, stiffly beaten
4 egg yolks   10-12 almond macaroons, crumbled
1 cup sugar   ½ pint whipping cream

Soften gelatin in ½ cup of the milk and set aside. Beat egg yolks and add sugar. Mix well. Add remaining milk. Pour mixture into top of double boiler. When mixture is hot, add gelatin, stirring constantly. Cook mixture until it begins to curdle. Remove from heat. Let cool slightly. Add vanilla. Fold in egg whites. Place macaroon crumbs around the bottom of a 1½-quart ring mold. Pour custard mixture into mold carefully so crumbs will not float to top. Allow to congeal overnight. Unmold. Fill center with cream which has been whipped and sweetened to taste. *A beautiful layered dessert. May also be served in parfait glasses.*

Easy Apple-Pecan Crisp

4 cups tart apples, sliced and
   sprinkled with lemon juice
¾ cup brown sugar, packed
½ cup sifted plain flour
½ cup rolled oats

¾ teaspoon cinnamon
¾ teaspoon nutmeg
½ cup butter, softened
½ cup pecans, chopped

Butter 8-inch square pan. Spread apples on bottom. Blend remaining ingredients until crumbly. Spread over apples. Bake at 350° until apples are tender and top is golden brown (about 30-45 minutes). Serve with whipped cream or ice cream. Serves 6.

The Rector's Cheesecake

Crisco
2 cups pecans, chopped
4 8-ounce packages cream cheese
   (room temperature)

1½ cups sugar
6 large eggs
2 tablespoons lemon juice

Grease sides and bottom of springform pan with Crisco. Sprinkle pecans on bottom and sides of pan so there will be an all-over crust when cake is removed from pan. Cream the cheese and sugar together. Add eggs one at a time, mixing until completely smooth, then add lemon juice. Bake at 450° for 35-40 minutes. Let cool. Keep refrigerated. Serves 10.

▼ May top with fresh strawberries or blueberries or Comstock blueberry or cherry pie filling.

Chocolate Fondue

2 tablespoons honey or
   light corn syrup
½ cup half-and-half
1 bar (8¾ or 9-ounces) milk
   chocolate, broken

¼ cup almonds or pecans,
   finely chopped and toasted
1 teaspoon vanilla
2 tablespoons orange liqueur

Heat honey and cream in ceramic or metal fondue pot over high heat. Lower heat and stir in chocolate pieces. Heat, stirring constantly, until chocolate is melted. Stir in nuts, vanilla and liqueur. Cool slightly. Let each person spear their choice of the following: angel food cake squares, apple wedges, banana slices, canned or fresh pineapple chunks, strawberries, mandarin orange sections, seedless grapes, tiny marshmallows, pears or popcorn. Yields 1½ cups.
Try this instead of ice cream and cake for a child's birthday party.

239

Mocha Baked Alaska

5 ounces (or squares) semi-sweet chocolate, cut into bits
4 tablespoons dark rum
2 tablespoons cold, strong coffee
5 egg yolks

1½ cups sugar
9 egg whites
2 pinches of salt
3 pints coffee ice cream, softened
confectioners sugar, sifted

Cake: Butter a 9-inch round cake pan. Line it with waxed paper and butter the paper. In top of a double boiler, melt chocolate with 2 tablespoons rum and 2 tablespoons coffee. Let cool. In a bowl, beat egg yolks until frothy. Beat in ½ cup sugar, ¼ cup at a time, and beat for several minutes, or until it ribbons when beater is lifted. In a bowl, beat 5 egg whites with a pinch of salt until they form stiff peaks. Add cooled chocolate mixture to the egg yolk mixture, combining well, and fold in ¼ of the whites, lightly but thoroughly. Pour the mixture over remaining whites and lightly fold the batter together until there are no traces of white. Pour batter into pan and spread it evenly with a metal spatula. Bake in a preheated moderate oven (350°) for 20 minutes. Turn oven off and let cake stand in oven for 5 minutes. Remove and cool 10 minutes. Turn out on rack and remove waxed paper. Chill cake.

Ice Cream: Beat ice cream until smoooth but not melted. Pack in 8-inch pie pan and freeze for 1 hour or until firm. Release ice cream on top of cake. Freeze overnight on a wooden board.*

Meringue: Beat 4 egg whites with pinch of salt until they hold soft peaks. Beat in 1 cup sugar, a little at a time, and beat until meringue is stiff. Lightly fold in 2 tablespoons rum. With a metal spatula, spread a thick layer of meringue over cake and ice cream. Sprinkle meringue with confectioners sugar and brown on wooden board in upper part of a very hot (500°) preheated oven for 5 minutes or until meringue is golden. Transfer Baked Alaska to cake platter and serve immediately. Serves 12.

*May be made several days ahead to this point.

Pots-de-Crème

1 6-ounce package semi-sweet chocolate bits
1 cup half-and-half cream
1 egg

1 teaspoon vanilla
pinch of salt
¼ cup good brandy or cognac

Put chocolate pieces in blender. Heat cream to boiling point. Pour cream over chocolate bits. Blend on high one minute. (Hold blender top on.) Turn off blender. Add egg, vanilla and salt. Reblend. Add brandy or cognac. Reblend. Let thicken a little and pour into pots-de-crème or ramekins. Chill. Serves 4-6.

❦ Flavor is enhanced if left overnight before serving.

Chocolate Mousse

6 ounces semi-sweet chocolate
2 tablespoons Kahlua
1 tablespoon orange juice
2 egg yolks
2 whole eggs

1 teaspoon vanilla
¼ cup sugar
1 cup whipping cream
garnish: whipped cream and
    chocolate shavings

Melt chocolate in Kahlua and orange juice over very low heat. Set aside. Put yolks and eggs in blender with vanilla and sugar. Blend 2 minutes at medium high speed. Add cream and blend 30 seconds. Add chocolate mixture and blend until smooth. Pour into bowl or small individual cups. Chill. Garnish. Serves 4-5.

Chocolate Mint Mousse

1 6-ounce package chocolate
    chips
¼ cup boiling water
4 eggs, separated
3 tablespoons crème de menthe

¼ pound butter, softened
1 tablespoon sugar
½ cup whipping cream, whipped
    and sweetened to taste

Put chocolate chips in blender. Blend until grated. Scrape sides. Add boiling water and blend until melted. Add egg yolks and crème de menthe. Blend again. Pour into mixing bowl. Beat in butter a little at a time. In another bowl, beat egg whites until soft peaks form. Add sugar and beat until stiff. Fold about ¼ of the egg whites into chocolate mixture. Fold in remaining egg whites. Pour into lightly oiled mold or bowl. Chill 4 hours or until firm. Dip in hot water to unmold.* Garnish with whipped cream. Serves 8.
*Can be prepared a day ahead. Add whipped cream at last minute.
This is a very rich dessert.

Coffee Mousse

1 cup strong coffee
½ cup sugar
1 tablespoon unflavored gelatin
½ cup cold water

2 eggs, beaten separately
1 teaspoon vanilla
½ pint whipping cream, whipped
nuts and whipped cream

Boil coffee and sugar until syrupy. Soften gelatin in water. Add to coffee mixture. Remove from heat. Add eggs one at a time. Add vanilla. Let cool until it begins to thicken, then fold in whipped cream. Put in mold and chill until firm. Serve topped with whipped cream and nuts. Serves 8.

Coffee Gel Dessert

2 envelopes unflavored gelatin
½ cup coffee liqueur
3 cups hot black coffee

¾ cup sugar
pinch of salt
whipping cream

Sprinkle gelatin over liqueur to soften. Add coffee, sugar and salt. Stir until mixture is clear. Pour into 8 individual molds or sherbet glasses. Chill until firm. Garnish with lightly sweetened whipped cream, squeezed from a pastry bag. Serves 8.

▼ May substitute a good brandy for coffee liqueur.
This is a nice light dessert to follow a heavy meal.

English Toffee Dessert

¾ cup sugar
½ cup whipping cream
¼ cup light corn syrup
2 tablespoons butter

½ cup Heath bars, broken
2 pints fresh strawberries,
   hulled
1 cup sour cream

Combine first 4 ingredients in saucepan. Boil for 1 minute. Remove from heat, stir in candy and cool.* Serve sauce over strawberries topped with sour cream. Serves 6-8.
*Sauce may be made well ahead and left to stand. Stir occasionally.

Frozen Mocha Toffee Dessert

8 ladyfingers, split
2 tablespoons dry instant coffee
1 tablespoon boiling water
1 quart vanilla ice cream,
   softened

4 chocolate-covered toffee bars,
   frozen and crushed (1 cup)
½ cup whipping cream
2 tablespoons white crème de cacao

Line bottom and 2 inches up sides of 8-inch springform pan with ladyfingers, cutting to fit. Dissolve coffee in boiling water. Cool. Stir coffee, ice cream and candy together. Spoon into pan, cover and freeze until firm. Before serving, combine cream and crème de cacao. Whip to soft peaks. Spread over top. Garnish with pieces of additional broken toffee bars if desired. Serves 8-10.

Cornelia's Mocha Log

Cake:
4 eggs
¾ cup sugar
¼ cup sifted plain flour
¼ teaspoon baking powder

¼ teaspoon salt
¼ cup cocoa
½ teaspoon vanilla
powdered sugar

Filling:
4 teaspoons dry instant coffee
2 cups whipping cream

½ cup sifted 4X powdered
   sugar

Beat eggs until very light in color. Add sugar gradually until thick. Sift dry ingredients together. Fold into egg mixture. Add vanilla. Pour into 10x15-inch jelly roll pan which has been greased and lined with waxed paper. Bake at 350° about 20-25 minutes. Turn hot cake out on a dish towel which has been sprinkled with powdered sugar, pull waxed paper off and roll cake up in towel. Chill several hours. Prepare filling by dissolving coffee in cream. Whip the cream. Add sugar. Unroll cake and spread with half of filling. Roll up jelly roll fashion and ice with remainder of filling.* Serves 8.
*This can be made a day ahead.
▼ Garnish with chocolate curls, cherries, chopped nuts and add holly at Christmas time.
Luncheon or dinner party dessert. Men adore it!

Chocolate Nut Bombe

1 quart coffee ice cream,
   softened
½ cup walnuts, chopped
1 quart chocolate ice cream
1 tablespoon brandy or
   white crème de menthe
1 pint vanilla ice cream

2 squares unsweetened chocolate,
   melted and cooled
¼ cup light corn syrup
1 egg
garnish: chopped walnuts
   (optional)

Line 2-quart mixing bowl with foil. Blend coffee ice cream and walnuts together. Pack this mixture on bottom and sides of bowl forming a shell. Freeze until firm. Pack softened chocolate ice cream over coffee-nut layer to form second shell. Freeze. Blend liqueur into softened vanilla ice cream. Pack in center of mold. Freeze several hours. Turn mold out onto cold tray or serving plate. Peel off foil. Return mold to freezer. Freeze overnight. Combine chocolate, corn syrup and egg in small bowl of mixer. Beat 3 or 4 minutes or until thick and fluffy. Quickly frost mold with chocolate mixture. Sprinkle top and sides with walnuts, if desired. Freeze 1 hour or until serving time. Serves 12.
▼ Pecans may be substituted for walnuts.

Ann's Ice Cream Bombe

Aunt Peg's Chocolate Sauce:

½ cup butter
2 squares unsweetened chocolate
¼ cup cocoa

¾ cup sugar
½ cup whipping cream
½ teaspoon vanilla

Bombe:

¼ cup dark rum
½ cup water
sugar to taste
2 3-ounce packages lady
   fingers, split

½ gallon vanilla ice cream,
   softened
1 quart orange sherbet,
   softened

Sauce: Melt butter and chocolate together. Add remaining ingredients, except vanilla. Bring to a boil over medium heat. Add vanilla. Let cool.

Bombe: Place a piece of wax paper on bottom of 2½-quart soufflé dish, casserole or charlotte mold. Mix rum, water and sugar. Dip each lady finger in rum mixture. Line bottom of mold, trimming lady fingers as necessary to cover well. Line the sides of mold with vertical lady fingers. Place half of vanilla ice cream on bottom of mold, spreading smoothly. Pour a thin layer of chocolate sauce over ice cream. Next add sherbet, spreading smoothly. Again, cover with a layer of chocolate sauce. Add remaining ice cream, spreading smoothly. Cover with waxed paper. Place in freezer for at least 4 hours.* When ready, unmold on serving platter. Serves 6-8.

*Can be prepared and kept frozen for several weeks.

Basic French Vanilla Ice Cream

6 egg yolks
2 cups milk
1 cup sugar
¼ teaspoon salt

1 vanilla bean, split lengthwise,
   or 2 tablespoons vanilla
   extract
2 cups whipping cream

Beat yolks and milk in top of double boiler until well blended. Stir in sugar, salt and vanilla bean (if extract is used, add after cooling). Cook, stirring constantly, over hot (not boiling) water until mixture coats a metal spoon. Cool, then cover. Refrigerate until well chilled. Stir in cream and vanilla extract, or if vanilla bean was used, remove it and scrape inside of bean into custard. Chill until ready to churn. Yields about 2 quarts.

Ice Cream Cake

20 lady fingers, split
2 quarts vanilla ice cream
1 6-ounce can frozen orange
   juice concentrate
2 10-ounce packages frozen
   raspberries
2 8¼-ounce cans crushed pineapple

1 tablespoon frozen lemonade
   concentrate
1 teaspoon almond flavoring
1 teaspoon rum flavoring
6 maraschino cherries, chopped
3 tablespoons blanched
   pistachio nuts, chopped

garnish: whipped cream, sugared strawberries and mint leaves

First layer: Line bottom and sides of a 9-inch springform pan with lady fingers. *Second layer:* Mix 1 quart softened ice cream with orange juice. Pour into pan and freeze until firm. *Third layer:* Put raspberries and pineapple in blender with lemonade concentrate. Blend. Strain. Freeze until partially frozen. Place in chilled bowl and beat slightly. Spoon over orange layer and refreeze. *Fourth layer:* Add almond and rum flavoring, cherries and nuts to remaining ice cream. Pour over raspberry layer. Freeze overnight. Remove from freezer 2 hours before serving and put in refrigerator. Garnish. Serves 12.
An excellent summer dessert.

Apricot Brandy Ice Cream

1¼ cups sugar
2 egg yolks, well beaten
¾ cup brandy

1 17-ounce can apricots, drained
   and mashed
1 quart half-and-half

Add sugar to egg yolks. Stir brandy into apricot pulp. Add sugar mixture and cream to apricot mixture. Churn.

Chocolate Chip Ice Cream

2¼ cups sugar
4 eggs, beaten
5 cups milk
4 cups whipping cream

4½ teaspoons vanilla
½ teaspoon salt
1⅔ cups semi-sweet chocolate,
   chopped or grated

Add sugar gradually to eggs. Beat until mixture is very stiff. Add remaining ingredients except chocolate. Mix thoroughly. Pour into gallon freezer. Churn about 15 minutes or until ice cream has frozen to a mushy consistency. Add chocolate. Churn until frozen. Yields 4 quarts.
▼Amount of chocolate can be reduced from 1⅔ to 1 cup if preferred.

French Chocolate Ice Cream

¼ cup sugar
½ cup water
1 6-ounce package semi-sweet
  chocolate pieces

3 egg yolks
1½ cups whipping cream,
  whipped

In small saucepan, bring sugar and water to a rapid boil. Put hot sugar mixture and chocolate pieces in blender. Cover and blend on high for 6 seconds or until smooth. Add egg yolks, cover and blend for 5 seconds. Stir mixture down if necessary. Fold chocolate mixture into whipped cream. Spoon into refrigerator tray and freeze for 2-3 hours or until frozen. Ice cream remains creamy without stirring. Serves 6.

Peach Ice Cream

12 peaches
2 cups sugar
1 14 or 15-ounce can sweetened
  condensed milk

2 quarts milk
1 8-ounce carton sour cream
2 teaspoons vanilla

Mix peaches and sugar together in blender. Add peach and sugar mixture to other ingredients and churn until frozen. Yields approximately 4 quarts.
▼ Bananas or strawberries can be substituted for the peaches.

Fruit Sherbet

2 ripe bananas, sliced
juice of 2 medium oranges
juice of 2 medium lemons
1½ cups sugar
1 cup milk

1 cup water
¼ cup maraschino cherries,
  chopped
3 tablespoons cherry juice

Combine bananas, orange and lemon juices in blender. Add remaining ingredients and blend well. Pour into 6-cup ice tray or 9x5x3-inch loaf pan. Freeze until firm. Remove and break into chunks in chilled mixing bowl. Beat until smooth. Return to freezer. Cover and freeze until firm. Yields 2½ pints.
▼ Prepare 1 day before serving.

Orange Ice

1 16-ounce can peaches, drained
1½ cups fresh orange juice and
   pulp

juice of 1½ lemons
1 cup sugar

Mash peaches with fork and add juices and orange pulp. Stir in sugar until dissolved. Pour in ice tray and freeze. Serves 5-6.
Light, refreshing dessert after a heavy meal.

Lemon Ice Cream

juice of 8-9 lemons
3 cups sugar

¾ pint whipping cream
1½ quarts whole milk

Mix all ingredients and churn in ice cream freezer. Serves 8-10.

Frozen Orange Cream

1 cup milk
1 cup whipping cream
1 cup sugar
juice of 1 orange

rind of 1 orange, grated
6 orange cups, halved and
   scooped out

Combine milk, cream and sugar. Stir until sugar is dissolved. Freeze until mushy, about 1 hour. Mix with orange juice and rind in mixer on medium speed for 3 minutes. Fill orange halves and freeze until solid, about 3 hours. Serves 6.

Grape Ice Cream

1 cup sugar
¼ teaspoon salt
4 eggs, beaten
4 cups milk, scalded
2½ cups sugar
1 cup milk

juice of 1 lemon
2 quarts unsweetened
   grape juice
1 quart whipping cream,
   slightly whipped

Add 1 cup sugar and salt to eggs. Slowly add scalded milk. Return to low heat, stirring constantly until mixture coats a wooden spoon. Remove from heat. Add 2½ cups sugar and milk. Let cool. When cold, add remaining ingredients. Pour into churn and freeze. Yields 1½ gallons.

Old-Time Chocolate Sauce for Ice Cream

3 squares unsweetened chocolate 1½ cups confectioners sugar
¼ cup butter or margarine 1 5.3-ounce can evaporated milk

Combine all ingredients in top of double boiler. Cover and heat over boiling water. Stir well when chocolate melts. Cook 30 minutes, stirring occasionally. Yields 1 pint.

▼ Can be refrigerated and reheated in double boiler each time before serving.

Dear's Chocolate Sauce

1 cup sugar ⅓ stick butter
2 heaping tablespoons cocoa 1 teaspoon vanilla
1 tablespoon cornstarch ½ cup nuts (optional)
½ cup milk vanilla ice cream

In a saucepan, mix dry ingredients together and stir in milk. Cook over low heat for 5-10 minutes, stirring only occasionally. Add butter and vanilla. Sprinkle nuts on top. Serve warm over ice cream. Yields 1 cup.

Peppermint Sauce

1 cup sugar ⅛ teaspoon peppermint flavoring
2 tablespoons cornstarch red food coloring
½-1 cup water old-fashioned peppermint candy,
¼ cup light Karo syrup broken into pieces

Combine sugar and cornstarch. Add water and Karo and place over low heat, stirring constantly until sugar is dissolved and mixture comes to a boil. Remove from heat. Add flavoring and several drops of food coloring. Cool. Add candy. Serves 12.

Orange Sauce

½ cup sugar 1 teaspoon fresh mint leaves,
½ cup orange juice finely chopped

Combine ingredients in saucepan. Cook until it comes to a full boil. Remove from heat. Chill. Yields 1 cup.

▼ Delicious served over sherbet garnished with mint sprigs and orange sections.

Lemon Whipped Cream Sauce
Byron Nelson, Masters' champion 1937 and 1942

1 cup sugar
½ cup lemon juice
2 tablespoons lemon peel, grated

3 eggs
1 cup whipping cream, whipped

Put sugar, lemon juice and lemon peel in top of double boiler. Place over direct heat, stirring constantly until sugar dissolves. Remove from heat. Beat eggs until blended. Add a little of hot mixture to eggs to warm them. Pour eggs into sugar mixture slowly, stirring constantly. Return to top of double boiler over simmering water and cook until thickened. Stir often. Remove and cool thoroughly. Fold in whipped cream. Chill. Serves 12.
This is excellent over pound cake or any fresh fruit.

Praline Sauce

2 cups dark Karo syrup
⅓ cup sugar
⅓ cup boiling water

1½ cups pecans, chopped
1½ teaspoons vanilla

Combine all ingredients. Bring to a boil. Remove from heat. Serve over vanilla ice cream. Yields 2½ cups.
▼ This can be stored in refrigerator for several weeks.

Brandied Butterscotch Sauce

¾ cup dark brown sugar, packed
dash of salt
½ cup water
1 tablespoon dry instant coffee

¼ cup brandy
1 14-ounce can sweetened
condensed milk
1 teaspoon vanilla

Combine sugar, salt and water in small saucepan. Bring to a boil, stirring constantly. Cook to 230° on candy thermometer. Melt coffee in brandy. Pour milk into bowl. Stir in hot syrup until blended. Pour in coffee-brandy mixture and vanilla. Stir. Pour into hot sterilized container or several small jars for gift giving. Serve warm over ice cream. Yields 2 cups.
▼ Stores on shelf or if opened, in refrigerator.

Cookies
and Candy
16

Dot's Butterscotch Brownies

1 16-ounce box light brown sugar
1½ sticks butter
2 eggs
2 cups plain flour

2 teaspoons baking powder
1 teaspoon salt
1 teaspoon vanilla
1 cup nuts, chopped

Melt brown sugar and butter together. Cool. Add eggs. Mix flour, baking powder, salt, vanilla and nuts together. Add to other mixture. Mix well. Bake in greased 9x13 pan at 350° for 30 minutes. Yields 25-30 squares.
Probably the best blond brownie you will ever eat!

Delicious Bars

2 sticks butter
1 cup dark brown sugar
1 egg yolk
2 cups plain flour

1 teaspoon vanilla
¼ teaspoon salt
15 1.2-ounce chocolate
     Hershey bars

Cream butter and sugar. Add egg yolk, flour, vanilla and salt. Put in greased 9x13-inch pan. Bake at 350° for 20 minutes. Remove from oven and top immediately with chocolate bars. Smooth with knife when melted. Let cool and cut into bars. Yields 3 dozen.

Oatmeal Crisps

1 cup sifted plain flour
¼ teaspoon salt
½ teaspoon baking powder
½ teaspoon baking soda
½ cup margarine
½ cup dark brown sugar, packed

½ cup white sugar
1 egg
1 tablespoon water
1 teaspoon vanilla
1½ cups oatmeal
½ cup nuts, chopped

Sift together flour, salt, baking powder and soda. Set aside. Cream margarine and sugars. Add egg and beat until fluffy. Add water and vanilla. Add ⅓ of oatmeal and ⅓ of flour. Mix well. Add remainder of oatmeal and flour in thirds. Mix well after each addition. Fold in nuts. Drop by teaspoonfuls onto greased baking sheet. Bake at 350° for 10-12 minutes or until light brown. Yields 4-5 dozen.

Chocolate Peppermint Sticks

Cookies:
4 eggs
2 cups sugar
1 cup cocoa
1 cup plain flour

½ teaspoon peppermint extract
1 teaspoon vanilla
2 sticks butter, melted

Frosting:
2¾ cups 10X powdered sugar
1 stick butter
½ teaspoon peppermint extract

milk
3 drops green food coloring
  (optional)

Coating:
2 1-ounce squares unsweetened
  chocolate

2 tablespoons butter

To make cookies, beat eggs and sugar together by hand until thick. Add cocoa and flour. Mix well. Add peppermint, vanilla and butter. Spread into a greased 11x17-inch pan. Bake at 350° for 15 minutes. DO NOT OVERBAKE. For frosting, beat powdered sugar and butter until creamy. Add peppermint. Add enough milk to obtain desired consistency for icing. Food coloring may be added if desired. Frost cookies with mixture. To make coating, melt chocolate and butter. Paint on frosted cookies with a pastry brush. Chill 10 minutes before cutting into fingers. Yields 96 cookies.

Date Nut Roll Cookies

Filling:
½ pound chopped dates
⅓ cup water

¼ cup sugar
1 cup nuts, chopped

Dough:
½ cup margarine
½ cup dark brown sugar
½ cup white sugar
1 egg, well beaten

½ teaspoon vanilla
2 cups sifted plain flour
½ teaspoon baking soda
½ teaspoon salt

Filling: Combine dates, water and sugar, and cook for 5 minutes. Add nuts. Let cool.
Dough: Blend margarine and sugars. Add egg and vanilla. Sift flour, soda and salt together. Add to other ingredients. Chill dough thoroughly and roll out as thin as possible. Spread filling on dough and roll like a jelly roll. Wrap in waxed paper and freeze. Slice thinly while frozen. Bake at 375° for 5-6 minutes or until light brown. Yields approximately 3 dozen.

Fruitcake Cookies

1 cup butter or margarine
1 cup dark brown sugar
3 eggs, beaten
3 tablespoons bourbon plus
  enough milk to make ½ cup
3 cups plain flour
1 teaspoon cloves
1 teaspoon cinnamon

1 teaspoon nutmeg
1 teaspoon baking soda
½ pound candied cherries, ground
½ pound candied pineapple, ground
½ pound dates
½ pound raisins
6 cups nuts, chopped

Cream butter and sugar. Add eggs. Beat in bourbon and milk. Sift flour with spices and soda. Blend into other ingredients. Add candied fruits, dates, raisins and nuts. Dough is stiff and hard to mix. Drop onto greased cookie sheet. Bake at 300° for 30 minutes. Yields approximately 6 dozen.

Date Bar Delight

½ stick butter
1 cup dark brown sugar
2 eggs
4-6 ounces dates, chopped
¼ cup pecans, chopped

½ cup plain flour
¼ teaspoon salt
1 teaspoon baking powder
½ teaspoon vanilla
powdered sugar

Cook butter and sugar together until smooth and blended. Cool. Add unbeaten eggs and beat. Add dates and nuts. Sift flour, salt and baking powder. Add to butter mixture. Stir in vanilla. Spread in 8x8x1-inch pan lined with brown paper. Bake at 350° for 25 minutes. When cool, cut into finger-shaped pieces and roll in powdered sugar. Yields 25-30 bars.

Spritz Cookies

¾ cup butter
½ cup sugar
1 egg yolk
1 teaspoon orange rind, grated

½ teaspoon orange extract
2-2¼ cups sifted plain flour
¼ teaspoon salt

Cream butter and sugar. Beat in egg yolk, then rind and extract. Sift flour and salt together. Gradually add flour mixture to other ingredients until of consistency to put through cookie press. Allow dough to come to room temperature. Put through cookie press onto ungreased cookie sheet. Bake at 425°-450° for 8-10 minutes.

▼ For chocolate cookies, add 5 tablespoons cocoa and use a whole egg.

Marbled Fudge Bars

Fudge:

1 cup margarine
4 1-ounce squares unsweetened
  chocolate
2 cups sugar
3 eggs

1 cup plain flour
½ teaspoon salt
1 cup walnuts, chopped
1 teaspoon vanilla

Marbling:

1 8-ounce package cream cheese
½ cup sugar

1 egg
1 teaspoon vanilla

To make fudge, melt margarine and chocolate in 2-quart saucepan over low heat. With spoon, beat in sugar and eggs until well blended. Stir in flour, salt, nuts and vanilla. Spread batter evenly in a greased 13x9 baking dish. For marbling, combine softened cream cheese, sugar, egg and vanilla in mixer. Beat at low speed until just mixed. Increase speed to medium and beat 2 minutes, scraping bowl occasionally. Drop mixture in dollops on top of fudge batter. Using tip of knife, lightly score top surface in a crisscross pattern. Bake at 350° for 40-45 minutes. Cool and cut into bars. Yields 3 dozen.

▼ May be refrigerated up to one week.

Melting Moments

Cookie:

½ pound butter or margarine
5½ tablespoons powdered sugar
1¼ cups plain flour

½ cup cornstarch
¼ teaspoon almond extract
¼ teaspoon orange extract

Glaze:

1 cup powdered sugar
1 tablespoon butter or
  margarine, melted

1 tablespoon lemon juice
1 tablespoon orange juice

Cookie: Cream butter and sugar in large bowl of electric mixer. Sift in flour and cornstarch. Mix thoroughly. Add flavorings. Mix well. Chill for 1 hour. Shape into balls the size of a walnut. Place on greased cookie sheet about 2 inches apart. Flatten to about ¼-inch with the bottom of a wet glass or the palm of your hand. Be careful not to get cookies too thin. Bake at 350° for 10 minutes. These cookies do not brown. Carefully remove from pan while warm.
Glaze: Beat all ingredients together. Spread over warm cookies. Yields 25 cookies.

▼ Keep in airtight container. Must be handled carefully to avoid breaking. This is a special party cookie and is not just to fill the cookie jar.

Jewel Cookies

1 stick butter
3 tablespoons 10X powdered sugar
1 cup sifted plain flour
1 teaspoon vanilla

1 cup pecans, ground or finely chopped
jam or jelly

Cream butter with sugar. Stir in flour to make soft dough. Add vanilla and nuts. Chill until firm enough to handle. Roll a teaspoon of dough at a time into marble size balls. Place 2 inches apart on ungreased cookie sheet. Make a hollow in center of each with thumb. Fill with ½ teaspoon jam or jelly. Bake at 300° for 20 minutes or until lightly browned. Remove from cookie sheet and cool completely on racks. Yields 3 dozen.

Martha's Kisses

2 egg whites
pinch salt
½ cup sugar
½ teaspoon vanilla

1 6-ounce package butterscotch bits
½ cup nuts, chopped

Preheat oven to 375°. Beat egg whites and salt until soft peaks form. Slowly add sugar and continue beating until stiff peaks form. Add vanilla. Fold in butterscotch bits and nuts. Cover cookie sheet with brown paper or aluminum foil. Drop by teaspoon onto cookie sheet. Put in oven, close door and turn off heat. Let kisses remain in oven until oven cools to room temperature, or about 3 hours. Yields approximately 36.

Peanut Butter Cookies

½ cup butter
½ cup peanut butter
½ cup white sugar
½ cup brown sugar
1 egg, well beaten

1¾ cups plain flour
¾ teaspoon baking soda
¼ teaspoon salt
½ teaspoon baking powder

Cream butter and peanut butter. Add sugars gradually, beating until fluffy. Add egg. Sift dry ingredients. Add to sugar mixture. This will be very stiff. With fingers, form into hickory nut size balls. Place on a greased cookie sheet 1½-2 inches apart. With tines of a fork which have been dipped in flour, flatten dough in a crisscross pattern to approximately ¼-inch thick. Bake at 400° for 8-10 minutes. Yields 3½ dozen.

Yummies

1 cup shortening
1 cup granulated sugar
1 cup light brown sugar
2 eggs
1 teaspoon baking soda
½ teaspoon baking powder
½ teaspoon salt
2 cups plain flour
2 cups oatmeal
2 cups Rice Krispies
1 cup pecans, chopped
1 teaspoon vanilla

Cream shortening and sugars. Add eggs and sifted dry ingredients. Mix well. Add oatmeal, Rice Krispies, nuts and vanilla. Drop by teaspoonfuls onto lightly greased cookie sheet. Batter will be very stiff and hard to drop. Bake at 300° for 25-30 minutes. Yields 5 dozen.

Bourbon Snaps

¼ pound butter or margarine, softened
½ cup sugar
¼ cup bourbon
1 cup sifted plain flour
¼ teaspoon nutmeg

Cream butter and sugar with mixer until fluffy. Add bourbon alternately with flour. Sprinkle in nutmeg and mix thoroughly. Chill 1 hour or more. Drop small amounts from teaspoon 2 inches apart on ungreased cookie sheet. Bake at 350° for 5 minutes or until slightly browned. Watch carefully. DO NOT OVERBAKE. Cool slightly before removing from pan. Store in air-tight container. Yields 2½-3 dozen.

Christmas Gingerbread Men
Mrs. Terry Diehl

½ cup shortening
½ cup sugar
½ cup molasses
1 egg yolk, unbeaten
½ teaspoon salt
½ teaspoon baking soda
1 teaspoon baking powder
1 teaspoon ginger
1 teaspoon ground cloves
1½ teaspoons cinnamon
½ teaspoon nutmeg
2 cups plain flour, sifted

Cream shortening and sugar together. Add molasses and egg yolk. Blend well. Add salt, soda, baking powder and spices. Slowly add sifted flour. Roll out dough and cut with a gingerbread man cookie cutter. Bake at 350° for 8-10 minutes. Decorate. Yields 2-3 dozen, depending on size of cutter.
May be used for tree decorations by making small holes in the top before baking. Their aroma fills the air throughout the holidays. My boys eat them right off the tree.

Love Notes (Lemon Cookies)
Mrs. Tom Watson, wife of 1977 Masters' Champion

Crust:
2 cups sifted plain flour
½ cup 4X powdered sugar

1 cup butter

Topping:
4 eggs, slightly beaten
2 cups granulated sugar
6 tablespoons lemon juice

1 teaspoon baking powder
¼ cup plain flour

Crust: Cut flour and powdered sugar into butter until mixture clings together. Press dough into 13x9-inch baking pan. Bake at 350° for 25 minutes. Cool to room temperature before putting on the topping. This is essential for a crisp crust.

Topping: Mix eggs, sugar and lemon juice together. When well blended, add remaining ingredients. Mix well. Pour over baked crust. Bake at 350° for 25 minutes. Sprinkle with powdered sugar. Cool completely, then cut into bars. Yields 2½ dozen.

Cream Cheese Cookies

1 3-ounce package cream cheese
1 cup butter (not margarine)
2 cups plain flour

½ cup sugar
1 tablespoon vanilla
chocolate chips or pecans

Soften cream cheese and butter. Blend well. Combine flour and sugar. Add to butter mixture. Add vanilla and mix well. Shape into small balls and place on ungreased cookie sheet. Press chocolate chip or pecan into each cookie. Bake at 350° for 12 minutes or until lightly browned. Yields 5 to 6 dozen.

Mother's Butter Cookies

1 cup butter
1 cup sugar
1 egg
1 teaspoon salt

1 teaspoon vanilla
2 cups plain flour
½ teaspoon baking soda
chocolate bits (optional)

Cream butter and sugar. Add remaining ingredients and mix well. Chill. Shape into small balls. Place on ungreased cookie sheet and press flat with tines of fork. Leave plain or decorate with sugar or chocolate bits. Bake at 350° for approximately 15 minutes or until lightly browned. Yields 9 dozen small cookies.

Thin Wafers

2 sticks butter or margarine
1 cup sugar
1 egg, separated
2 teaspoons vanilla

2 cups sifted plain flour
⅛ teaspoon salt
½ cup pecans, finely chopped

Cream butter and sugar. Add egg yolk, vanilla, flour and salt. Spread thinly with spatula on 2 large ungreased cookie sheets. Dough will not run. Beat egg white and spread for glaze. Sprinkle with pecans. Bake at 250° for 1 hour. Cut into rectangles while hot. Yields 3 dozen.
A delightful cookie!

Aunt Nan's Gingersnaps

1 cup cane syrup or molasses
½ cup sugar
6 tablespoons shortening
2 tablespoons buttermilk
4 cups plain flour
1 teaspoon baking soda

1 teaspoon salt
1 teaspoon ground cloves
1 teaspoon ground nutmeg
1 teaspoon ground ginger
1 teaspoon cinnamon

Bring syrup or molasses to a boil. Add sugar, shortening and buttermilk. Set aside. Sift flour with remaining ingredients. Mix all ingredients together. Chill until consistency to roll out. This is a very stiff dough which is hard to roll out. Roll as thinly as possible. Cut with round cookie cutter. Place on ungreased cookie sheet. Bake at 350° for 8-10 minutes. Watch closely. Yields 15 dozen 2-inch cookies.

Rocks

1 cup sugar
⅔ cup butter
2 eggs
1½ cups plain flour
1 teaspoon cinnamon
1 teaspoon ground cloves

1 teaspoon vanilla
1 pound seeded raisins
1½ pounds nuts, chopped
1 teaspoon baking soda
1 teaspoon water

Cream sugar and butter. Blend in eggs. Add flour, cinnamon, cloves, vanilla, raisins and nuts. Mix well. Batter will be very stiff. Dissolve soda in water and add to other mixture. Drop from teaspoon onto greased cookie sheet. Leave a little space between for spread. Bake at 250° for 30-40 minutes. Store in tin box. Yields 5-6 dozen.

Chinese Drops

3 sticks butter
¾ cup sugar
3 cups plain flour

1½ teaspoons vanilla
2 cups nuts, chopped
confectioners sugar

Cream butter. Add sugar and beat until fluffy. Blend in flour. Stir in vanilla and nuts. Dough will be very stiff. Roll into balls about the size of a walnut. Place on ungreased cookie sheet. Bake at 350° for 15-20 minutes. Cool. Roll in confectioners sugar. Yields 6 dozen small cookies.

Orange Candy

2 cups sugar
1 cup milk
3 tablespoons orange juice
pinch of salt

pinch of baking soda
rind of 1 orange, grated
3 cups pecans, chopped

Combine sugar, milk and juice. Boil to soft-ball stage or until candy thermometer registers 240°F. Remove from heat. Add salt, soda and orange rind. Beat slightly. Add pecans and beat. Pour onto greased pan or slab. Let cool and cut into squares.

Caramel Candy

1 cup sugar
1 stick butter
½ teaspoon salt

1 14-ounce can condensed milk
1 cup nuts, chopped
1 teaspoon vanilla

Melt sugar and butter over low heat until caramelized to a golden brown. Add salt and milk. Stir constantly until a hard ball can be formed in water. Add nuts and vanilla. Beat until cool. Pour into pan. Let stand in refrigerator at least 30 minutes before cutting. Yields about twenty 1-inch squares.

Holiday Bonbons

1 16-ounce box 4X powdered
   sugar
¼ pound butter
¾ cup pecans, finely chopped

4 tablespoons (exact) bourbon
   (not blended whiskey)
8 ounces semi-sweet chocolate
1 teaspoon paraffin

Cream sugar and butter. Mix in pecans and bourbon. Roll into small balls and chill 30 minutes. Melt chocolate and paraffin over hot water in double boiler. Dip each ball into chocolate using a fork or teaspoon. Put on waxed paper and chill at least 2 hours. Wrap separately in waxed paper or candy paper cups. Keep in cool place. Yields 4 dozen.

Christmas Orange Pecans

1½ cups sugar
½ cup water
grated rind of 1 orange

3 tablespoons orange juice
pinch of salt
12 ounces pecan halves

Boil sugar in water until mixture spins a long thread when tested in water. Remove from heat. Add orange rind, orange juice and salt. Beat a few times. Add pecans and beat until creamy. Pour onto waxed paper and separate.

Never Fail Fudge

3 cups sugar
¾ cup margarine
⅔ cup evaporated milk (5.3 ounces)
1 12-ounce package semi-sweet
   chocolate chips

1 7-ounce jar marshmallow creme
1 cup nuts, chopped
1 teaspoon vanilla

Combine sugar, margarine and milk in a heavy 2½-quart saucepan. Bring to a boil, stirring constantly. Continue boiling 5 minutes over medium heat, stirring constantly to prevent scorching. Remove from heat. Stir in chocolate. Continue stirring until melted. Add marshmallow creme, nuts and vanilla. Beat until well blended. Pour in greased 13x9-inch pan. Cool and cut into small squares. Yields about 4 dozen pieces.

Peanut Logs

1 12-ounce jar crunchy peanut butter
1 cup margarine
2 cups graham cracker crumbs
1 pound confectioners sugar
1 teaspoon vanilla
1 cup nuts, finely chopped
1 4-ounce bar paraffin
1 12-ounce package semi-sweet chocolate chips

Mix first 6 ingredients well. Hand roll into logs about size of little finger. Melt paraffin and chocolate chips in top of double boiler. With a fork, dip logs one at a time into chocolate mixture. Place on waxed paper to dry. Yields 100 or more.

▼ Better if logs are made one day, refrigerated, and dipped the next day. May be kept several weeks in a tin.

Stella's Mint Wafers

2 egg whites
1 6-ounce package chocolate mint bits
⅔ cup sugar
¾ cup pecans or English walnuts, chopped

Beat egg whites until stiff peaks form. Add remaining ingredients. Mix well. Drop by teaspoon on lightly greased cookie sheet. Put in preheated 250° oven. Turn oven off immediately. Leave overnight without opening oven. Yields 25-40.

▼ One 6-ounce package semi-sweet chocolate bits and 2 to 3 drops of peppermint extract may be substituted for chocolate mint bits.

Pickles, Preserves, Relishes

17

Bread and Butter Pickle

4 quarts (approximately 8
  pounds) medium cucumbers
6 medium white onions, sliced
2 green peppers, sliced
3 cloves garlic
⅓ cup coarse salt

5 cups sugar
1½ teaspoons turmeric
1½ teaspoons celery seed
2 tablespoons mustard seed
3 cups cider vinegar

Do not pare cucumbers. Slice thin. Add onions, peppers, whole garlic cloves and salt. Cover with cracked ice. Mix. Let stand 3 hours. Drain well. Combine remaining ingredients in large kettle. Add cucumber mixture. Heat just to boiling point. Seal in hot sterilized jars. Yields 8 pints.

Curry Slices

8 cups (2½ pounds) cucumbers
  thinly sliced
1 medium onion, thinly sliced
1 tablespoon plain salt
2 cups cider vinegar
1⅓ cups sugar
1 tablespoon curry powder

2 teaspoons mixed pickling
  spice
1 teaspoon celery seed
1 teaspoon mustard seed
½ teaspoon pepper
1 green pepper, cut in
  thin strips

Place cucumbers and onion in large bowl. Sprinkle with salt and cover with ice water. Let stand 3 hours. DRAIN WELL. Combine remaining ingredients in a large kettle and heat. Add drained cucumbers and onion. Heat just to boiling. Seal in sterilized jars. Yields 3 pints.

Pickled Okra

2 pounds small okra (or
  enough to fill 5 pint jars)
5 pods hot red or green peppers
  or 1¼ teaspoons dried hot pepper
5 cloves garlic, peeled

1 quart white vinegar
½ cup water
6 tablespoons plain salt
1 tablespoon celery seed

Wash okra. Pack in 5 hot sterilized jars. Place 1 pepper pod (or ¼ teaspoon hot pepper) and 1 garlic clove in each jar. Bring remaining ingredients to a boil. Pour over okra, spooning some celery seeds into each jar. Seal jars and let stand 8 weeks before using. Yields 5 pints.

▼ For a milder pickle, add ¼ cup sugar to vinegar solution. Dill seed may be substituted for celery seed.

Sliced Artichoke Pickle

3 pounds cabbage, chopped
1 quart white onions, chopped
6 green peppers, chopped
1 gallon water
1 cup plain salt
2 quarts cider vinegar
6 cups sugar

¾ cup plain flour
1 12-ounce jar prepared mustard
1 tablespoon black pepper
2 tablespoons turmeric
3 tablespoons mustard seed
4 quarts Jerusalem artichokes,
cleaned and thinly sliced

Soak cabbage, onions and peppers overnight in mixture of water and salt. Place in refrigerator if possible. Drain well. Spread on paper towels to dry. Make a paste of vinegar, sugar, flour, mustard and spices. Over medium heat, stir constantly until thickened (about 10 minutes). Add drained vegetables and cook until wilted (about 15 minutes). Add artichokes. Cook 2 to 5 minutes until artichokes are heated. DO NOT BOIL. Fill sterilized jars and seal. Yields 14 to 16 pints.

▼ Can substitute brown sugar for white.

Pat's Squash Pickle

4 quarts small yellow squash,
thickly sliced
6-8 medium onions, chopped
4 medium green peppers, chopped
¼ cup plain salt

3 cups white vinegar
5 cups sugar
1½ teaspoons mustard seed
1½ teaspoons celery seed
1 teaspoon turmeric

Combine squash, onions and peppers in large container. Sprinkle with salt. Cover with ice cubes. Let stand 3 hours. Drain well. In large pot, make a syrup of remaining ingredients. Heat well. Add vegetables. Bring to a full boil. Fill sterilized jars, leaving ½ inch at top. Seal and turn jars upside down to cool. Yields about 5 quarts.

Mustard Pickle

2 heads cauliflower
6 bell peppers
1 head cabbage
3 pounds white onions
1 gallon water
2 cups plain salt
½ gallon white vinegar

3 pounds sugar
3 tablespoons mustard seed
1 tablespoon black pepper
1½ cups plain flour
1 tablespoon turmeric
1 12-ounce jar prepared mustard
1 pint dill pickles, sliced

264

Chop vegetables and soak overnight in mixture of water and salt. Drain vegetables and pat dry with paper towels. In large pot, pour ⅔ of vinegar and all the sugar over drained vegetables. Bring to a boil. Combine mustard seed, black pepper, flour, turmeric, prepared mustard and remaining vinegar. Add this mixture and pickles to vegetables. Stir well. Boil 5 minutes. Seal in sterilized jars. Yields 12 to 14 pints.

Green Tomato Dill Pickle

Pack into each sterilized quart jar:

firm green tomatoes cut into fourths	1 hot green pepper
1 clove garlic	2 teaspoons dill seed or
1 stalk celery	1 head fresh dill

Liquid for 8 quarts:

2 quarts water	1 cup coarse kosher salt
1 quart cider vinegar	

Cook together 5 minutes. Pour into packed jars and seal. Let pickle stand for 4 weeks. Yields 8 quarts.

Cucumber Crisps
(or Green Tomato Pickle)

7 pounds cucumbers, sliced ⅛ inch thick	4½ pounds sugar
2 gallons cold water	1 teaspoon celery seed
3 cups lime	1 teaspoon salt
2 quarts white vinegar	1 teaspoon whole cloves
	1 teaspoon pickling spice

First Day: Soak cucumbers in mixture of cold water and lime for 24 hours. Stir carefully occasionally. Use a large enamel or crockery pot (not metal).
Second Day: Drain and cover with clear water. Soak for 4 hours in clear, cold water, changing water each hour. Let stand in cold water until night. Drain. Make a syrup of remaining ingredients. Bring to a boil. Pour over cucumbers. Let stand until morning.
Third Day: Cook for 45 minutes to 1 hour. Seal in sterilized jars. Yields 8 pints.
▼ May substitute 7 pounds sliced green tomatoes for cucumbers. May add green food coloring to syrup if desired.

Pickled Peaches

1 gallon peaches, peeled*	1 ginger root
6-8 cups sugar	3 sticks cinnamon
2 cups water	1 tablespoon whole cloves
3 cups cider vinegar	1 tablespoon allspice

*If many peaches are to be peeled at once, put the peeled peaches in the following solution until ready to use: 1 gallon water mixed with 2 tablespoons vinegar and 2 tablespoons salt.

Boil 3 cups sugar, water and spices for 3 minutes. Add 10 to 12 peaches at a time and simmer until tender. Remove peaches and add remaining peaches. Simmer until tender. Return other peaches to pot and let stand in syrup 12 to 24 hours. Pack peaches in sterile quart jars. Add remaining sugar to liquid. Boil until desired thickness. Pour over peaches and seal. Yield depends on size of peaches.

▼ For spicier version, stud each peach with several cloves and add a piece of cinnamon stick to each jar.

Pear Pickle

1 pint cider vinegar	1 tablespoon whole cloves
1 cup water	2 sticks cinnamon
1½ pounds sugar	5 pounds hard pears
1 tablespoon ginger root	1 lemon, sliced

Make a syrup of vinegar, water and sugar. Tie all spices in cheesecloth and add to syrup. Peel and quarter pears and add with lemon to syrup. Bring to boiling point. Cook until pears can be pierced with a toothpick. Remove from heat. Allow to stand overnight. Pack pears in sterilized jars. Heat syrup, pour over pears and seal. Yields 6 to 8 pints.

Watermelon Rind Pickle

1 pound lime	1 teaspoon cinnamon
10 pounds watermelon rind	1 tablespoon allspice
4 or 5 pieces ginger root	½ gallon cider vinegar
1 tablespoon whole cloves	6 pounds sugar

Prepare lime as directed. Peel and soak rind overnight in lime water. Drain. Cover with salt water. Boil 2 minutes. Drain. Cover with water. Add ginger. Boil 20 minutes. Drain. Tie spices in bag. Make syrup of vinegar, sugar and spices. Add syrup to rind. Boil 20 minutes longer. Place rind in sterilized jars. Boil syrup 20 minutes longer, then fill jars with syrup and seal.

Hot Pepper Jelly

¾ cup hot peppers, ground
1¼ cups green peppers, ground
1½ cups white vinegar
6½ cups sugar

juice of 1 lemon
1 6-ounce bottle Certo
red or green food coloring

Remove seeds and veins from peppers and grind or chop fine in blender. May use some of the 1½ cups vinegar with the peppers in the blender. Mix all ingredients except Certo and red or green food coloring. Cook on low heat 45 minutes. Bring to a rolling boil and boil 1 minute. Remove from heat and let stand 5 minutes. Add Certo and either red or green coloring. Stir well. Seal in sterilized jars. Yields 6 to 7 half pints.
Serve with pork or lamb. May spread on cream cheese and serve with crackers.

Sherry Jelly

4 cups very dry sherry
6 cups sugar

1 6-ounce bottle Certo
paraffin

Mix sherry and sugar in top of double boiler. Place over boiling water. Stir until sugar is dissolved. Remove from heat. Stir in Certo with wooden spoon. Pour into glasses. Cover with ⅛-inch hot paraffin. Makes 8-10 half-pints.
For a nice Christmas gift, fill sherry glasses or Irish coffee cups and cover with paraffin. Press a design into paraffin for a special touch.

Peach Preserves

4 pounds ripe peaches
3 pounds sugar

juice of 2 lemons

Peel and cut peaches into eighths. Place in large pot or kettle. Add sugar and lemon juice. Let stand 4-6 hours. Simmer very slowly and cook until syrup becomes thick (about 1 hour depending on peaches). Stir occasionally with wooden spoon to prevent sticking. Skim foam when necessary. Pour into sterilized jars and seal. Yields 4 to 6 pints.
For spiced peach preserves, tie loosely in cheesecloth bag 2 sticks cinnamon, 6 whole allspice, 8 cloves, 1 blade mace, ½ ginger root. Discard after peaches are cooked.

Pear Preserves

8 pounds pears   5 pounds sugar
1 lemon, thinly sliced

Peel pears. Chip into pieces about the size of a large pecan half. Scatter lemon slices over pears and cover with sugar. Let stand overnight stirring occasionally. Next day, bring pears to a boil stirring often. Cook over medium heat stirring often until syrup drips in 2 parallel drops from the side of a spoon. Ladle into hot, sterilized jars and seal. Yields 6-8 pints.

Chili Sauce

24 large ripe tomatoes   1 tablespoon salt
6 medium onions, chopped   1 clove garlic, minced
6 sweet green peppers, chopped   ¼ teaspoon ground cloves
2 red peppers, chopped   1 teaspoon allspice
1 cup sugar   1 teaspoon mace
2 cups cider vinegar   1 teaspoon cinnamon
1 tablespoon celery seed   1 tablespoon prepared
1 tablespoon mustard seed   horseradish

Peel and quarter tomatoes. Place all ingredients in a large preserving kettle. Place over low heat. Bring to a boil, stirring occasionally to prevent sticking. Cover and let cook on low heat 2 to 3 hours or until mixture is quite thick and no longer watery. Pour into sterile jars. Seal while very hot.
Serve with meats and fish or as a sauce for meat loaf or omelets. Also good with fried eggplant and fried green tomatoes.

Mixed Corn Relish

1 teaspoon turmeric   1 medium head cabbage,
1 teaspoon celery seed   finely shredded
2 tablespoons dry mustard   4 medium white onions,
½ cup salt   finely diced
2 cups light brown sugar   4 sweet green peppers,
1 quart cider vinegar   finely diced
12 ears yellow corn, cut   4 sweet red peppers
   from cob   finely diced

Mix spices, salt, sugar and vinegar. Combine with vegetables. Cook over low heat about 1 hour, stirring occasionally until slightly thickened. Relish thickens as it cools. Pack while hot into sterilized jars. Seal at once. Yields 20 cups.

Artichoke Relish

5 quarts Jerusalem artichokes, cleaned and chopped
2 gallons water
2 cups plain salt
3 pounds white cabbage, chopped
1½ pounds onions, chopped
6 large green and red bell peppers, chopped
¾ cup plain flour

1 24-ounce jar French's mustard
½ gallon cider vinegar
3 pounds sugar
2 tablespoons turmeric
2 tablespoons celery seed
3 tablespoons mustard seed
1 tablespoon black pepper
1 tablespoon hot sauce or more to taste

First Day: Soak artichokes overnight in 1 gallon water and 1 cup salt. In a second container, soak cabbage, onion and bell peppers in 1 gallon water and 1 cup salt. *Second Day:* Drain artichokes. Spread on large towel to drain thoroughly. Drain vegetables. Spread a second large towel to drain thoroughly. In a mixing bowl, combine flour and mustard carefully. Avoid lumping. Stir until mixture is smooth. In a large (at least 10 quart) kettle, mix vinegar, sugar, turmeric, celery seed, mustard seed and pepper. Bring to a boil. Add cabbage, onions and bell peppers. Bring mixture back to a boil and cook for 10 minutes over medium heat. Reduce to low heat. Dip out about a cup of hot liquid and add to flour mixture. Mix well. Add thinned flour mixture to vinegar and vegetables. Stir thoroughly until well mixed. Add hot sauce (and pimientos if used) and artichokes. Increase heat. Stir until mixture is about to boil (about 5 minutes). Seal in sterilized jars. Yields 17-18 pints.

▼ If red bell peppers are not available, use 1 4-ounce jar chopped pimientos.

Granny's Pear Relish

½ bushel green pears
12 large green peppers
12 small hot peppers
24 medium white onions
1 large bunch celery
1 9-ounce jar mustard

5 cups sugar
1½ quarts cider vinegar
1 tablespoon turmeric
2 tablespoons salt
1¼ ounces pickling spice, tied in cheesecloth

Grind pears, peppers, onions and celery through food chopper, using coarse blade. Drain off juice. Mix mustard, sugar, vinegar, turmeric and salt. Add pickling spice. Bring mixture to boil. Add vegetables. Cook slowly 20 to 30 minutes. Discard pickling spice. Seal in sterilized jars. Yields 12 to 16 pints.

▼ Add 12 more hot peppers for a very hot relish.
Excellent garnish for pork, poultry and hot dogs.

Cranberry Chutney

5 tangerines
2 cups fresh cranberries
1 large tart apple
½ cup good orange marmalade
½ cup cider vinegar
1 cup water (less if using
   brown sugar)
1½ cups sugar

2 teaspoons ginger
¾ teaspoon cinnamon
1 tablespoon curry powder
¼ teaspoon ground cloves
dash allspice
½ cup white raisins
dash salt

Peel tangerines, removing all white membranes and strings. Leave transparent membranes intact so sections will not disintegrate. Cut sections in half. Remove seeds. Wash cranberries and drain well. Peel, core and dice apple. Combine all ingredients in a saucepan. Bring to a boil over medium heat. Reduce heat to low, cover pan, and simmer for 30 minutes, stirring occasionally. Seal in sterilized half-pint jars. Yields 6 to 8 half pints.

Chutney
Mrs. Gene Sarazen, wife of 1935 Masters' Champion

9 pounds pears (weigh after
   peeling and cutting up)
2 pounds sultana raisins
6 large green peppers, chopped
6¼ pounds sugar

1 teaspoon salt
1 quart cider vinegar
2 tablespoons whole cloves and
   3 sticks of cinnamon, tied
   in bag
¾ pound crystallized ginger

Combine all ingredients in large kettle. Cook slowly for 1½ to 2 hours until rich and thick. Put in sterilized pint or half-pint jars and seal.
Serve with lamb or curry.

Apple Relish

6 cups apples, peeled and
   chopped
2 green peppers, chopped
2 red peppers, chopped
1 cup onion, chopped
1 teaspoon dry mustard

½ cup cider vinegar
¼ teaspoon turmeric
1 cup water
1½ cups sugar
1 teaspoon salt

Combine all ingredients. Cook on low heat for 45 minutes. Seal in sterilized jars. Yields 6 to 8 pints.

INDEX

Here are some interesting garnishes or decorations to try:

Frosted grapes: Boil 1 cup granulated sugar and 1 cup water 5-10 minutes or until syrup consistency. Let cool until barely lukewarm. Dip washed and dried grapes in syrup, then in granulated sugar. Transfer to cooling rack to dry for 1 hour. Garnish ham or poultry platters, or use on desserts with grape or ivy leaves.

Chocolate leaves: Melt semi-sweet chocolate. Using a pastry brush, paint the top side of camellia or similar leaves with the chocolate, covering the entire leaf down the stem. Place in freezer to harden. When hard, peel chocolate off. May use to garnish whipped cream.

Chocolate curls: Warm a milk chocolate bar, still wrapped, by placing on a warm spot just until soft, not melted. Unwrap and pare lengthwise with a vegetable peeler, pressing lightly, to form a curl. Lift curl with a toothpick to a plate and chill until hard.

Cabbage bowl: A red cabbage, hollowed out, makes a colorful container for dips, especially for raw vegetables.

Olive crabs: Enlarge the holes in pitted large black olives with the point of a knife. Insert three-inch pieces of scallion, carrot or celery, and fringe the ends with a sharp knife. Put in ice water to flare.

Cucumber catfish: Use an unpeeled cucumber. One fourth forms the head, with gills cut in the sides and half-round radish slices inserted for eyes; the center half is sliced in rounds for the body; the tail consists of the final fourth with the skin cut back from the stem end and shaped into points.

Vegetable Bouquet

Beet or turnip roses: For beets, parboil large beets for 10 minutes or until skins slip off. Cool. Carve into rose shape with a sharp knife. Beginning at the lower end, cut petal-shape scallops (much as you would a radish). Then, just above this row of petals, pare a ¼-inch strip around the beet to cause the next row of petals to be slightly indented. Start from a point ¼-inch above and midway between 2 petals of first row, cut down and in until knife touches tops of first row of petals. Continue around to form second row of petals. Again pare off a ¼-inch strip and make another row of petals. Continue until rose is complete. For turnips, pour boiling water over white turnips and let stand for 5 minutes. Peel and follow procedure for beets. Keep in ice water.

Onion chrysanthemums: Peel a medium red onion. Cut each layer of the onion into thin slivers vertically from the pointed end down, leaving the bottom attached. Place in ice water to crisp and flare the petals.

Vegetable daisies: With a sharp knife, cut tiny V-shaped wedges from the edge of a round slice of carrot, white turnip or cucumber. Put a small round or contrasting color in center, as carrot on white, ripe olive or black grape on color. Secure the center to the flower with a toothpick.

Grapefruit container: Cut off one third of a grapefruit and discard. From the remaining piece, scoop out about half the center. Tie fresh parsley together to make a tight bouquet to fit into grapefruit. Stick strong toothpicks into bottoms of small beet and turnip roses, carrot curls, vegetable daisies and onion chrysanthemums and arrange on parsley.

Cauliflower centerpiece: Using toothpicks, stick turnip daisies, carrot daisies and tiny whole beets on large head of cauliflower. Leave green leaves on cauliflower. This is a pretty garnish for meat trays.

Pickle fans: Thinly slice a medium-size cucumber pickle or gherkin lengthwise to within ⅓-inch of end. Spread to form fan. These may also be secured with toothpicks onto a cauliflower centerpiece.

METRIC CONVERSION TABLES

Liquid Measure:

1 tsp.	= 5 c.c.		1 c.	= about ¼ liter
1 T.	= 15 c.c.		1 qt.	= about 1 liter
1 oz.	= 30 milliliters			

To determine liquid measure multiply

The number of:	By	To Get
ounces	30	milliliters
pints	0.47	liters
quarts	0.95	liters

Dry Measure:

1 oz.	= about 28 grams
1 lb.	= about 454 grams

To determine dry measure multiply

The number of:	By	To Get
ounces	28	grams
pounds	0.45	grams

4 ozs. = ½ c.
8 ozs. = 1 c.

Food Measurements:

Sugar:
1 T = 15 grams
1 c. = 240 grams

Salt:
1 T. = 15 grams

Rice:
1 c. = 240 grams

Flour:
¼ c. = 35 grams
1 c. = 140 grams

Butter:
1 T. = 15 grams
½ c. = 125 grams

Since 1928, the members of the Junior League of Augusta have been improving the quality of life in their community through their volunteer efforts. They have provided the financial aid and manpower to implement programs concerning child advocacy, historical preservation, drug abuse, domestic violence, the arts and public education.

Proceeds from the sale of the Junior League's two cookbooks are directed to those programs and to a better tomorrow.

Second Round, Tea-Time at the Masters ® is the companion cookbook to *Tea-Time at the Masters* ®. It offers not only outstanding recipes but also a nostalgic look at the world's most prestigious golf tournament, the Masters.

Through the pages of *Second Round* ®, you can experience the awe and devotion that past winners feel for the Masters® Tournament and relive great moments from its colorful history while creating sumptuous delights.

Treat yourself to a *Second Round* ® or delight someone with a gift of both cookbooks. For your convenience, order forms are provided on the following pages.

The word "MASTERS®" is registered in the U.S. Patent and Trademark Office as a trademark and service mark of Augusta National, Inc., Augusta, Georgia.

Additional copies of *Tea-Time at the Masters®* may be obtained by sending $18.95 plus $4.00 each to cover postage and handling (Georgia residents add $1.60 sales tax) to the following address:

Tea-Time at the Masters®
P.O. Box 40058
Augusta, Georgia 30909

Tea-Time at the Masters®
P.O. Box 40058
Augusta, Georgia 30909

Please send me_____ copies
    Tea-Time at the Masters®   @ $18.95 each _____
    Postage and handling (within continental U.S.)   @   4.00 each _____
        Each additional book   @   2.00 each _____
    Georgia residents add 7% sales tax   @   1.60 each _____
Please send me_____ copies
    Second Round, Tea-Time at the Masters®   @ $16.95 each _____
    Postage and handling (within continental U.S.)   @   4.00 each _____
        Each additional book   @   2.00 each _____
    Georgia residents add 7% sales tax   @   1.47 each _____

    Gift Wrap (optional)   @   1.00 each _____
                              TOTAL ENCLOSED $ _____

Name _____
Address _____
City_____State _____ Zip Code_____

Make checks payable to *Tea-Time Publications*.
Or call 1-888-JLT-TIME toll free to charge your order.

Credit Card #_____ Exp. Date_____
Signature _____

Tea-Time at the Masters®
P.O. Box 40058
Augusta, Georgia 30909

Please send me_____ copies
    Tea-Time at the Masters®   @ $18.95 each _____
    Postage and handling (within continental U.S.)   @   4.00 each _____
        Each additional book   @   2.00 each _____
    Georgia residents add 7% sales tax   @   1.60 each _____
Please send me_____ copies
    Second Round, Tea-Time at the Masters®   @ $16.95 each _____
    Postage and handling (within continental U.S.)   @   4.00 each _____
        Each additional book   @   2.00 each _____
    Georgia residents add 7% sales tax   @   1.47 each _____

    Gift Wrap (optional)   @   1.00 each _____
                              TOTAL ENCLOSED $ _____

Name _____
Address _____
City_____State _____ Zip Code_____

Make checks payable to *Tea-Time Publications*.
Or call 1-888-JLT-TIME toll free to charge your order.

Credit Card #_____ Exp. Date_____
Signature _____

I would like the following individuals to receive information about **Tea-Time at the Mast** and **Second Round Tea-Time at the Masters®**

Name_____ | Name_____
Address_____ | Address_____
City_____State_____Zip_____ | City_____State_____Zip_____

I would like to see **Tea-Time at the Masters®** and **Second Round Tea-Time at the Mast** in the following stores in my area.

Name_____ | Name_____
Address_____ | Address_____
City_____State_____Zip_____ | City_____State_____Zip_____

I would like the following individuals to receive information about **Tea-Time at the Mast** and **Second Round Tea-Time at the Masters®**

Name_____ | Name_____
Address_____ | Address_____
City_____State_____Zip_____ | City_____State_____Zip_____

I would like to see **Tea-Time at the Masters®** and **Second Round Tea-Time at the Mast** in the following stores in my area.

Name_____ | Name_____
Address_____ | Address_____
City_____State_____Zip_____ | City_____State_____Zip_____